LUCRECIA THE DREAMER

SPIRITUAL PHENOMENA
TANYA LUHRMANN and ANN TAVES, Series Editors

KELLY BULKELEY

LUCRECIA
THE DREAMER

PROPHECY, COGNITIVE SCIENCE,

AND THE SPANISH INQUISITION

STANFORD UNIVERSITY PRESS
STANFORD, CALIFORNIA

Stanford University Press
Stanford, California

©2018 by the Board of Trustees of the Leland Stanford Junior University.
All rights reserved.

Printed in the United States of America on acid-free, archival-quality paper

Library of Congress Cataloging-in-Publication Data

Names: Bulkeley, Kelly, 1962- author.
Title: Lucrecia the dreamer : prophecy, cognitive science, and the Spanish Inquisition /
Kelly Bulkeley.
Other titles: Spiritual phenomena.
Description: Stanford, California : Stanford University Press, 2018. |
Series: Spiritual phenomena | Includes bibliographical references and index.
Identifiers: LCCN 2017018397 | ISBN 9780804798242 (cloth; alk. paper) |
ISBN 9781503603868 (pbk.; alk. paper) | ISBN 9781503604483 (epub; alk. paper)
Subjects: LCSH: León, Lucrecia de, 1568—Prophecies. | Women prophets—Spain—
Biography. | Fortune-telling by dreams—Spain—History—16th century. | Dreams—
Religious aspects—Christianity. | Inquisition—Spain. | Cognitive science. | Psychology,
Religious.
Classification: LCC BF1815.L46 B85 2018 | DDC 154.6/3092—dc23
LC record available at https://lccn.loc.gov/2017018397

Designed by Bruce Lundquist
Typeset at Stanford University Press in 10/15 Baskerville

For others like her

CONTENTS

TABLES, FIGURES, ILLUSTRATIONS, AND MAPS

NOTE ON TRANSLATIONS

Unless otherwise noted, the dream texts presented here have been trans-lated by Professor Eva Nuñez of Portland State University, drawing on Spanish transcriptions of the original Castilian manuscripts currently preserved and available for public study in Madrid in the National His-torical Archive of Spain. The transcriptions of the dreams appear in María Zambrano, Edison Simons, and Juan Blázquez Miguel, *Sueños y procesos de Lucrecia de León*. The original, handwritten manuscripts and other materials related to the trial are preserved at the National Histori-cal Archive in the following files: legajos 3712–3713, 3703, 3077–3082, 2085, 2105/1, 115/23, and 114/10. All other dream texts and trial tran-scripts quoted in the following pages have been translated by specialists in the language and culture of early modern Spain, including Richard L. Kagan, María V. Jordán, Roger Osborne, and Henry Kamen.

LUCRECIA THE DREAMER

INTRODUCTION

This is the story of a young woman who was violently persecuted because of her dreams. The fact that she dreamed frequently and vividly from an early age does not make her especially unusual since every society, from ancient times to the present day, has its share of such gifted people. What makes her story remarkable and historically significant is that she focused her dreaming abilities on gaining insights into the most pressing dangers facing her country. She was born a big dreamer and then, with the help and guidance of various supporters, she amplified her oneiric powers to new levels of visionary intensity.[1]

For that, she was condemned as a traitor and a heretic.

Her name was Lucrecia de León. Born in 1568 in Madrid, Spain, she was the oldest of five children raised in a family of modest economic means. Her father worked as a banking administrator in the royal court of Philip II, the "Most Catholic King." Philip controlled the largest empire in history up to that time, covering twice as much territory as ancient Rome did at its peak. Lucrecia grew up in the capital city of this burgeoning global imperium during a time known as the Siglo del Oro, or the "Golden Age," of Spanish history.[2] As her parents and neighbors later testified, Lucrecia was an active dreamer from early childhood. In the fall of 1587, when she was not quite 19, she mentioned one of her odd dreams to a family friend visiting her house. This friend later described the dream to a nobleman, Don Alonso de Mendoza, who was known to be deeply interested in mystical theology and apocalyptic omens. Curious to hear more, Don Alonso arranged to record Lucrecia's dreams on a daily basis. For the next three years he collected her dreams, analyzed them in relation to passages in the Bible, and showed them to other people concerned about the future of Spain. Public interest in Lucrecia's dreams grew, and so did the disapproval of Church authorities whose job it was to guard against political dissent and unorthodox spirituality. In 1590, the king ordered the Inquisition to arrest Lucrecia. Now 21 years old and several months pregnant, she was brought to the Inquisition's secret prison in the nearby city of Toledo and tried for heresy and treason. The carefully recorded collection of her dreams became a primary source of evidence against her.

Despite her humble origins, and in defiance of the most powerful ruler on earth, Lucrecia insisted to the end that her dreams did not violate her Catholic faith and she had done nothing wrong in sharing them with others.

During her trial, questions about Lucrecia's dreams became the focal point of the investigation: Was she making the dreams up? Were other people making them up for her? Was she possessed by the Devil? Was she deluded by the empty nonsense of her private fancies? Or could she really be a prophet, a genuine religious visionary?

Vexing questions about the spiritual ambiguities of dreaming echo throughout the history of religions, not just in 16th century Catholicism. Every religious tradition has struggled with the bewildering multiplicity of dreams, trying to find a reliable means of distinguishing between true revelations and deceitful fantasies.[3] An acute epistemological tension seems inherent in oneiric experience. Some dreams appear trivial and pointless, while others are clearly meaningful and relevant to waking life. No outside observer can verify the accuracy of another person's report of a dream, which leaves the door open to conscious and/or unconscious fabrications. Yet every culture has stories, often embedded in its most sacred texts, of intense and transformative dreams that have given people a profound feeling of connection with the divine. This means that dangers lurk in both directions, either by mistaking a truly revelatory dream as nonsense, or by treating a mundane dream as a heaven-sent message.

The Spanish Inquisition's trial of Lucrecia de León provides a dramatic case study of this age-old conflict between traditional religious authority and the spiritual dynamism of dreaming. The surviving court documents from her trial enable us to witness, in unusually close detail, this young woman's efforts to navigate through the life-and-death conflict between her strict Catholic faith and the prophetic potency of her nocturnal imagination. A new study of Lucrecia's life holds the promise of illuminating one of history's most impressive yet unheralded expressions of visionary dreaming.

Dream Research and the Cognitive Science of Religion

A great deal of information about Lucrecia's background already exists, thanks to the work of historians such as Richard Kagan, Roger Osborne, and María Jordán.[4] They have shown that her dreams provided an outlet for expressing bold political ideas that would otherwise be forbidden from a young, uneducated woman of her modest social class. Kagan introduces his book by asserting that "the real importance of these dreams lies in their social and political criticism of Philip's Spain."[5] Jordán has explained the importance of Lucrecia's case by saying, "dreams were particularly effective vehicles to convey political information and to place it in a tangible narrative form accessible to an audience across a broad social spectrum."[6]

This historical-political approach leads to important insights. But it leaves unexplored a central mystery of Lucrecia's story. Since the Inquisition's trial more than 400 years ago, no one has closely studied Lucrecia's dreams *as dreams*, as authentic expressions of her nocturnal imagination.[7] From a purely historical perspective it does not matter whether her dreams were real or not, because the same political themes could be effectively communicated either way. Indeed, the safest scholarly approach might be to assume they were *not* real dreams, to avoid the risk of being duped by made-up fantasies. I will argue, to the contrary, that it does matter, a great deal, whether or not we take Lucrecia seriously as a dreamer. If we recognize her dreams as the creative products of her mind during sleep, not fabricated fictions from the waking state, it makes an enormous difference in how we understand her dramatic rise and harrowing fall as a religious visionary.

This approach is supported by new scientific research on the functioning of the brain-mind system,[8] particularly in relation to dreaming and religious experience. These findings help to highlight the meaningful patterns in the reports of Lucrecia's dreams, patterns that are consistent in many ways with current knowledge about mental activities in sleep. If we assume from the outset that her reports are mere fictions, then modern research on dreams has no relevance. But if, instead, we begin by tentatively accepting the possibility that Lucrecia was telling the truth about her experiences, then we can benefit by using the latest findings in the science of dreaming to analyze her reports and form a reasoned assessment of their authenticity and significance.

cog. sci.

An important resource in this study is the cognitive science of religion (CSR).[9] Psychological approaches to religion have a long history reaching back more than a century to the pioneering investigations of William James, Sigmund Freud, C. G. Jung, and others.[10] Recent developments in cognitive science and evolutionary theory have opened up new vistas in our understanding of religion's many roles in human life. Researchers in CSR have studied the neurophysiology of fire-walking rituals in rural Greece,[11] the use of mental imagery in prayer among American Evangelical Christians,[12] and the memory systems that facilitate the spread of spirit possession beliefs among Afro-Brazilian healing cults.[13] Cognitive approaches have been applied to everything from meditation and trance states to beliefs about the soul, God, and other supernatural beings.[14] The researchers pursuing these projects all share the central conviction that scientific psychology has important implications for the study of religion. This was certainly the approach of James, Freud, and Jung, each of whom was deeply versed in the best neuroscience of his day. Thanks to 21st century advances in research technology, we now have a wealth of detailed evidence about how the mind works, which allows us to expand and improve on the pioneering efforts of those earlier psychologists of religion.

New scientific knowledge about human cognition can be enormously helpful in the study of religious phenomena, and not just in present-day contexts. Some researchers have begun to apply CSR methods to individuals, texts, and traditions from earlier times in history.[15] The working hypothesis is that scientifically verified facts about the evolutionary development of the human brain enable us to make reasoned inferences about the experiences of people who lived long ago. As John Tooby and Leda Cosmides put it in "The Psychological Foundations of Culture," "our modern skulls house a stone age mind."[16] The basic psychological architecture of our species took shape several hundred thousand years ago, and it has remained largely the same ever since. This means that modern knowledge about the workings of the mind can give insights into the lives of people from other historical eras by referring to the innate mental predispositions shared by all members of our species.

Turning the method around, this also means that historical studies can reveal aspects of mental functioning that have relevance for present-day scientific theories about the nature of the human psyche.[17] Along these lines, I will argue that the dreams of a person who lived more than four hundred years ago can tell us something important about the cognitive potentials of the dreaming imagination in people's lives today, despite the vast gulf of time, language, and religious sensibility separating her world from our own.

Of course, a CSR approach to history can easily be abused if one yields to the temptation to project modern beliefs and expectations onto the lives of people from the distant past. Many scholars have criticized Freud, Jung, and their immediate followers on exactly this point. For Freudians the problem came in trying to apply psychoanalytic ideas about sexuality to past cultures where family relations and childrearing practices differed from those of 20th century Europe. For Jungians the difficulties arose in trying to map Jung's theory of universal archetypes onto the complex and widely varying myths of non-Western traditions. Both Freudian and Jungian practices of interpretation tended to exaggerate the psychological similarities across cultures while ignoring or downplaying the crucial differences. They imposed modern concepts of explanation onto the lives of people from non-modern settings, without taking into account how those people explained their own experiences, using their own ideas and concepts.[18]

Can a CSR approach do any better? If properly deployed, yes. The models generated by CSR have more scientific evidence to support them than Freudian or Jungian theories originally had, with more precise ways of distinguishing between mental qualities that are culturally contingent and those that seem to be universal features of the way our brains have evolved.[19] To be clear, this does not give CSR researchers an interpretive carte blanche. Each case requires a careful study of the unique combination of influences and forces at play. It is easy to do this kind of research badly, and hard to do it well.

his model

One of the early practitioners of the psychological study of history was Erik Erikson, a 20th century psychoanalyst who wrote biographies of Mahatma Gandhi, Martin Luther, and others.[20] Erikson described his approach as a kind of "triple bookkeeping" in which he examined the life of his subject from three angles: physiological, psychological, and sociological.[21] By taking all of these influences into account—the functioning of the body, the development of the mind, and the social framework of the community—Erikson was able to sort through the multiple strands of biographical information and formulate an insightful picture of the person's life and impact on the world.[22] Following Erikson, I will explore these three dimensions of Lucrecia's life and try to integrate them into an accurate portrait of her life and experiences as a dreamer.

A fourth dimension of biographical bookkeeping will also be considered in Lucrecia's case—the *religious* dimension, in recognition of the powerful role the Roman Catholic Church and its theological teachings played in the development of her dreaming imagination. In late 16th century Madrid, Roman Catholicism was the supreme and unquestioned faith of all loyal subjects.[23] Lucrecia's world was steeped in religious imagery, language, and behavior to a degree scarcely conceivable for people in modern Western societies. The largest buildings in her neighborhood were churches and monasteries. The biggest gatherings she attended were religious processions and services. The most beautiful art she saw was religious art. The rhythms of her daily life and the daily lives of everyone in her local community revolved around religious rituals, ceremonies, and celebrations. A careful reckoning of these influences should be included in any attempt to understand her dreams and how they impacted the people around her.

Lucrecia's story is more than an obscure curiosity of Spanish history. Her powers of dreaming were unusual, but not unique. Other people in various places and times, including people today, have experienced similar phenomena. Perhaps everyone has the potential for such dreams, given the right circumstances. Lucrecia's dreams highlight latent abilities within the human psyche that are real, powerful, and potentially valuable, although they may appear threatening to traditional religious and political authorities. I will speak of her in the pages to come as a *prophetic dreamer*, in a way that does not rely on supernatural causes or magical explanations. Prophetic dreaming, as the term will be developed here, is a natural process in which the cognitive capacities of the sleeping mind work to simulate highly realistic visions of future possibility. Recent findings in scientific psychology can shed new light on Lucrecia's cultivation of an extraordinarily powerful capacity for future-oriented dreaming—so powerful that it shook the throne of the mightiest king in the world.

PART I

THE LIFE AND TRIAL OF A DREAMING PROPHET

Spain in the 16th Century

HISTORICAL
PROLOGUE

508 BCE 🔁 The Rape of Lucretia

Although we know few details about Lucrecia de León's parents, we do know they chose to give their first child the name of a legendary young woman of ancient Rome who was renowned for the supreme purity of her feminine virtue. A name is not destiny, of course. But it reflects something important about the parents' heritage and values, and it hints at their expectations for their child's future. In this case the parents' choice of a name unknowingly foreshadowed a path leading to violence, tragedy, and rebellion against the highest authorities of the state.

The first recorded version of Lucretia's story appears in Livy's *The Early History of Rome*, composed at the beginning of the 1st century CE, in which Lucretia plays a pivotal role in the overthrow of the Tarquin monarchy, leading to the founding of the Roman Republic.[1] According to Livy, Lucretia was the wife of a young nobleman named Lucius. While Lucius was away on a military campaign, Lucretia received a visit from Prince Sextus Tarquinius, the son of the king who ruled over Rome. In the middle of the night, when everyone else in the house was asleep, the prince silently entered Lucretia's room, brandished his sword, and raped her. The next day, after the prince's departure, Lucretia sent an urgent call for her husband and father. They came at once and asked if she was all right. She replied, "No. What can be well with a woman who has lost her honor?"[2] She told them what the prince had done to her, and she begged them to avenge her death. Too shocked by the prince's horrible crime to react, they did not realize what was coming next. She went on, "as for me, I am innocent of fault, but I will take my punishment. Never

ILLUSTRATION 1. *Tarquin and Lucretia*
An oil painting by the Italian artist Titian, commissioned by Philip II and completed in 1571; now in the Fitzwilliam Museum in Cambridge, England.

shall Lucretia provide a precedent for unchaste women to escape what they deserve."[3] With those words, she brought out a hidden dagger and thrust it into her chest, dealing herself a mortal wound.

As her husband and father wailed in grief, Brutus, one of their kinsmen, made a fateful vow. He drew the bloody dagger out of Lucretia's lifeless body and held it aloft, crying, "By this girl's blood—none more chaste till a tyrant wronged her—and by the gods, I swear that with sword and fire, and whatever else can lend strength to my arm, I will pursue Lucius Tarquinius the Proud, his wicked wife, and all his children, and never again will I let them or any other man be King in Rome."[4] The dagger was passed from one man to the next, each of them swearing the same oath. From there they took Lucretia's body to the public market-place, where a large crowd gathered to view her corpse and hear Brutus describe her shameful defilement and lamentable death. The rape and suicide of Lucretia became the spark for a revolution that overthrew the Tarquinian monarchy and opened the way to a new form of republican self-government for the Roman people.

Myth, legend, and factual events are mixed together in this story, which Livy recounted five hundred years after it supposedly happened. We cannot be sure that there really was a woman named Lucretia whose death became a cause for rebellion. But we do know the Roman people *believed* that during a key moment in their history such a woman actually lived and died as Livy described, and we also know her story remained a source of wonder and admiration for many centuries afterward. Ovid, a contemporary of Livy's, wrote a dramatic version of Lucretia's death in his compendium of Roman mythology, *The Book of Days* ("Then she stabbed herself with a blade she had hidden, and, all bloodied, fell at her father's feet. Even then she took care in dying so that she fell with decency, that was her care even in falling"[5]). In *The Divine Comedy*, Dante's sweeping cosmological poem composed in early 14th century Italy, Lucretia occupied an honored place in Limbo, the outermost circle of hell, reserved for famous pagans without sin who were born before the time of Christ. As Dante began his downward descent into the Inferno, he first passed through a gate into a blooming green meadow where he found an impressive gathering of the "master souls of time"—Hector, Aeneas, Caesar, Brutus, Lucretia, and all the other great heroes of ancient Rome.[6]

The story of Lucretia's virtuous self-sacrifice would have been familiar to many people in the Roman Catholic world of late 16th century Spain.[7] Parents who chose this epic figure as a namesake for their firstborn daughter would have forever connected her to an ancient paragon of feminine purity, a haunting example of absolute commitment to the values of family honor and sexual subservience.[8]

711 CE 🐎 The Rape of La Cava

The historical setting of Lucrecia de León's life was shaped by another well-known tale of a chaste young lady betrayed and sexually assaulted by a royal lord. The earliest legends of the Spanish people focused on an incident that occurred in the 8th century, when the Iberian peninsula was ruled by a Christian Visigoth king named Rodrigo.[9] Rodrigo lived in a splendid palace in Toledo, the ancient capital. One day the king noticed the unusual beauty of a maiden in the queen's entourage. Known as La Cava, she was the daughter of Count Julian, a Visigoth nobleman who had entrusted her care and protection to the king. Rodrigo's desire for the young woman reached unbearable proportions, and heedless of his royal responsibilities he ordered her to appear in his private chambers. Despite her pleas and protests Rodrigo raped La Cava, and then forbade her speaking about it with anyone. She went to her father anyway and told him of her disgrace and dishonor. Furious at Rodrigo's brutal violation of his daughter, Count Julian plotted a terrible revenge. He secretly negotiated with Rodrigo's enemies, the Muslim armies from across the Mediterranean Sea in North Africa, and helped them invade the peninsula from the south. Rodrigo's army was slaughtered, Toledo fell without a fight, and frightened Christians scattered into the wild mountainous regions of the north.

This was the beginning of al-Andalus, the period of Islamic rule over the Iberian peninsula lasting more than seven hundred years. In many ways it was a time of tremendous cultural progress in science, philosophy, art, architecture, and education. However, from the perspective of the exiled Christians, the Muslim conquest represented a shattering defeat and humiliating loss of God's favor. They blamed their shameful plight on the moral weakness of the king.[10] God had turned away from them because Rodrigo had failed to uphold the sacred duties of a Christian monarch. If only the Christians could find a leader of pure religious faith and dignity, they believed they could regain what was lost and restore their privileged place in the Lord's favor.

Just a few years later, between 718 and 722, the first battle was fought in what came to be known as the Reconquista, the Christian war to regain control of Spain. A small group of Christians led by the Visigoth nobleman Pelayo emerged from a hidden cave in the northern mountains to attack and defeat a much larger Muslim force at the town of Covadonga. For the next several hundred years the northern-based Christian armies battled fiercely against the Muslims, pushing the invaders farther and farther south, each victory encouraging their belief that God's favor was returning.

The legend of La Cava and Rodrigo remained a central narrative during the Reconquista, and over time the moral center of the story shifted from Rodrigo's betrayal to La Cava's seductiveness. As documented by historian Patricia Grieve, medieval versions of the story transformed La Cava into the culprit, not the victim, and emphasized her irresistibly lustful overtures toward Rodrigo. In the process, female desire was turned into a political and religious threat of cataclysmic proportions. Grieve says, "in the story's later, more misogynistic manifestations, beginning in the sixteenth century, she [La Cava] used her sexuality shamelessly, tempting the man who was powerless against such seduction. . . . For all intents and purposes, she is the Eve of Spain, a Helen of Troy with a Christian moral dimension added to her."[11]

One of Lucrecia's dreams makes a specific reference to Rodrigo, so she was familiar to some extent with the legend of La Cava and its message about the dangers of unbridled female sexuality.[12] She was also familiar, as every Spanish Christian would be, with the heroic Pelayo and his divinely blessed crusade in quest of their people's redemption. All three of these mythic characters from the early history of Spain helped to shape the development of Lucrecia's dire dreams of her country's future.

1469 🔊 The Marriage of Isabella and Ferdinand

One of the great puzzles of European history is how Spain, a small and undistinguished country on the outer fringe of the continent, managed to rise in a few short decades to became the largest imperial power the world had ever known. The seeds of this improbable ascent were first sown in 1469, when Isabella, an 18-year-old princess of Castile, chose to marry her second cousin Ferdinand II, the 17-year-old King of Aragon and Sicily. During their thirty years of rule together Isabella and Ferdinand forged a nation of bold, aggressive, and extremely religious people who were confident that God intended them to rule the world. And for a glorious, bloody period of about a century, they did exactly that.

None of this was apparent in 1469, however. The immediate result of Isabella's marital choice was international outrage and civil war. The other suitors for her hand—Prince Charles of France and Prince Alfonso V of Portugal—were furious at her reckless and headstrong decision, which she made despite the opposition of her older half-brother Enrique, the king of Castile. Many noble families stayed loyal to Enrique in denouncing the marriage, while others pledged their support to Isabella and her new spouse. The outcome of their power struggle was in doubt for ten war-torn years, until the military forces of Isabella and Ferdinand finally prevailed and consolidated all the Christian realms under one joint monarchy. Thus began an amazingly prosperous reign that launched Spain on its course toward the imperial heights of the Siglo del Oro.

Once their royal legitimacy and governing authority had been established, Isabella and Ferdinand devoted themselves to the task of fighting the Muslim forces in the southern province of Granada. The Reconquista had successfully liberated many northern towns and regions of the country (León became Christian again in 856, and Toledo was taken back in 1086), but progress had ground to a halt, and there was a real danger the tide of military momentum would turn again. Granada remained a Moorish stronghold whose rulers were becoming increasingly brazen in their cross-border attacks on nearby Christian towns. Like all Christian rulers in Europe, Isabella and Ferdinand were anxiously aware of Ottoman Turkish armies pressing hard from the east. If the Turks formed an alliance with the Moors in Granada and launched an invasion of the Iberian peninsula from the south, the Spanish Christians would be quickly overwhelmed. Isabella and Ferdinand came to the grim conclusion that there was only one way to secure the future safety of their people: they must destroy the Muslim kingdom of Granada.

The ensuing savagery and slaughter inflamed passions on both sides, as bloody attacks were followed by even bloodier reprisals. While Ferdinand led the troops in the field, Isabella worked on gathering intelligence, devising strategy, and boosting morale. To keep her people united and motivated, the queen emphasized the religious justification for the fight. Their cause was God's cause, she insisted, the cause of good against evil. By driving the Moors from Spain they were purifying the land of infidels and restoring the ancestral rule of Christians after more than seven centuries of shameful Muslim occupation.

By 1492, the Reconquista was complete. The Moors in Spain were finally defeated, and Isabella and Ferdinand triumphantly entered their capital city of Granada and took possession of the Alhambra, the famed palace of Muslim rulers for hundreds of years. The crusade that Pelayo had launched in the early 8th century had finally reached a victorious conclusion.

In that same year, to guarantee the religious purity they had fought so hard to achieve, the queen and king announced the Edict of Expulsion, a royal decree banishing the practice of the Jewish religion and ordering all Jews to leave the country. No more chances were to be taken with non-Christians living in Spain. Anyone who was not a true and actively practicing Catholic was banished under threat of execution.

The fall of Granada and the Edict of Expulsion would be enough to mark this as a pivotal year in Spanish history. But equally as important for the country's future was Isabella's decision in late 1492 to provide financial support and royal sanction for an expedition led by Cristobal

Colon, whom we know as Christopher Columbus, in search of a western trade route to the Far East. The astounding success of his expedition—he discovered the "New World" of Central and South America—opened up vast new horizons for Spain to acquire territory, seize treasure, and spread the Catholic faith. The queen took special interest in the latter goal. As soon as Columbus returned from his first voyage and reported his amazing discoveries, Isabella began planning for his next expedition, with an emphasis on taking advantage of the religious opportunities when encountering non-European populations:

> Isabella gave him [Columbus] specific instructions for the trip. The first and most important point—and the one that she most fully elaborated—called for the religious instruction of the Indians, whom she said Columbus should "by all ways and means . . . strive and endeavor to win over," to convert them to "our Holy Catholic faith," teaching them Spanish so they would understand the religious instruction they would receive. To that end, she sent a contingent of twelve priests to begin the missionary work.[13]

Isabella and Ferdinand led their people in a nearly seamless transition from the national task of fighting Moorish invaders to the international task of colonizing the New World. The same principles that enabled their ultimate victory in the Reconquista—religious fervor and military ferocity—were now applied to the imperial settlement of overseas territories in the Americas. Although no one yet knew the full magnitude of all the riches waiting to be plundered, it already appeared to the Spanish people that God was rewarding them for their religious devotion by giving them a fresh new continent to rule. They threw themselves into the colonizing mission with gusto.

1478 🦌 The Spanish Inquisition

Not all Spaniards were happy with the doctrine of *limpieza*, or blood purity, as the ultimate test of Christian faith and national loyalty. Many of the old noble families of Spain had long relationships with both Muslims and Jews, financially and by marriage, and they opposed the expulsion of people purely on the grounds of their religious beliefs. The Spanish nobility were certainly not pluralists in the modern sense of the term, but their self-interest led them to tolerate non-Catholics as long as they obeyed the laws like everyone else.

This opened a social space for the *conversos*, Jewish people who had renounced their old faith and proclaimed their acceptance of the Catholic Church and its teachings. The large number of *conversos* would seem to represent a victory for Catholicism, but instead it generated resentment and suspicion among the public. Many of the new converts, now officially Christians like everyone else, took the opportunity to fill lucrative government jobs that were previously forbidden to them as Jews. Many other *conversos* continued to practice their old religion despite a public pretense of Catholicism. The "old Christians" of pure blood were outraged by the privilege and hypocrisy of the *conversos*, and they demanded action from Isabella and Ferdinand in their royal capacity as defenders of the faith. So in 1478, the queen and king empowered a special agency—the Tribunal del Santo Oficio de la Inquisición (Tribunal of the Holy Office of the Inquisition)—and gave it the task of investigating people accused of religious subversion.

As the Spanish empire grew, so grew the power of the Inquisition. Both were driven by the same goal of asserting absolute Catholic control over the greatest possible range of physical and spiritual territory. The officials of the Inquisition would have more than one hundred years to hone their craft before Lucrecia de León came to their attention.

The legal framework of the Inquisition derived from ancient Roman law and its emphasis on personal confession as the surest proof of criminal guilt.[14] Witness testimony was important, but a confession by the accused was the best way to assure everyone involved that justice had been done. In practice, this encouraged the use of extreme measures, including gruesome forms of torture, to coerce people under investigation to admit the truth of the charges against them, thus settling the case in a definitive manner. In Rome the worst crime of all was treason, a crime against the state, and it was punishable by death. The Spanish Inquisition merged political treason with religious heresy as the most heinous of misdeeds. To rebel against the Church was equivalent to rebelling against the state, and it deserved thorough investigation, with the guilty parties receiving the harshest punishment. This line of thinking fueled the Inquisition's aggressive and ever-expanding drive to root out religiously deviant behavior wherever it might be found.

It served the Inquisition's mission to foster a general sense of anxious vigilance and paranoia among the populace. The seemingly limitless power of the Inquisition made this easy to accomplish. Its agents could arrest people without warning, seize their property, and jail them in isolation for an indefinite time. Automatically presumed guilty on secret charges, the arrested individual was not told what the accusations were or who had made them. Instead the Inquisitors demanded that the accused people confess all their sins and name any accomplices who helped them in their heretical activities. The process was conceived as a rough but necessary form of pastoral care: the accused person had strayed from God's laws, and it was now the job of the Inquisition to bring the wayward individual back into alignment with the Church. If torture was required to achieve this goal, that was the choice of the accused, and it was performed with the same bureaucratic precision that governed all aspects of the Inquisitorial system.

The vast majority of prisoners were found guilty and punished in a public ceremony known as an *auto de fé*, or "act of faith," usually held in a large town plaza to maximize attendance by the local residents. The heretics, wearing white penitential robes and caps (*sanbenitos*), were paraded through the streets and then brought before the assembled crowd. After their crimes were read aloud they were forced to repent their sins and accept their punishment—a punishment intended to save their souls, even if it meant whipping, hanging, or burning their bodies.

1527 ⇗ The Birth of Philip II

King Philip II, the great-grandson of Isabella and Ferdinand and heir to a vast imperial domain, played a central role in Lucrecia's dreams. The dangers he faced as ruler of Spain, especially toward the end of his forty-year reign, provided much of the raw material for her dreaming imagination.

Through a tangled web of royal scheming, marital maneuvering, and fortuitous pregnancies, Isabella and Ferdinand's third child, Juana, inherited the Spanish crown. In 1498, Juana married Prince Philip I, the son of the Hapsburg emperor Maximilian I of Austria. The combination of their royal domains was initially intended to create a stronger defense against their mutual enemy, France. But the full might of the military machine known as the Holy Roman Empire emerged only when their oldest son, Charles, assumed the throne and became the king of Spain (Charles I) in 1516 and Holy Roman Emperor (Charles V) in 1519. By this time Spanish ships had established a regular stream of commerce with the Americas, bringing back huge quantities of looted gold and silver that Charles used to fund his mercenary troops in various battles around the empire, including fights with the brutal Ottomans in the east, the heretical Protestants to the north, and the rebellious Comuneros in Spain itself. The Comuneros were a group of traditionalists centered in Toledo who were angry at Charles for spending too much time away from Spain, lavishing his attention on the cosmopolitan cities of the Netherlands and Italy while wasting money and lives in foreign wars that mattered little to the Spanish people.[15] Their protests were fruitless; Charles sent a military force into Castile in 1521 to destroy the Comuneros' rebellion and execute its leaders.

Charles relied heavily on the Inquisition to help him maintain control in Spain while he pressed ahead with warfare on other fronts. Some of the most horrendous massacres of *conversos* by the Holy Office occurred during his reign.[16] Ensuring religious purity at home made it possible to concentrate his efforts on combating threats to religious purity abroad.

When his son Philip was born, Charles carefully groomed the boy as his successor. As a child Philip was cared for primarily by his mother, Isabella of Portugal, and tutored intensively in academic and military subjects. In 1543, at the age of 16, he assumed command of Spain on behalf of his father. This experience gave Philip early and valuable training in the practical arts of governing. From the start he ruled in a thoughtful and measured fashion, never acting rashly or impulsively, always seeking as much information as possible before making a decision. On one point, however, Philip never hesitated: his trust in the Inquisition. Charles made sure his son understood the importance of the Inquisition as guardian of the faith and defender of domestic security, and throughout his life Philip fully supported the Holy Office and its heretic-hunting pursuits.

In 1545, Philip married Princess Maria of Portugal, but she died in childbirth after bearing their son, Carlos. In 1554, at his father's strategic behest, Philip journeyed across the English Channel to London, where he married the English Queen, Mary Tudor. In so doing, Philip added the title King of England to what would become a lengthy list of royal appellations. Charles had long hoped to combine Spain, England, and the Netherlands into one cohesive Catholic realm. The union of Philip and Mary finally transformed that vision into a reality. At last, the emperor felt confident he could successfully transfer power to his son. In 1556, Charles abdicated the throne and granted the majority of his vast territories, including Spain, to Philip.

Despite his father's best intentions, Philip II's reign began in crisis and despair. All the riches plundered from the Americas were not enough to support Charles' endless wars, and Philip quickly realized the empire's finances were in a catastrophic condition.[17] Just a few months into his rule, Philip was forced to declare bankruptcy so he could restructure the huge debts Charles had incurred before abdication. Then, in 1558, came a double loss: his father died, and so did his wife, Queen Mary, who passed away without leaving Philip any heirs. This meant the English crown passed from Mary to Princess Elizabeth, a Tudor and a Protestant. Meanwhile, the Inquisition arrested several groups of people in Spain and accused them of being secret Protestants—a shocking infiltration of heresy into the heart of his homeland. Suddenly Philip found himself a widower, fatherless, financially ruined, and religiously threatened from within and without.

1561 ᴣ A New Capital City

Philip's plan to assert greater control over his many domains started with the creation of a new center of imperial authority. For centuries the kings and queens of Spain had moved the royal court from one city to another every few months so they could visit their subjects, settle local disputes, confirm loyalties, and levy taxes. In 1561, Philip decided the growing power and expanse of his territorial holdings required the building of a permanent capital with the grandeur to rival any other city in Europe. For this purpose he chose Madrid, at that point a modest town of about nine thousand inhabitants with a settlement history going back to Roman times, located in the middle of the Iberian peninsula along the Manzanares river.[18] Like his father, Philip was enchanted by the art and architecture of Italy and the Netherlands, and he wanted to create a similar aura of magnificence here in the center of Spain. His designs were aided by a new influx of silver from the Americas, which strengthened the royal finances and gave him the resources to move ahead quickly with an ambitious plan of grand construction projects.[19]

In short order the forests surrounding Madrid were cut down to provide space for urban expansion and raw material for new buildings. The population grew rapidly with the sudden arrival of thousands of construction workers, court officials, diplomats, priests, bankers, and merchants, along with the royal family and all their servants and attendants. By the time Lucrecia was a teenager, the city's population was approaching eighty thousand people.[20] All the money Philip spent on glorious palaces and magnificent churches did not, however, include an adequate system of infrastructure to provide sanitary living conditions for so many inhabitants, nor much of a public safety system to protect ordinary people from crime. The filthy streets and sewage stench of Madrid became legendary, and nights were a dangerous time of lawless violence and shadowy misbehavior.

The arrangements in Madrid worked well for Philip, in any case. He built several smaller palaces in the country outside the city where he routinely went to enjoy hunting, horse riding, and other noble pursuits. He also started construction on an immense monastery that he initially planned as a tomb for his father's remains. Known as San Lorenzo de El Escorial, or just El Escorial, the monastery became one of the greatest religious structures in Christendom. Designed jointly by the king and his royal architect, Juan Bautista de Toledo, it was placed in a barren

ILLUSTRATION 2. *Philip II*
An oil painting by the Italian artist Sophonisba Angussola, completed in 1565; now in the Prado Museum in Madrid, Spain.

mountainous region thirty miles away from Madrid. The Escorial would eventually house the king's enormous collection of religious art and sacred relics. The more Philip aged, the more time he spent at the Escorial as a refuge from the pressures of court and a means of rejuvenating his faith.

Philip had time to focus on architectural plans for his capital city and the Escorial because one of Spain's worst threats had been temporarily neutralized. A peace treaty with France had just gone into effect, and as part of the agreement Philip had married 14-year-old Princess Elisabeth of Valois, daughter of King Henry II. The new security of Spain's northeastern border with its historic rival allowed Philip to concentrate his military efforts on fighting back the Ottoman Turks in the Mediterranean, who were attacking Christian merchant vessels and plundering coastal cities. During these sea battles the Spanish naval forces continued to grow in size, skill, and tactical experience, giving Philip a much stronger hand to play in other conflicts—which were soon in coming.

1568 ⚓ Philip Besieged

Just like his father, Philip gave abundant military support to the Roman Catholic Church in its holy war against the Protestants. But the fight did not go well. Large swaths of northern Europe were already lost to the heresies of Luther and Calvin. Elizabeth, the Protestant Queen of England, was growing in power, and religious rebels in the Netherlands were refusing to obey the Spanish troops occupying their towns. Mass violence broke out in 1566 during the Beeldenstorm, or "Iconoclastic Fury," that convulsed cities all over the Netherlands, with Protestant mobs destroying Catholic churches, statues, and monuments while local authorities stood by and watched. Suddenly a threat of heresy had transformed into a full-scale revolt in one of Philip's most cherished imperial realms. The prospect of losing this region, his father's favorite, to the Protestants was intolerable, and the king sent a message to the Pope promising immediate action: "you can assure His Holiness that rather than suffer the least injury to religion and the service of God, I would lose all my states and a hundred lives if I had them, for I do not intend to rule over heretics."[21]

Philip's response to the problem was straightforward: more troops, more repression, more executions. Unfortunately, these measures had the opposite effect to the one intended. The rebellion became an open, ugly, and very costly war, requiring the deployment of enormous resources in a distant and hostile land. The king's leading military commander, the Duke of Alba, had proven his ability to impose enormous suffering on the Dutch population, but he had also proven his failure in preventing the Protestant revolt from spreading and gathering strength. By 1568, Philip could no longer avoid the realization that the only way to preserve his rule over the Netherlands was a long and brutal military occupation.

The same year also witnessed a violent revolt in Granada by the *moriscos*, Moorish people who had converted from Islam to Catholicism. Like the Jews who became *conversos*, the formerly Muslim *moriscos* had found ways to assimilate into Spanish society. But tensions following the Reconquista had never really gone away, and in 1568, vicious fighting broke out in cities throughout southern Spain, threatening once again to reverse the Christian gains and give the Turks an opening for invasion. Philip sent troops to Granada to destroy the rebellion and subdue the population by any means necessary.

The worst blows for Philip in this tumultuous year were personal. His succession plans had always centered on his son Carlos, born from his first marriage. But Carlos, now 23 years old, had become increasingly erratic and mentally deranged over time, to the point of disrupting court business and interfering with the king's military commanders. Philip finally decided to arrest Carlos and forcibly confine him in isolation in his royal quarters. Six months later, from causes still unknown, Carlos was dead.

Then, just two months after that, Philip's wife Elisabeth, whom by all accounts he had truly grown to love, died in childbirth. She had borne the king five children, only two of whom survived, both daughters. Philip, now a widower three times over and with no male heirs, once again found himself on the brink of financial ruin and at war with heretics inside and outside the country. It must have seemed in 1568 that nothing had improved since he took over the throne from his father twelve years earlier.

But Philip could look to the future with some confidence, knowing he had several valuable resources at his disposal. The seemingly endless flow of treasure from the Americas gave him financial flexibility and room for political maneuvering. His naval forces were growing in size, strength, and experience, developing into a major military asset that would enhance the king's power in several regions of his empire. And Philip always knew he could depend on the Inquisition. As many historians have noted, the total number of people executed by the Holy Office diminished toward the end of the sixteenth century. This did not, however, mean the Inquisitors had lessened their pursuit of heretics. On the contrary, it meant the Inquisition had succeeded in stamping out the worst deviations from Catholic orthodoxy and imposing a strict system of control over the country's religious beliefs and practices. The Inquisition could now turn its gaze to subtler forms of heresy, less obvious but for that reason more dangerous to church and state.

CHAPTER 1

EARLY LIFE

1568, October ⤞ The Birth of Lucrecia

Ana Ordoñez, wife of Alonso Franco de León, gave birth to their first child in October of 1568. I have already discussed one of the few known facts about the couple: their choice of a name for their daughter. Alonso originally came from Valdepeñas, a small town in southern Spain only recently liberated from the Muslims in the final push of the Reconquista.[1] Born in the 1540s, Alonso was proud of being an "Old Christian," a Spaniard of pure blood with no "taint" of Jewish or Muslim ancestry. This suggests that Ana, too, was an Old Christian; Alonso would not likely have chosen a wife from any other background. He worked in the court as a *solicitador*, a kind of legal advisor operating between the royal government and the bankers of Genoa (then a prosperous city-state in Italy) who financed Philip's imperial ventures. Although Alonso probably did not have a university education, his work required a great deal of administrative knowledge and awareness of current international affairs. It put him in the thick of Madrid's political and economic discussions, giving him much familiarity with the inner workings—and weaknesses— of Philip's empire.

Ana Ordoñez was born around 1550 in a small town in northern Spain, where the Reconquista would have driven out the Moors many centuries earlier. This background might have burnished her Old Christian credentials in Alonso's eyes. Nothing is known of how the two of them met, but they were already married and living in Madrid when Lucrecia was born. Alonso's work required long periods of travel away from Madrid, so he was not always present to enforce his paternal authority, giving Ana more latitude than a wife usually had for making decisions about the family.

The young couple rented an apartment on the first floor of a modest, newly built house near the center of Madrid, in the parish of San Sebastián. The owner of the house was Lady Jane Dormer, also known as the Duchess of Feria, an English expatriate and well-connected member of the Spanish social elite who played a key role in the later development of Lucrecia's prophetic career.[2] The Leóns' apartment was not large, but it afforded enough space for Lucrecia to have a bedroom of her own with a window looking onto the street. The neighborhood of San Sebastián was filled with recently constructed buildings that provided housing for the city's surging population, and it attracted a diverse and dynamic group of residents. Among the Leóns' neighbors were artists, craftsmen, merchants, and shopkeepers, along with minor court officials and members of various religious orders. The Augustinian convent of La Magdalena (Mary Magdalene) stood directly across the street from Lucrecia's bedroom window. The great playwright Félix Lope de Vega y Carpio, known today as Lope de Vega, was born in the parish in 1562, six years before Lucrecia, and the two of them very likely attended the same worship services in the San Sebastián church.

As noted earlier, Madrid's public infrastructure did not develop nearly as fast as its population. Water for the growing number of residents came from streams, wells, and the modestly sized Manzanares river. Ana's domestic tasks likely included carrying water from one of these sources back to their house on a regular basis. The major avenues of Madrid—the ones most traveled by the king and his retinue—had cobblestone surfaces, but most of the city's streets were bare dirt pathways worn into dusty ruts and grooves by the frequent traffic of people, carts, and horses and other domestic animals. As for sewage and waste disposal, most people used chamber pots to relieve themselves in their homes, after which they emptied the contents out of their windows into the street. The hot, arid climate of central Spain meant that there were few rains to cleanse the streets of accumulated waste, creating a constant health hazard for the city's population. The dangers were especially acute for pregnant women and young children, whose mortality rates were alarmingly high. No one knew the sad truth of this more than King Philip. His family always received the best medical care available at the time, yet three of his wives died in childbirth or soon thereafter, and only four of the eleven children they bore him survived beyond the first few years of life.

Alonso, Ana, and their infant daughter would not have had an easy or comfortable existence in the Madrid of 1568. But in many ways their timing could not have been better. The city was rapidly transforming itself into the wealthy center of a mighty global empire. They set down roots in Madrid at just the moment when a dramatic burst of urban growth was taking off and Spain's international power was soaring toward its zenith.

1571 🦓 The Battle of Lepanto

As much trouble as he had with the Protestants and *moriscos*, Philip faced a threat of an entirely different order from the Ottoman Turks, whose naval forces were wreaking havoc throughout the Mediterranean and threatening to overwhelm the Christian lands to their empire's west. In 1570, the Turks seized control of the island of Cyprus, a protectorate of the Italian city-state of Venice. Philip and the other Catholic rulers realized the time had come to confront the Ottoman forces before they launched a full-scale invasion of Europe.

After lengthy preparations and intricate tactical maneuvering, the two great navies finally met on October 7, 1571, in the Gulf of Lepanto off western Greece. Each side had more than two hundred vessels loaded with cannons and archers, and also well-armed troops ready to leap aboard enemy ships and engage in hand-to-hand combat. The fighting lasted all day, and by sunset the outcome was clear. The Catholic League forces had crushed the Ottoman fleet, seizing or destroying almost 90 percent of their vessels and killing, injuring, or capturing more than 30,000 Turks. The Catholics suffered the loss of 8,000 troops and only ten galley ships.[3]

Even though the Ottomans rebuilt their fleet a year later and continued to harass Catholic coastal holdings in the Mediterranean, their westward push had been decisively blocked at Lepanto. Most importantly, the Ottoman aura of invincibility had been shattered. After countless years of terrifying and seemingly unstoppable Ottoman expansion, the Catholic forces had finally defeated the Turks in a major battle.

When the news finally reached Philip, he reacted with great joy and gave abundant thanks to God. According to historian Henry Kamen, "over the next few days all Madrid exploded in an orgy of celebration."[4] Lucrecia, who was three years old at the time, may have had a dim awareness of the triumphant revelry consuming the city. Her parents would certainly have joined in the public festivities organized by the king to commemorate the battle. He and the people of Madrid were celebrating not only a military success but a religious revelation of their national destiny. The miraculous result of the battle was interpreted as the latest and most powerful sign yet that God was on Spain's side, supporting Philip's imperial mission and encouraging him and his subjects to continue their aggressive efforts to expand the domain of the Roman Catholic faith. As historian J. H. Elliott put it, "the spectacular victory of the Christian forces at Lepanto in 1571 was to epitomize for contemporaries all that was most glorious in the crusade against Islam. It was an eternal source . . . of grateful wonder to the millions who saw in it a divine deliverance of Christendom from the power of the oppressor."[5]

One of the Spanish soldiers wounded during the fighting was a poor 24-year-old wanderer from a rural Castilian family, Miguel de Cervantes. A proud volunteer in Philip's army, the future author of *Don Quixote* was shot three times during the Battle of Lepanto, and permanently lost the use of his left hand. For the rest of his life he considered his injury a badge of honor and a noble reminder of his participation in "the grandest occasion the past or present has seen, or the future can hope to see."[6]

Cervantes' life has more than coincidental relevance for the study of Lucrecia's dreams. He was another highly creative resident of her neighborhood in Madrid, living from 1582 to 1585 in the same parish of San Sebastián where Lucrecia's family dwelled (during the period when he was aged 35 to 38 years old and she was aged 14 to 17). We do not know if they ever met, but their daily lives surely overlapped within the bustling community of their parish. Many of the narrative themes that make *Don Quixote* so distinctive and powerful also appear in Lucrecia's story: the dangerous interaction of dreaming and waking, the ambiguous symptoms of madness, the shifting boundaries of religious heresy, and the tragic dignity of staying true to a heartfelt belief about what is right and just. Cervantes wrote *Don Quixote* about the cultural world of late 16th century Spain, the same culture that shaped Lucrecia's waking existence and dreaming imagination.

1570s ⇗ A Time of Wonders

Cervantes' great novel centers on a Spanish gentleman whose mind becomes so addled by reading books of chivalry that he decides to become a knight himself and sets out in search of adventures like those found in the 16th century stories called "histories." Part of the novel's satire involves making fun of people like Don Quixote who believed in the literal truth of everything written in these books. Spain's most popular story of this kind, *Amadís of Gaul*, was first published in the early 1500s and featured a courageous and indestructible knight who journeyed to magical lands, battled wizards, rescued damsels, fought dragons, and heroically defended the Christian faith. Throughout the 16th century Spaniards read *Amadís* and other chivalric stories with great enthusiasm, just as Cervantes described in *Don Quixote*. Did they believe the stories were historically accurate? Perhaps some of them did, but their views of reality may have been more complex and sophisticated than that. Everyone living in Spain at this time had good reasons for keeping an open mind about extraordinary events and unexpected wonders. In addition to stories about Amadís and other epic heroes, they were also hearing incredible firsthand reports from New World *conquistadors* that rivaled anything in the books of chivalry: brave Spaniards sailing through uncharted waters, discovering pagan temples filled with gold and silver, and defeating huge enemy armies with miraculous ease. The stories from the Americas were no less fantastic than Don Quixote's beloved tales of knights and giants. This was a time when anything seemed possible, especially for those who stayed true to God and Spain.

The Catholic Church made sure this sense of expanded reality stayed within theologically acceptable boundaries. In contrast to the Protestants and their iconoclastic attacks on art, Roman Catholic teachings after the Council of Trent in 1563 reaffirmed the importance of artistic imagery as a legitimate means of stimulating people's faith in God and educating the public about Church doctrine. The same idea applied to other physical expressions of divine presence, such as shrines, relics, and holy festivals—they were all acceptable as long as they did not violate official Church teachings.[7] Although primarily intended to protect against inappropriate artistic content, the Church's rules allowed people to approach the divine via special kinds of sensory experience. The creative power of the visual imagination was thus free to express itself within these closely monitored boundaries. Art, especially visual art, was accepted by Catholic authorities insofar as it served a holy purpose.

For people living in late 16th century Madrid the primary source of marvels and wonders was the Bible itself, filled with supernatural beings, miraculous events, and magical powers going far beyond the ordinary sphere of daily life. At a time when failure to believe in such things could have life-or-death consequences, people were strongly motivated to make a public show of accepting the seemingly impossible phenomena described in the Bible. Yet fear alone did not shape their expansive worldview. Many people of the late 16th century saw the incredible rise of Spain's global power as an inspiring sign of God's active presence in their lives and divine support for their national cause. The strength of the empire became a convincing theological proof of God's existence.

Not everyone felt so optimistic, however. Many people of deep religious faith held much darker views of the heavenly signs. Apocalyptic anxieties grew during this time, not only in Spain but throughout Europe. After decades of bloody religious warfare, deadly plagues, and vicious foreign attacks, more and more people came to believe they were living in the end times as foretold in the biblical Book of Revelation, the final days of earthly destruction before the divine judgment that would send them to heaven or hell. Those who held these beliefs took an eager interest in any omens or portents that might indicate God's will for the future.

Around this time, Lucrecia began to dream. She was 6 or 7 years old, according to testimony from her mother and other neighbors, putting the date between 1574 and 1575. The first of her four siblings had just been born, so she was no longer the only child in the house. Perhaps Lucrecia had dreams at earlier ages, but this was the first time when others began to notice. Soon thereafter she gained a reputation in the neighborhood as someone with a highly active dreaming imagination.

We do not know what exactly Lucrecia heard or learned about the traditional dream beliefs of her culture, so we cannot be sure whether or not these beliefs directly influenced her experiences. However, she was raised in a densely populated neighborhood in the capital city of an international empire that took great pride in its historical heritage, so it seems reasonable to presume that she became familiar over time with a set of commonsense ideas about dreaming shared for centuries among the people of medieval and early modern Europe.

Included among these ideas were the following: dreams can be caused by supernatural entities, both good and evil; some dreams offer accurate glimpses of the future; other dreams reflect nothing more than the natural functions of the body; strong emotions or preoccupations in waking life can prompt dreams revolving around those concerns; a few dreams express valuable insights about social or political concerns, especially in times of collective crisis; dreams can help in the treatment of people with mental and physical illnesses; interpreting dreams is difficult and potentially dangerous.[8]

These ideas did not constitute a formal theory of dreaming. Rather, they expressed the general assumptions held by many people at this time, assumptions that had historical roots reaching far back into classical antiquity and the earliest civilizations of Mesopotamia.[9]

The most influential model of dreaming during this era was devised by Macrobius, a Roman scholar of the late 4th and early 5th centuries.[10] Born as a pagan, Macrobius converted to Christianity and wrote several works about philosophy, religion, and language. His most popular and long-lasting book was the *Commentary on the Dream of Scipio*, in which he outlined a five-category system of dreams.[11] First was the *insomnium*, a dream rooted in mundane physical experiences, with no meaning or significance. Second was the *visium*, which occurs in the spectral state between waking and sleeping, and which seems meaningful but is actually false and insignificant. Third was the *somnium*, which occupied a middle position between the deceptions of the first two categories and the revelations of the higher two. A *somnium* may have some truth, but only in ambiguous, veiled forms that require interpretation. Fourth was the *visio*, a true revelation about something in the mundane physical world. And fifth was the *oraculum*, the clearest and most trustworthy type of dream, usually involving a visitation from an otherworldly character: "A parent, or a pious or revered man, or a priest, or even a god clearly reveals what will or will not transpire, and what action to take or to avoid."[12]

Beyond this typology, Macrobius actually said very little about the nature and functions of dreaming. Most of the *Commentary on the Dream of Scipio* has nothing to do with dreams, focusing instead on lengthy discussions of cosmology, astronomy, and Neo-Platonic philosophy. And yet for the next one thousand years, this text would be regarded throughout Europe as the primary authority on dreaming.[13]

Why was there virtually no innovation or development in Western dream theory for such a long period of time? One major reason was the anxious hostility of Christian church officials toward dreaming. In the early years of the tradition, dreams were actually welcomed as expressions of God's presence in people's lives, especially for converts (newly born to the faith) and martyrs (about to die for the faith).[14] But the more institutionalized the Christian Church became in its policies and doctrines, the less it cared about dreaming, and the more suspicious it became of people who did show interest in their dreams. Many of the early Christians who were cast out of their churches as heretics (the Gnostics, the Montanists, the followers of Simon Magus) were accused of believing in the revelatory power of their own dreams.[15] Church authorities soon decided to forbid "divination by dreams" as a pagan practice comparable to astrology and necromancy, possibly indicative of witchcraft. A specific prohibition against using books of dream interpretation was included by Gratian, a 12th century theologian, in his widely used legal text known as the *Decretum*.[16]

Despite the official attitude of hostility and skepticism, many Christian laypeople could not help but take a lively interest in their own dreams and the dreams of other people in their tradition. Even Church authorities had to admit the Bible was filled with inspiring examples of heaven-sent dream revelations. Stories of the great interpreters Joseph and Daniel encouraged people to heed their dreams for possible glimpses of things to come. Many Catholic saints had powerful dream experiences during the course of their lives, indicating that revelatory dreaming had not ended in biblical times but still remained possible for people of true faith in the present day.[17]

Again, we cannot be sure how many of these beliefs and practices directly influenced Lucrecia or her family. But we do know they lived in the profoundly pious Catholic community of late 16th century Madrid, which makes it very likely they faced the same conflict as other Christians throughout Europe at this time. Historian Steven Kruger has described the medieval dream dilemma as follows: "the dreamer who believes in the possibility of both divinely-inspired and demonic dreams thus finds him- or herself in a difficult position, both attracted to and repelled from dreams. The only possible response is one of extreme caution, taking care neither to believe nor to distrust dreams too easily.[18]

It can hardly be surprising, given this fearful and uncertain religious context, that Lucrecia's parents sensed problems ahead. Lucrecia later testified to the Inquisition that "since I was small and began to understand these dreams, my parents beat me for talking about them."[19]

1580, October 🐎 The Death of Queen Anna

Portugal, Spain's Iberian neighbor to the west, fell into a bitter and destabilizing political crisis in 1578 when its ruler, Sebastian I, died without leaving an heir. Philip eventually decided he should end the chaos by asserting his own claim to the Portuguese throne, and he began assembling an army to march on Lisbon and settle the matter. In 1580, he, his wife (Queen Anna), and his military leaders gathered in the town of Badajoz, near Spain's western border, to review an impressive assembly of 47,000 troops ready to invade Portugal and lay siege to its capital city.[20]

Meanwhile, a deadly strain of influenza had broken out and was spreading rapidly across Spain, causing hundreds of deaths in Madrid and elsewhere.[21] The king and many of his advisors fell ill, too, as the epidemic struck people throughout the country.

Lucrecia, who was 12 years old at the time, had a dream about a royal funeral procession in Badajoz. We know of this dream because her father described it during his testimony to the Inquisition.[22] Given that Alonso was the person most adamantly opposed to his daughter's prophetic career, his account has a high degree of credibility. He told the Inquisitors that he asked Lucrecia if the funeral in her dream was for the king, and she said no, it was not. For some reason this reply angered Alonso. He ordered her to stop having such dreams and threatened to punish her if she continued to do so. This was not the first nor the last time her father expressed extreme hostility toward her dreaming. Yet Alonso also told the Inquisitors he could not help feeling amazement when a few weeks later Queen Anna died in Badajoz, another victim of the epidemic.

It seems unlikely Alonso would make up a story like this in front of the Inquisition, so we can reasonably assume the dream was related by Lucrecia as he said it was. That does not necessarily imply it involved some kind of supernatural prediction. Lucrecia would have known in waking life about people getting sick and dying in Madrid and elsewhere, and she probably knew, given her father's close involvement with the court, about Philip's campaign against Portugal and his base of operations in Badajoz. The dream did not specify when the funeral would occur or who among the royal family would die, although she had apparently ruled out the king himself. This allowed a large degree of interpretive freedom in applying the dream to several possible candidates from the royal family.

In any case, his daughter's experience clearly unnerved Alonso. The disturbing impact of this dream on him and anyone else who heard about it (which may have included Lucrecia's mother, her siblings, and other people in the neighborhood) should not be underestimated. Lucrecia was now marked as having a strange and uncanny ability that touched on the vital concerns of the nation. It was one thing to have vivid dreams; it was quite another to have seemingly prophetic visions of death in the royal family. A girl who dreamed of such lofty affairs put herself and her family at potentially grave risk.

1586–1587 🐦 The Royal Palace

Lucrecia and her four younger siblings all survived through childhood, something of a demographic miracle. The León family still lived in the same apartment, which must have started to feel crowded as the children grew, although Lucrecia continued to have her own bedroom. She never received any formal education, and she spent most of her time helping her mother with housework and performing small paid jobs in the neighborhood. Despite a lack of schooling, she had many sources of information that shaped her understanding of the world and influenced her dreams. Simply listening to what the adults talked about in her own home would have been immensely educational. The Leóns' living room was a vibrant node in Madrid's wide-ranging network of political gossip. The family hosted a constant stream of neighbors, friends, relatives, and visitors who shared news from the court and around the world. Alonso's work put him in close touch with bankers from Italy and other parts of Europe, and in his better moods he explained aspects of the empire's finances to Lucrecia. Ana's sister lived in Mexico, and she asked people traveling back from the colonies to visit the León household; they would have brought both messages and reports of the New World. A child who paid close attention to these discussions could learn a great deal about global affairs and royal intrigues, even with no formal education and little ability to read or write.

The renewed Catholic emphasis on religious art encouraged the display of beautiful paintings and statues in public spaces all over the city, several of which appeared in Lucrecia's dreams. She and her mother made regular visits to the numerous churches, shrines, and other places of worship spread throughout Madrid, especially the famous black-and-gold statue of Nuestra Madre de Atocha. These visits exposed Lucrecia to the profound piety and cultural dynamism of the city, which had become a gathering place for religious leaders and preachers from all over the empire.

Nothing, however, would have made as big an educational impression as her work in the royal palace between 1586 and 1587. Now 18 years old, Lucrecia had matured into a beautiful and sociable young woman, with brown hair and dark eyes. Lady Jane Dormer, the Leóns' landlord, may have provided the initial contact within the palace that enabled Lucrecia to gain a position as an assistant to the governess to Prince Philip, heir to the throne and the last of Queen Anna's five children still alive. The prince was born in 1578, so he was ten years younger than Lucrecia, about the same age as her youngest sibling. The fact that she was considered suitable for such a job indicates she must have had a good reputation, a presentable appearance, and enough tact and discretion to behave properly within the private residence of the royal family.[23]

Little is known of what exactly she did at the palace, but her work provided an excellent opportunity for direct, firsthand observation of life inside the court. The outer chambers of the palace held offices and meeting rooms for government business, usually crowded with clerks, diplomats, and petitioners from all over the realm. Lucrecia passed through this teeming throng each day to reach the restricted interior chambers where Philip and his family lived. The lavish furnishings and personal comforts of the royal residence must have seemed like an alien world compared to the dusty, reeking streets of the parish of San Sebastián.

All was not well, however, inside the plush private quarters of the palace. The king projected a public image of supreme confidence, but hidden behind the reassuring façade was a depressing and dysfunctional reality. Philip was nearing 60 years of age, increasingly frail and pain-ridden, and showing worrisome signs of the gout that would eventually kill him.[24] His son, the future Philip III, though a good-natured child, had only a moderate intellect and little aptitude for the governing duties that awaited him. His daughter Isabella, born from his third wife and now 20 years old, languished in the palace as she waited in vain for the consummation of a marital union arranged by her father when she was an infant.

How much of this royal family drama Lucrecia witnessed we do not know, but what she did learn clearly gave her a low opinion of the king. The seeds of her fierce dream criticism of Philip were planted during these months of working in the most intimate chambers of the royal palace.

CHAPTER 2

A RECORD
OF DREAMS

1587, September 🐟 Piedrola

In addition to absorbing the orthodox religious teachings she heard
at church from priests and theologians, Lucrecia also interacted with
many other people interested in exploring unconventional dimensions
of spiritual experience. Neighbors introduced her to healers, astrologers,
visionaries, *beatas*, and a plethora of "street prophets" who preached in
public about the dangers of failing to heed God's commands.[1] For three
or four years the León family had a *morisca* boarder living with them
in their apartment building, a Muslim woman who apparently talked
with Lucrecia about Islamic dream teachings.[2] Don Guillén de Casaos, a
friend of Ana's sister from the New World, became a frequent visitor to
the León household, and he took an avid interest in discussing astrology,
prophecy, and other unusual spiritual phenomena with Lucrecia. People
all over Madrid talked in reverential tones about the famous mystics active in their midst—Teresa of Ávila, Sor María de la Visitación, Juan de
Dios, and Miguel de Piedrola.[3]

The latter, commonly known as the "soldier-prophet," played an especially significant role in Lucrecia's life, both in waking and dreaming.
An orphan raised by a priest in northern Spain, Piedrola grew up to
become an itinerant soldier, fighting in Philip's armies in several cam-
paigns. He was frequently captured and held in enemy prisons, and during these times he began to perceive divine voices that encouraged his
efforts to escape. Over the years he gained greater access to the voices,
visions, and dreams that provided him with supernatural information.
After retiring from armed service, Piedrola roamed the streets of Madrid

wearing his military uniform and preaching about the dangers facing Spain and the failure of King Philip to defend his people.

His warnings found a receptive audience at a time when people were becoming increasingly concerned about a new threat from the north: Francis Drake, the English sea captain and privateer (i.e., pirate) whose warships were ravaging Spain's Atlantic coast with virtually no resistance from Philip's security forces. In the spring of 1587, Drake and his marauding fleet not only plundered Cádiz and several other port cities, they also disrupted Spain's commercial shipping traffic with northern Europe, casting a pall of uncertainty over the country's finances and stoking fears that the aging king was unable to protect his realm. How, people anxiously wondered, could the greatest empire in the world be so vulnerable? What could be done to stop further attacks by Drake? Piedrola gave a simple answer: the king should listen to his advice. The soldier-prophet claimed he had special heavenly teachings to impart directly to Philip to guide his rule during these perilous times.

Piedrola persuaded many people at the highest levels of the Church, government, and society that his visions could lead Spain through the coming crisis to ultimate salvation. After Drake's humiliating rampage along the Atlantic coast (the English mockingly referred to it as "singeing the King of Spain's beard") and a worrisome rise in poverty due to the collapsing economy, Piedrola's urgent calls for political reform became a rallying point for those who wanted Philip to act more forcefully.

In the summer of 1587, the Cortes, or legislative council, of Castile created an official commission to investigate Piedrola and his divine revelations about Spain. Piedrola's supporters proposed that he should be officially established as the country's first "Royal Prophet." His detractors, however, questioned the old veteran's sanity and accused him of consorting with demons. During the investigation several theologians asked Piedrola about the source of his divine knowledge. He avoided giving a straight answer, insisting the authority of his revelations elevated him beyond the control of the Church or government. When pressed to say more about the specific content of his supernatural insights, Piedrola refused to share them with anyone but the king himself.

At some point during these discussions, the soldier-prophet crossed the line from tolerable dissent to arrogant blasphemy. Philip could put up with him no longer. On September 18, the investigation was suspended and the Inquisition arrested Piedrola, transporting him immediately to Toledo, where he was charged with the heresy of promoting ideas contrary to the Catholic faith. His supporters in Madrid were furious. The arrest of Piedrola gave them further proof that Philip had badly strayed from the path of a righteous Spanish king.

According to Martín de Ayala, a neighbor of the Leóns who testified during Lucrecia's trial, he once arranged for Lucrecia to meet Piedrola at the soldier-prophet's residence in a Madrid monastery. Nothing is known of their conversation, but the meeting indicates she was indeed familiar with Piedrola and his teachings and had direct contact with other people who followed him. As Lucrecia's later dreams made clear, his sudden arrest by the Inquisition deeply worried her, and those feelings would have been amplified by the outrage of other Piedrola supporters.

One afternoon in late September, the León household received a visit from a young man named Juan de Tebes. Juan was a member of Ana's extended family and an administrative assistant in the Church. The conversation turned to Lucrecia's strange dreams, and Juan asked her what she saw in them. She demurred and said they were nothing more than nonsense from the Devil. When he urged her to describe something she had dreamed, Lucrecia mentioned a recent one about a man who resembled Piedrola. In her dream this man was spewing wheat out of his mouth, followed by a stream of milk. She could recall the image vividly, even though its meaning seemed obscure.

A few days later Juan mentioned her dream to his superior, Don Alonso de Mendoza. Don Alonso came from one of the oldest and most powerful families of the Spanish nobility (his brother Bernardino was a close confidante of Philip and the king's chief diplomat to England and France, essentially serving as Spain's Secretary of State), and he currently held a high position in the Catholic hierarchy of Toledo. An ardent supporter of Piedrola, Don Alonso had a long history of curiosity about unusual spiritual phenomena, including apocalyptic visions and prophecies. When he heard about Lucrecia's dream he immediately sent her an invitation to meet him at a church in Madrid so he could inquire about her experience in more detail. This urgent request from a powerful nobleman must have surprised Lucrecia and her family, and perhaps alarmed them given Don Alonso's close association with the Inquisition's latest and most infamous prisoner. But someone from Lucrecia's modest background could hardly refuse a personal overture from an eminent member of Spain's ruling class. Chaperoned by her mother, she met with Don Alonso a few days later and told him about her dreams.

The nobleman found her story captivating. Just when Piedrola's cause seemed lost, along came a new source of revelatory visions to guide Spain's future. Soon after this meeting, Don Alonso introduced Lucrecia to his friend Fray Lucas de Allende, the director of a large Franciscan monastery in Madrid and another powerful religious official interested in mystical experiences and omens of the future. When Fray Lucas first met her, Lucrecia said, "I am the girl Don Alonso told you about, and I have so many dreams and visions about the loss of Spain that I do not know what to do."[4] Intrigued, Fray Lucas agreed to help investigate her experiences.

Don Alonso approached Lucrecia and her family and told them he wanted to study her dreams more closely. To do so he needed a written record, and since neither she nor her mother knew how to write, Don Alonso arranged for Fray Lucas to serve as Lucrecia's confessor so she could share her dreams with him in a private and religiously sanctioned context. Lucrecia's father may have resisted this plan at first, but Don Alonso's offer of financial gifts for the family plus his assurances about the theological validity of his interest seem to have persuaded her parents to agree. Thus began a process lasting several months in which Don Alonso and Fray Lucas visited the León household each morning to carefully record any dreams Lucrecia might have remembered from the previous night.

Fray Lucas's involvement began on a deeply unsettling note. After several weeks of transcribing her dreams he was startled one morning when she dreamed of the monastery where he lived; in the dream she saw a part of his personal chambers that neither she nor any other woman had ever visited in waking life.[5] Shocked and frightened by the thought of where a dream like this might lead, Fray Lucas immediately destroyed all the reports he had transcribed so far, and told Don Alonso he would no longer participate in the project. Although Fray Lucas dismissed Lucrecia's dreams as nothing more than a girl's silly fantasies, his actions were rather excessive if he truly thought the dreams held no more significance than that. The opposite seems more likely—the clairvoyant quality of Lucrecia's dream struck Fray Lucas as too close for theological comfort, and he worried about the potentially heretical consequences of continuing to encourage a person with such strange abilities.

Don Alonso rushed from Toledo to Madrid to persuade Fray Lucas to reconsider. From the nobleman's perspective Lucrecia's uncanny dream of Fray Lucas's cell was compelling evidence *in favor* of pursuing their study, not breaking it off. This was precisely the kind of phenomenon Don Alonso wanted to explore in more detail. He reassured Fray Lucas that everything they did was motivated by a legitimate religious interest in determining whether her dreams were spiritual or demonic in nature.

Fray Lucas reluctantly agreed to return to his transcription duties, and Don Alonso spoke with Lucrecia about the dreams that had been destroyed, asking her how much of them she could still remember.

1587, November ⇖ The Perilous Future of Spain

Don Alonso's request brought out several important features of Lucrecia's dream recall. To begin with, there was a *lot* of material to be recalled. As she and her parents discovered early in her childhood, Lucrecia had an unusually active dreaming imagination: "*I wake up the moment my eyes are closed.*"[6] She remembered a dream almost every morning, often describing it in so much detail that Don Alonso was amazed and impressed by the mental faculties enabling her to retain such elaborate images from the sleep state.[7] The nobleman also noticed her frequent use of complex religious terms and concepts in her dreams, and he found it puzzling—"the language of her dreams was different from that of her natural, ordinary speech."[8] He pondered the "mysterious" urgency of her need to share the dreams: "after she has had a dream and this has not been written within a day or so, she is very nervous on account of her strong desire to tell it and have it written."[9] Unfortunately for Don Alonso's project, her recall was usually temporary: "once the dream is dictated and transcribed, it is erased from memory, as if she had never dreamed or imagined it."[10]

The best she had to offer of her previously transcribed dreams were some fragments. The earliest dream she could recall for him came from November 7, with scenes of an enemy army attacking Toledo and an injury to Álvaro de Bazán, the Marquis of Santa Cruz, the famous admiral and leader of the mighty Spanish navy known as the Armada. Other dreams from that month included references to the plague, a new Comuneros' rebellion, an Ottoman invasion, a monastery like the Escorial consumed by flames, and a hearth fire in the royal palace suddenly dying out. Two of the dreams, from November 23 and 25, portrayed Francis Drake and the English defeating the Marquis of Santa Cruz and the Spanish navy.[11]

These recollections fueled Don Alonso's enthusiasm about pursuing a closer study of Lucrecia's dreams, and he urged her to let him resume the practice of transcribing them each morning. For a brief time, it seems, she hesitated. Her former confessor, a priest named Fray Gerónimo de Aguiar, counseled her to stay away from Don Alonso and refrain from telling anyone about her dreams. No good could come of it, he said, and eventually the Inquisition would take notice. But Fray Lucas, her new confessor, assured Lucrecia that she could tell him her dreams with no fear of any negative consequences: "the Inquisition has no interest in these dreams unless you believe in them; they are not against the faith."[12]

The idea that one could *believe* or *not believe* in one's dreams played an important role in her trial, as we shall see. In this usage, to believe (*creer*) indicated more than just taking dreams seriously; it reflected a deeper acceptance of their autonomous authority as a source of spiritual insight, which led to the sin of idolatry. The first of the Ten Commandments of

Moses warned people not to worship false gods or treat anything from within the created world as having ultimate value. To believe in dreams in this way—by worshipping or idolizing them—was unquestionably sinful. People who strayed in that direction were endangering their souls and threatening the religious supremacy of the Church.

The conflict over whom to follow, the old confessor or the new, appeared directly in Lucrecia's dreams, and it was there that her decision emerged. In one of the fragments from November she listened to competing arguments from her "companions" (who are discussed in the next chapter), as they debated the reasons why she should heed the advice of Fray Lucas or Fray Aguiar. At the conclusion of reporting this dream, Lucrecia announced that she had been ordered *not* to reveal everything to Fray Aguiar. She never said who gave the order, but she treated it as a final decision. Based on this inner sense of guidance, she decided to trust Fray Lucas and Don Alonso, thus taking the fateful step of allowing them full access to the nightly products of her dreaming imagination.

CHAPTER 3

THE THREE
COMPANIONS

1587, December ᷤ The Dangers of Prophecy

With a heightened sense of dedication and purpose, Don Alonso and Fray Lucas resumed their system of recording Lucrecia's dreams. Fray Lucas visited the León household each morning to write down her reports of dreams from the previous night. He then sent the transcriptions to Toledo where Don Alonso made a "fair copy" (a new, cleanly written text) of several dreams for better study and analysis. They continued this method for four months, and the fair copy dreams represent the most complete and legible texts available in the archives.[1] They were not the first dreams Lucrecia had, nor were they last, but they came during a crucial time in her development, just before the unusual nature of her dreaming experiences became more widely known.

The first full report in the series offers a microcosm of the recurrent themes, images, and characters found throughout her dreams during this time.

> The first of December of this year [1587], the Ordinary Man came to me, and calling me said: "Stick your head out of the window," which I did, and I heard a great noise and asked him: "What noise is this I hear?" He answered: "You will soon see." And then I saw coming from the east a cart pulled by two bulls or buffalos (so they said they were called), in which I saw a tower, on the side of which there was a dead lion, and on the top of which was a dead eagle with its breast cut open. The wheels of this cart were stained with blood, and as it moved it killed many people; and many men and women, dressed as Spaniards, were

tied to the cart. They were shouting that the world was ending. Not hav-ing ever seen anything like this, I asked: "What vision is this?" The Ordi-nary Man told me that he could not tell me (although he showed signs that he wanted to). In this instant, the Old Fisherman appeared, and I asked him: "Why have you left the seashore and come here?" He responded that it was necessary to come because this man wanted to tell me about this vision, and it should not be known until the third night. I saw that he was carrying a palm leaf, which it seemed he was creating right there. I asked him: "Who is this palm leaf for?" He said: "For the new king who will be to God's pleasing. I will give it to him, but for the moment I cannot say any more." And then I woke up. . . .

Lucrecia's dreams often began in the normal setting of her home; she would be looking out her bedroom window, and then something fantastic and otherworldly would happen—she would journey to a far-away land, or see an amazing sight in the street, or go the royal palace for an intimate conversation with the king. El Hombre Ordinario (the Ordinary Man) was a nearly constant presence in her dreams, and so was El Viejo (the Old Man), also known as El Pescador (the Old Fisher-man). A third figure, known as the Young Fisherman or the Lion Man, also appeared frequently. These three "companions" usually appeared in a coastal setting, on a beach or a cliff overlooking the ocean, hence her surprise in this dream at seeing them in the city rather than at the seashore. Many other dreams besides this one included strange animals, bloody violence, apocalyptic warnings, and a variety of allegorical sym-bols. The emotional tone was often negative: fear of the enemies besieg-ing Spain from all directions, and despair at the inability of the king to safeguard his people.

This first report highlights Lucrecia's unusual capacity for self-awareness and metacognition (that is, high-level mental functioning) during her dream experiences. Almost every one of her dreams in-cluded sophisticated thought processes and features of conscious reflec-tion and social intelligence. When she said, "I wake up the moment my eyes are closed," she was not just speaking poetically; she was trying to

describe the highly conscious quality of her dreaming. As a result, many
of her dreams had at least two levels of activity. At one level she witnessed and/or engaged with elements of the dream world, and at another level she analyzed and interpreted the events occurring on the first
level. She often spoke at length with her three companions about the
meanings of her ongoing dreams, although these mysterious men rarely
gave her a straight answer and often argued among themselves. During these digressive discussions the three companions would occasion-
ally mention Don Alonso, Fray Lucas, and other people in Lucrecia's
waking life, either to correct their mistaken interpretations or comment
on their behavior. This added another level of awareness and cognitive
complexity to her experiences.

As the dreams went on, night after night, they began to interweave
with each other in unpredictable temporal loops, going back to images
from previous dreams and looking forward to the appearance of new
images in future dreaming. A core concern here and throughout the
series was the fate of the king and the question of who would replace
him on the throne (having observed the crown prince up close, Lucrecia
apparently had little confidence in the official succession plan). The Old
Fisherman's magically appearing gift of a palm leaf, a common Christian symbol of spiritual victory, indicated that Philip's reign must end so
a new king with true religious faith could lead Spain to a better future.

The next night she dreamed this:

> The second of December of this year, I had the same vision as the night
> before. There was also a man holding a sword in his hand on top of the
> two buffalos, with one foot on top of each, dressed with red clothing on
> top and blue on the bottom. When the Ordinary Man saw him with me,
> he said "True Justice." I saw that all the carnivorous birds came closer to de-
> vour the dead eagle's chest, placed on the castle, and its heart was open.
> I said: "Why do those birds devour that eagle?" The Ordinary Man re-
> sponded: "All these birds are carnivorous, and as they see this eagle dead,
> they all come to devour it. Remember these words I have told you, and tell
> them to everyone. Now tell me what you think about them." I answered

him that I am not a woman of intelligence, and I do not know how to talk about these things. Nevertheless, he insisted on me answering him. I said that if this eagle is the king, as you have already told me so, then I guess that once he dies, many infidels will come to take away the best he has. And without any reply, he looked at me and crossed himself. Then he said: "My friend walks very fast because he has cast his nets in the sea, and I want to go where he is." He left with these words, and then I woke up. . . .

During her trial the Inquisitors asked for a more detailed description of the Ordinary Man. She told them he had the physical appearance of John the Baptist as she had seen him commonly portrayed in church paintings around Madrid: a slender young man clothed in animal skins, with bare arms and legs and a God-haunted face. When she referred to him as *ordinario* she did not mean plain, dull, or uninteresting. Far from it. Rather, she meant he was a regular, expected visitor in her dreams. An ordinary dream for Lucrecia typically included the presence of this extraordinary character.

Calling him John the Baptist may have satisfied Don Alonso and the Inquisitors, but it did little to explain the Ordinary Man's perplexing words or behavior, and it conflicted with his comment in the next dream (December 3rd), in which he spoke about John the Baptist as a separate person. The Ordinary Man's unusual knowledge and power made him seem more than human, but he never claimed to be an angel or spiritual being. Despite Lucrecia's best efforts to persuade him to explain the images in her dreams, he always maintained a stubborn independence that usually left her with more questions than answers. He could be secretive, impatient, irritable, evasive, and judgmental, but his essential benevolence toward Lucrecia never wavered. As the dreams proceeded he gave the impression that he was training her to discover more of her power for herself. This dream of December 2nd had that kind of initiatory quality. Even though she worried that an uneducated woman had no business pursuing such matters, the Ordinary Man encouraged her to trust her intuitive understanding of the imagery and tell others about its significance.

ILLUSTRATION 3. *St John the Baptist*
An oil painting by the Spanish artist Bartolomé González y Serrano, completed
in 1621; now in the Szépművészeti Múzeum, Budapest.

The next dream followed up on the promise from December 1st about revealing more information on the third night. First, the Ordinary Man showed her an astrological omen of death for the king:

> The third of December of this year, the Ordinary Man appeared and said to me: "Wake up, tonight you will have to see more things," and looking out of the window in my house, I saw the sky had turned red as blood, and I asked him: "How is the sky like that?" He answered: "This means that your king will die in a year when there is a lunar eclipse lasting three nights, followed within fifteen days by the appearance of a bloody red comet with a white tail; as it disappears, your king will die." I asked him: "How come this could happen that way?" He answered me: "Would you like me to give you a sign like Saint John the Baptist to the angel? Another night I will tell you what the red star represents." Then I saw coming the cart drawn by the buffalos from the previous nights. It stopped in front of my window, and the Ordinary Man, close to me, said: "Go, it is time to start the battle!"

After this, a large flock of crows and rooks descended upon the dead eagle from the previous night and ate its heart, cheered on by a brown eagle who eventually swooped down to devour the flesh of the dead lion. Suddenly a huge host of pigeons arrived and tried to block the other carnivorous birds from their grisly feast. A vicious fight ensued in which all the pigeons were slaughtered, and then the crows and rooks flew away. As the dream continued, Lucrecia asked for help in understanding:

> I asked the Ordinary Man: "What is this? You promised to tell me, and tonight is the third night." And he answered: "I cannot do so, as the Old Fisherman has to tell you, and he has not come tonight; it is not something we can discuss now, but I will let him know, as he promised to tell you." Then he disappeared and I woke up when it was three o'clock in the morning and soon after I fell asleep again (which does not usually happen since I began having these dreams). I heard a voice (it seemed to be the Old Fisherman's voice) and he said: "I was coming to see you, however, because you are tired, I will not reveal the dream to you; tomorrow I will show you because we are indeed men that tell the truth." And

without seeing and hearing him anymore, and not being able to respond
to him, I woke up again. . . .

Lucrecia could never fully make sense of the complicated and contentious relations between the three companions. They seemed to have
plenty of things to do besides show up in her dreams, and when they
did appear they often fell to bickering among themselves. Still, all three
of them demonstrated a concern to help Lucrecia develop her ability to
recognize the spiritual dimensions of the images being revealed to her.

The next night she was ready for more, and the following morning
she reported one of the longest dreams in the written collection. The first
scene made a lasting impression on her, and it called into question Fray
Lucas and Don Alonso's whole enterprise of recording her dreams for
insights into the future of Spain:

The fourth of December of this year the Ordinary Man came to me and,
used to talking to me directly, he informally addressed me, calling me girl;
and he reminded me of his promise and asked me how I was feeling. I
answered him that I was a little bit anxious, without any particular reason.
He told me that I should imagine what I should see, and he asked me to
get dressed. I got dressed, and he took me by the hand (as he usually
does), and he took me flying to the east and placed me on top of a tower
and told me: "You are now in the highest tower of the world and now,
look around! You have plenty to see from here!" I saw all the planet with
lots of rivers flowing everywhere, and while I was looking at it, he came
down from the tower, and stood on the floor, and said: "Now you need
to come down, find a way to come down." I responded to him that I did
not know how, I would have to stay there and, as the sun was rising and
facing the tower, the sun was burning my face, and soon my face would
be black, and I would not feel like staying in this place. He asked me to
come down; he forced me to come down and prevented me from staying
there. I answered by saying that he was a strange man. Realizing that he
did not want to come up to help me, I started to come down, grabbing
the walls and the narrow battlements with my hands in an effort to slide
down. When I reached the middle of the tower, I saw how the tower wall

disappeared from there on down, folding itself inside in such a way that there was an empty space from there to the floor. Then I saw that there was nothing for me to grab on my way down. I said: "I am going to hurl myself down." After I said this, by my side, I saw a masked man with clothes of black damask print and irons on his feet, bound in chains. He took me by the hand and helped me down to the floor where the Ordinary Man was standing, and as I saw him laid in irons, I asked him: "Are you Piedrola?" He did not answer my question, but he said: "Be careful with whom you share your visions and dreams, because look at me!"

The dream accurately portrayed the current condition of the soldier-prophet—a prisoner of the Inquisition, held captive in a Toledo prison. He, too, had once gazed over the earth from a lofty prophetic perch, elevated far above the realm of ordinary mortals, but now he had fallen into isolation and darkness, and all he could do was warn those who came after him to be more careful. In the dream Lucrecia struggled with the awkward descent down from the top of the tower, but she eventually managed to reach the floor with the help of the man in chains. This suggested the importance of his cautionary example as she tried to navigate the perils ahead.

As the dream continued, the prisoner in chains disappeared and the Ordinary Man took Lucrecia by the hand to the seashore, where they engaged in a peculiar conversation with the other two companions. She extended a friendly greeting to the Young Fisherman, but he brusquely responded, "Do not ask me anything as you do not want to do what I say." The Old Fisherman lamented their inability to tell her everything they knew, but the Young Fisherman dismissed such concerns, saying she was getting plenty of information from them.

Feeling increasingly confused, Lucrecia exclaimed, "What is happening?" When they avoided answering, she demanded they tell her the meaning of vision of the cart drawn by the buffalos. Finally, the Old Fisherman explained it to her: the buffalos symbolized life, the cart was death, and the bloody wheels represented the deadly damage the king (the dead eagle) had done to the common people. The crows and rooks were infidels who would plunder the kingdom once he died, and the brown eagle was the new king who would rescue Spain at last and restore justice to the land.

Having elucidated these allegorical symbols for her, the Old Fisherman abruptly changed the subject and offered to take Lucrecia on a journey to see what was happening in England. She accepted the invitation, but first pressed the companions to say more about their identities. As usual, they turned her question around in a way that only deepened the mystery:

> I responded to him that I would be happy to go there [England], but I needed to know who he was before departing. He said: "Who did Don Alonso tell you were brothers and fishermen [from the Bible]?" I replied to him James and Saint John. Then he kept asking: "Are there others that are brothers and fisherman?" I responded: Saint Andrew and Saint Peter. They laughed, repeating these last two names, and asked the Ordinary Man (who was there by my side) to take me off to England.

This exchange muddied rather than clarified the identity of the other two companions. The dream accurately reflected Don Alonso's keen interest in this question, which he considered vital to establishing the divine provenance of Lucrecia's visions. But the companions seemed to find amusement in the nobleman's clumsy attempts to graft a biblical template onto their characters. Their mockery reflected the general contempt these three dream figures evinced toward Lucrecia's interpreters in waking life. Don Alonso, Fray Lucas, and the others who eventually joined the cause could never quite grasp the full creative potency of Lucrecia's dreams—or the profound threat the dreams posed to their safety.

Through the month of December 1587, Don Alonso did his best to keep up with the heavy flow of her recall. He analyzed Lucrecia's dreams in relation to other prophetic texts from the Bible, especially the apocryphal second book of Esdras and its vision of the death of a royal eagle. The dreams certainly had religious themes, but many of their recurrent features had nothing to do with Christianity. Lucrecia dreamed repeatedly about dangers to Spain, the death of the king,[2] the scheming of Francis Drake and Queen Elizabeth in England, and threats to the Spanish navy led by the Marquis of Santa Cruz. In a dream on December 14, she saw a terrible vision of war on the sea and woe for Spain:

> I saw two strong fleets fighting a fierce battle. Because I had seen them fight before, I knew that one was the fleet of the Marquis of Santa Cruz, the other of Drake. This battle was the fiercest and loudest of all those I had seen in other dreams. Previously, I had seen them fighting in a port; this one was on the high seas and lasted all afternoon because before it began I heard a clock strike one; it lasted three hours, until sunset. Once the sun was down, I saw the defeated fleet of the Marquis of Santa Cruz fleeing toward the north, having lost many of its ships and men, and I saw Drake's fleet returning to England to take on more troops. I saw Drake writing letters, asking for more men. He also wanted to forward a request for troops to the Great Turk, but one of his knights said, "Do not send it, the men we have are enough to secure victory." And with this I woke up.[3]

A dream sequence that Don Alonso found especially significant occurred on December 16th and 17th, when Lucrecia tried to gain interpretive help from the least forthcoming of her companions:

> The sixteenth of December of this year the Ordinary Man came to me and took me to the seashore where the two fishermen were, and I saw that the Lion Man was without his lion and was painting the tree (that he showed me the previous night) from the island with very vivid colors. He told me: "Girl, why do you call me 'fisherman'? I have never been fishing." I answered him: "I have seen you with your friend bringing the nets ashore; I thought you both were fishermen." He responded: "No, there was a time when I used to go fishing, however, I did not go for fish." After he finished saying that, from the same place where we were, I saw the city with the tower (the one I saw in my previous dream) was burning; and the fire was huge, it was not the fire from brick fireplaces; the fire had a black and thick smoke. And both were coming towards Spain. . . . I asked the Lion man: "Who was burning there?" He said that it was not important to tell me now, some other time they will tell me.

The Lion Man seemed more interested in painting the dream images, which he did several more times during the series, than he was in guiding Lucrecia toward a clearer understanding of their meaning. Don Alonso found it fascinating that a dream character wanted to paint the images of the dream while still in the dream, and he arranged to have paintings made in waking life of the images painted by the Lion Man. This added a paradoxical new dimension to Lucrecia's experiences—who exactly was studying whom?

Don Alonso tried to push the process a step further by instructing Lucrecia to make a specific request of her inscrutable companion. The next night, her dream included this scene:

> I said to him [the Lion Man]: "Don Alonso asked me to tell you that, although he would do what you ordered him to, to reveal these visions as he understood them, he would rather have you reveal them to me because he noticed that you do it better than him as in this past dream; therefore, he wishes that you do so. Tell me now: What was burning in that fire in the city of England?" He said: "That fire and smoke you saw coming from it towards Spain means that a big evil will come to destroy it. A lot of people will die in it." Placing himself in front of the Old Fisherman and the Ordinary Man, he said to them: "Take this woman with you as I have nothing else to do with her, and give me back my ink and paper." After they gave them to him, he started to paint all the dreams from previous nights with great skill and very bright colors.

The companions usually complied with a repeated request for answers, but they did so grudgingly, always giving the impression they knew more than they were willing to say directly. Don Alonso's eagerness to push for specific information made it harder for Lucrecia to follow their initiatory guidance and maintain a mutually trustworthy relationship with them. Worse, it signaled a troubling new development in the process of recording her dreams. No longer satisfied with studying the dreams as she reported them, Don Alonso had begun trying to influence and guide the dreams himself. His approach shifted from observing to experimenting, from listening to manipulating. As the many potential uses of her gift dawned on him, he began to regard her in more instrumental terms, as a means to a higher end. This became a growing source of tension between them as time went on. Some of these feelings may be discerned in the report from the 31st of December, her last dream of 1587:

> The Lion Man said: "I want to show you a vision." And he showed me a woman well dressed up in our clothes and there were four men around her. They looked from the royal palace because of their manners and good clothing. They pulled this woman's hair, and she was very quiet without moving a finger; they shaved all her hair and when she was bald, they took off her dress until she was naked. After this they wanted to molest her and she defended herself, and the four men hurt her many times with their cold swords.

Troubled, she asked the Lion Man, "Who is this woman?" and he replied, "I do not want to tell." He made a few more evasive comments and then she woke up, with this disturbing image of male sexual aggression and female vulnerability still vivid in her mind.

1588, January ⇜ From Third to First Person

Among the many omens, portents, and heavenly signs that people were pondering at this time, Lucrecia's dreams were unusual in their dire specificity. Even with all the strange symbols and puzzling comments from the companions, the dreams pointed directly and unambiguously to King Philip as the cause of Spain's bleak prospects and the ultimate target of God's coming wrath. Other people who claimed spiritual gifts—street prophets, *beatas*, and astrologers—generally refrained from providing too much detail about the future, lest they arouse the ire of those authorities most invested in the continuation of the current regime. Lucrecia and her oneiric companions were fully aware of these dangers, but the same cannot be said of Don Alonso. By now he felt absolutely convinced of her prophetic powers, and he began sharing her dreams with other people in his extensive social network, offering her nocturnal visions as fresh evidence of Spain's impending doom.

As Richard Kagan has astutely noted, Don Alonso made a crucial change to the transcription process at this point.[4] The earliest dream reports had been recorded in the third person—e.g., *"She went to the seashore where she met the Ordinary Man"*—but now Don Alonso revised the previous texts so that everything was expressed in the first person, as Lucrecia originally described the dreams to Fray Lucas—*"I went to the seashore where I met the Ordinary Man."* Henceforth this became the standard style for recording her dreams. This shift removed the editorial distance between the dreamer and the scribe, giving the reports a greater personal immediacy that Don Alonso evidently felt would attract more attention to their prophetic claims.

One person who seemed especially attracted was Don Guillén de Casaos, the León family friend and former governor of the Yucatan colony in New Spain. Don Alonso and Fray Lucas were senior Church officials, but Don Guillén was a veteran soldier, free to regard not just Lucrecia's dreams but also Lucrecia herself, with inclinations of a romantic nature. Such sentiments would not be inappropriate, given her age and their social circumstances. In fact, Lucrecia had made it clear, both in waking and in her dreams, that she did eventually want to get married. In her dream of December 29th she mentioned her reluctance to become a celibate seer, telling the Lion Man, "I do not want to be one of those [prophets] you said, I want to be married." Lucrecia was already older than her mother had been when she married and had her first child, so her desire was both normal and timely for a young woman of her age. In this context the frequent visits of Don Guillén to the León household took on the quality of a courtship, which could hardly have gone unnoticed by Lucrecia or her parents.

Meanwhile she continued dreaming, with Fray Lucas dutifully recording what she told him each morning. The apocalyptic themes continued to predominate, although the mystery of the ultimate source of the dreams only deepened. In her report of January 5th, the Ordinary Man took her to Constantinople to see the Turks gathering their weapons, and then to England to observe Drake and his men arming themselves. Afterward he took her to the seashore to join the other two companions, where she saw a coffin with three crosses floating in from the sea. The Old Fisherman asked if she knew whom the crosses represented, and she said she did: The king's son Carlos, his wife Elizabeth (both of whom died in 1568, the year of Lucrecia's birth), and Philip himself. But when Lucrecia asked a question of her own ("Why are they coming in this way?"), she received a conflicting reply from the companions:

> The Old Man replied: "It is not good to give too many details about everything." And the Lion Man said: "Well, God has brought this here in front of us to see it, God wants this to be explained."

The conflicts between the three companions increased as the imagery of her dreaming became more violent. Further omens about the king appeared a week later, and this time Lucrecia herself found the death and destruction almost too much to bear:

> The twelfth of January of this year [1588] the Ordinary Man came to me and I saw that he was bringing a Cross in his hand; he carried the Cross to the Palace and placed it in a tower with a view, and I said to him: "Why are you placing the Cross in this part?" He answered me: "Because his death is close." And I saw a blood river, coming from the area of the stables; this river was surrounding the Palace, flowing with serpents and snakes—that I have seen in other visions—and with lots of crows, squawking with their beaks in blood. Three men came out of this river and looted the Palace and cut many children's and old people's heads off. When I saw this, it hurt me so much that I started to cry aloud. The Ordinary Man said to me: "Do not be sad, do not cry because these things that God does, he does them to teach us a life lesson, so you should not be in sorrow."

The God of Lucrecia's dreams was a vengeful deity, willing to inflict terrible suffering to promote the cause of true faith. She, in her human frailty, could not help feeling sympathy for those who died so horribly. The Ordinary Man instructed her to ignore such emotions and accept God's control over all things, including the punishment of heretics and other unfaithful people. From justly deserved destruction will come divine salvation.

Many of her dreams revolved around threats to Toledo, the religious heart of Spain. That would be the location of the final, apocalyptic battle for the country's future. All Spain's enemies would surround the city walls, and the only hope would come from those few brave and faithful Christians who foresaw the dangers ahead and made preparations to fight back. Lucrecia's dreams anticipated that just as in the beginning of the Reconquista in the early 8th century, when Pelayo led his small band of warriors out of a cave in the northern mountains to fight the Moors, there would be a need for another heroic rescue of the Spanish people. Her last report of the month added a powerful new symbol to emphasize her special role in this process:

> The thirtieth of January of this year the Ordinary Man came to me bringing a mirror in his hand and I asked him: "Why do you bring this mirror?" He answered: "You are the mirror where all these people are reflected, as you warn them to win what they have lost. Look here! What kind of people do you see here in this mirror?" I saw many armed people and I asked: "If I am the mirror, how can I see these people?" He answered: "Do not you understand? Do you not see that they are going to see themselves through you?" I asked him: "Who are these people?" He answered: "Look here where they are coming from!" And I saw up to 500 men coming from La Sopeña.

In Lucrecia's dreams, La Sopeña was a cave where the defenders of Spain would gather in secret and prepare themselves for battle.[5] The dream went on to describe these men marching to Toledo where they broke the siege surrounding the city and sent Spain's enemies fleeing in panic. Lucrecia reported that during the battle:

> I heard a voice that said: "Bless one of the wounded enemies!" He [Fray Lucas] did so and the enemy recovered and asked to be baptized, and Fray Lucas came back and baptized him and took him to La Sopeña to recover fully. Fray Lucas thanked God because the church was back in place and they went to La Sopeña. With the noise, Ursula Beltran appeared outside, and she angrily shouted: "I am tired of taking care of

the people inside and now you bring me foreigners!" Fray Lucas replied: "This man is Christian." When Ursula Beltran heard that, she hugged him with lots of love.

Ursula Beltran was a neighbor and friend of the León family.[6] Her harried demeanor suggested she may have been a hard-working mother of several children like Ana Ordoñez. Her presence in the dream evoked a sense of reassuring familiarity and compassion otherwise lacking in the grim scenes of wartime carnage and religious purification. Whenever Lucrecia heard a disembodied voice in her dreams it seemed to carry an extra degree of spiritual authority, and in this case the auditory message emphasized the importance of welcoming new people into the faith, even if they were "foreigners."

After the victory at Toledo, the Ordinary Man closed the mirror in which Lucrecia had seen all these events. He brought her back to the companions for a celebration and a promise of her own future prosperity:

> He directed me to the seashore where the two companions were and when we arrived the Old Fisherman called me: "Mirror!" And the Lion Man called me: "Star!" I asked them: "Why are you calling me these names?" They replied: "Do you not think that you deserve them? You will enlighten people with your words and will guide them along the path that was revealed to you, because you and the one that has given Mass many times will see faraway lands. When you are twenty-seven years old and come back to find the land you thought lost, you will find it full of flowers and trees." And then I woke up. . . .

Some of these details remain obscure, such as the exact identity of "the one that has given Mass many times" and "the land you thought lost." The general meaning of the dream, however, came through clearly enough. The prophetic mirror of Lucrecia's night visions forecast a climactic struggle for the soul of Spain, a struggle that could be won only by a well-prepared, well-hidden group of the truly faithful.

CHAPTER 4

ESTA NEGRA
SOÑADORA

1588, February 🦎 The Vicar of Madrid

Don Alonso had many virtues, but discretion was not one of them. Still angry over the unjust imprisonment of Piedrola, the nobleman took it upon himself to inform anyone who would listen that another prophetic visionary had arisen to chastise the king and warn of Spain's impending doom. His fascination with Lucrecia's case blinded him to the possibility that Church officials and royal authorities might regard her dreams with rather less enthusiasm than he did.

In her dream of February 2nd, Lucrecia described going to the sea-shore and engaging in a complex discussion with the three companions about the interpretation of various religious symbols. During their conversation the Lion Man made a blatantly treasonous claim about the future of Philip's monarchy, and followed it with an ominous allegorical image:

> The Lion Man said to me: "Listen! How big is God's mercy with all of you, as he warns you as he did with all the patriarchs from the past! . . . . It has been foreseen from ancient times that the Austrian Monarchy will not continue to reign because God wants to create a new world, and the lineage from the past [before the Austrians] will be raised up and exalted. . . . I will show you a vision." And he showed me a knight with an unsheathed sword in his mouth and with one foot in a stirrup and the other on the ground, and his horse had a mouthful of oat straw. I saw that the one riding it said: "Because there is no manger for it." The Lion Man added: "This is to make you understand that you should not linger at the table because your enemies are coming soon, as time will show you."

The reference to the Austrian monarchy touched on the long-simmering resentment of many Spaniards toward Philip's connection with the Hapsburg dynasty, centered in Austria. This royal line extended to Philip from his father, Charles V, and his grandfather, Philip I, a Hapsburg lord. The revolt of the Comuneros in the 1520s foreshadowed these tensions, as local Spanish people demanded their independence from the international entanglements of the Hapsburg family. Why, they asked, should ordinary Spaniards pay taxes and provide young men as troops for pointless wars in faraway places? Charles had used military force to suppress these protests, but the deep-seated anger toward the Hapsburgs never disappeared. On the contrary, it seemed to flare up again toward the end of the 16th century as Philip II struggled to maintain control over his sprawling and costly empire while the Spanish people suffered plagues, famines, and ruinous taxation. It would be very dangerous to give voice to such rebellious sentiments, even in the context of a dream, because they directly challenged the supreme authority of the king. The Lion Man was playing with fire.

The vision of the knight and the horse drew its imagery from the chivalric tales of heroism and adventure familiar to everyone from the time. In Lucrecia's dream the knight stood in a position of alert anticipation, sword unsheathed, ready to vault into the saddle and sally forth. The horse was eating some dry grass, which the knight evidently felt required an explanation. The horse's behavior resulted from the lack of a manger, the normal place where a knight's steed would rest and feed. This suggested that now was not the time for such homely comforts, a point reiterated by the Lion Man in his commentary on the vision. With their enemies fast approaching, the people of Spain must be prepared to rise up and take immediate action to defend their country and their faith.

The dream ended with some cryptic counsel from the Old Fisherman. After urging Don Alonso to behave more secretively, he made a final prediction:

> "The Holy Spirit will visit you in your Sopeña to help you out and support you. And during the whole month of April you will know about bad news regarding the Marquis of Santa Cruz. Then you can gather quickly." Then I woke up. . . .

From her first remembered fragment in early November, Lucrecia's transcribed dreams had expressed a constant anxiety about the welfare of Álvaro de Bazán, the first Marquis of Santa Cruz. He was a prominent nobleman from Granada whose family had fought bravely during the Reconquista. He enlisted in the king's navy at an early age and distinguished himself in the Battle of Lepanto in 1571 and again during the invasion of Lisbon in 1580, when the ships under his command destroyed several enemy vessels. After this, the marquis became the most famous admiral in the Spanish navy, and Philip appointed him Commander by Sea for the Expedition of England—the leader of the Armada, a huge fleet of warships brought together for the holy mission of crossing the English Channel, landing an invasion force, and dethroning the heretical Queen Elizabeth. For many years Philip had worked with the Marquis of Santa Cruz on plans for the Armada's assault on England, driven by an increasingly urgent desire to reestablish Catholic predominance in Northern Europe and stamp out Protestant dissent.

The marquis was currently in Lisbon, making final preparations for the Armada's departure, which he told the king would occur in mid-February.[1] At the time of Lucrecia's most recent dream, no one in Madrid would have known that the marquis had become sick with a mysterious illness.

Meanwhile, Church officials in Madrid decided to launch a formal investigation into alarming reports of a girl whose dreams involved violent threats to the king. Public interest in these disturbing dreams had reached a point where the local religious authorities suspected a possible conspiracy against the social order. On February 10, the lead investigator, Juan Baptista Neroni, whose official title was Vicar of Madrid, began questioning people in Lucrecia's neighborhood about her character, her political and religious beliefs, and the dreams she had told them.

That night, Lucrecia had a dream of apocalyptic horror:

The tenth of February of this year the Ordinary Man came to me and told me: "Go out if you want to see how they are burying all those dead people left in Spain." I saw going towards Madrid a big dragon with a huge body and stomach, so big that he took all the street space where he was, which was in front of the door to my house. I do not know if his body was standing up or if he was lying down on the street. I could not see if his feet were holding him up. I saw that his body was very black and full of scales, with no wings; his head, the size of a ram, had horns similar to those of a deer, each ending in seven antler points, and very black eyes; his tongue, sticking out of his mouth, was extremely long and very red; his neck was very long, and he was blowing very black smoke through his mouth as if it was coming from a big fire with no flames. He had his head towards the west and his tail towards the east; it was so long that he had it rolled around many times. I thought the tip of his tail could reach the sky. I saw this dragon walking on the streets of Madrid, crawling, and with his horns he was lifting and throwing back all the corpses that filled the streets and those people that were on the streets. I saw that some of these corpses were on his body, entangled in his body shell, and he pushed them away with his own tail and put them in piles. And those that did not crash into his body disappeared high in the sky with a bright light. In this way, with this plan, it happened as in the bread mills, that the wheat chaff is thus separated to one side and the grain to the other. This is how I saw it or understood it. Once he had a pile with those that he pushed with its tail, he crawled on top of the pile (almost as when a hen puts herself on top of her many eggs or chicks, she seems to get bigger to cover them all), in the same way this dragon spread all over them. And raising his head to the sky, waving his tail, he roared as do bulls and lions. . . .

Dragons represented the supreme embodiment of evil in both chivalric stories and the biblical book of Revelation. In Lucrecia's case it would be an apt symbolic expression of the persecutory forces gathering around her. The dragon in her dream seized control of her home city with a primal, irresistible ferocity. Those he did not kill and fling away, he smothered beneath him. Curiously, Lucrecia's metaphorical comments about the dragon's behavior—like a mill separating wheat from chaff, like a hen incubating her eggs—seemed to hint at the seeds of new life beyond the apparent finality of the ungodly beast's domination.

By now news had reached Madrid that the Marquis of Santa Cruz was sick. This filtered into Lucrecia's dream two nights later in an experience that seemed to prepare her for the challenges ahead:

> The twelfth of February of this year the Ordinary Man came to me and took me to the seashore where the two companions were, and the Lion Man said to me: "What did Don Alonso tell you?" I answered him: "If you think it is a good idea that they should prepare some weapons for me to go and fight." He replied: "You will not need them. It is enough with that Cross you will wear." Then the two companions disappeared, leaving me alone with the Ordinary Man, who took me to England, a place that I found in good spirits, as it was known that the Marquis of Santa Cruz was sick. At that moment, I saw that Drake received a letter . . . which warned that they had already chosen a General Captain for the Armada and if the Marquis was not boarding it, the English would win more easily.

A dream like this would have accurately reflected the acute anxieties felt by many government officials in Madrid who knew how difficult it would be to replace the Marquis of Santa Cruz with another competent leader of the Armada. The English would indeed rejoice if he were not at the helm of the fleet.

Meanwhile, the Vicar of Madrid had conducted enough interviews with Lucrecia's neighbors to conclude beyond any doubt that her dreams were actively provoking people to question the king's authority. On February 13, he arrested Lucrecia and brought her to the house of another Church official, where she was held for ten days and repeatedly interrogated about her dreams. The vicar brought in several theologians to study her case and offer counsel about what to do with her. Lucrecia insisted that she simply told people what appeared in her dreams, without any intention of inciting rebellion. She told the vicar that if the dreams "were from the Devil, pray to Our Lord to remove them, and if they were from God, then she did not deserve them."[2]

The theological specialists were not impressed by her claims of innocence. A group of them reported to the vicar on February 14 that she "does not have the spirit of prophecy but rather one of trickery and sedition."[3] In a longer report the theologians condemned her in the strongest terms, asserting that her dreams did not come from God, nor from ignorance, nor from her own vanity:

> They do not even come from the Devil, who might have pretended to use this little woman to upset Spain and disrupt plans for the holy Armada against England. . . . This evil dreamer [*esta negra soñadora*] does not want these things to be told to our king, our lord, to whom it would matter if these things were from God. Rather she tells them to the common people in order to stir them up.[4]

The report concluded that because of her vague and self-contradictory answers about the sources of her dreams, Lucrecia was not a prophet. In fact, she was a social menace and an instigator of treasonous activities, and she should be turned over to a civil court for punishment. Traitors usually received the death sentence, carried out by secular officials who were not bound by the Church's rules for the humane treatment of prisoners. Lucrecia's dreams had suddenly brought her to the very edge of a potentially fatal precipice.

Fortunately, another eminent theologian evaluating the case gave the vicar a somewhat more favorable report.[5] He found that her dreams were not fraudulent, nor were they the products of divine causation. Instead, the dreams emerged from a "vertiginous spirit," meaning Lucrecia was mentally unstable, lacking control over her own faculties, and vulnerable to dangerous influences. In the view of this theologian she deserved not punishment but the purifying ritual of exorcism.

At some point during these proceedings two things happened that changed the course of the investigation. First, Don Alonso finally arrived from Toledo, and as soon as he reached Madrid he mobilized legal countermeasures to block the vicar's prosecution and gain Lucrecia's release. Second, the news came from Lisbon that the Marquis of Santa Cruz had died. This startling turn of events gave Don Alonso fresh material to use in arguing that Lucrecia did indeed have a prophetic gift. He went over the head of the vicar and appealed directly to Archbishop

Gaspar de Quiroga, the Inquisitor General of Spain, and showed him the meticulously recorded dream reports in which Lucrecia repeatedly anticipated misfortune for the Marquis of Santa Cruz. We do not know what, exactly, persuaded the supreme head of the Inquisition to order Lucrecia's release, but in short order he did so, ruling that neither punishment nor exorcism was required but, instead, more careful evaluation of her dreams. Archbishop Quiroga declared Lucrecia free to leave the Church's custody on the condition that she take up permanent residence in the secluded house of a women's religious order, where Don Alonso would be able to continue his study of her experiences.

The Vicar of Madrid was outraged. In spite of the clearly damning evidence he had found of traitorous behavior, his prisoner would be set free. Bitter over losing control of the case to Don Alonso and convinced that Lucrecia was a dangerous fraud, he gave her one last warning before releasing her. He brought her before Pedro de Valle, a veteran investigator with the Inquisition, and said to him, "Here is the prophet; look at her." Valle approached Lucrecia, took her head between his hands, and said, "I have undone many prophets with these hands."[6] The vicar ordered her to remain at her home and say nothing about her dreams until a suitable convent could be found to take her.

The ordeal was not yet over. Lucrecia's father had been traveling when she was arrested, and when he returned home he became furious with her for dishonoring the family name. He refused to let her go to a convent, insisting he would not tolerate any further scandal or domestic disruption. He called Don Alonso a madman and told him to stay away from his child and stop interfering with her life. He directed his greatest ire toward Lucrecia herself, and he left her with no doubt about the harsh consequences of any further disobedience: "Daughter, in my family nobody has ever believed in superstitions, because dreams are only dreams, and if you believe in them I will give the order to have you killed."[7]

In the space of about a week, Lucrecia was threatened with death no fewer than three times—by the civil authorities, the Inquisition, and her own father. This must have been a terrifying experience, and one that could not have failed to impress her with the extremely dangerous nature of her situation. The message coming from all sides was crystal clear: she was risking her life whenever she shared a dream.

It would have been easy to stop at this point, break off her relations with Don Alonso, remain at home with her family, and never say anything more about her nocturnal reveries. That would surely have been the safest and most sensible thing to do.

Yet Lucrecia did not stop. She continued dreaming and telling other people about her dreams. Don Alonso, whose excitement about her prophetic abilities had reached a fever pitch, was certainly encouraging her to continue, and so perhaps was her mother, in appreciation for the alms given by the nobleman to the León family. But the only way to explain what happened after her encounter with the Vicar of Madrid is that Lucrecia herself decided to continue following the path that was unfolding in her dreams each night. No one else could force her to do so. Indeed, there was sharp pressure on her to stop immediately. Rather than bowing to that pressure, Lucrecia chose to honor the urgent intensity of the visions that flowed through her mind during sleep.

Something did change, however, after this encounter with Church authorities. Lucrecia became more guarded in her dealings with Don Alonso and Fray Lucas, more assertive in her interactions with the three companions, and more independent in making decisions about her life. Her dreams reflected these changes, which began with two reports from her time as a prisoner of the Vicar of Madrid.[8] In the first she had an unusually contentious exchange with the Ordinary Man:

The seventeenth of February of this year the Ordinary Man came to me saying: "How come you do not do your work? Why are you such a coward in this little matter when you know what the angel and I have confessed to you?" I replied: "I am not afraid of anybody. How do I know who you are?" He answered: "Oh, shame on those that know the truth and deny it, scared away from other humans like them, knowing there is the Light from above that will judge all of us; it will know all our thoughts of fear that you have had about these troubles. Come with me, even though I am angry with you when I see that you are not involved enough in these matters."

He took her to the royal palace, where the king sat with his ears covered and his eyes staring out at a forest. Lucrecia, Don Alonso, Fray Lucas, Don Guillén, and an unknown man took turns speaking to the king. Lucrecia spoke last, and she declared that the Devil was not the cause of her dreams and she trusted in the justice of God who judges all. Then a host of demons appeared and attacked the unknown man, followed by an angel who spoke in praise of trumpets that sound loudly and often. Lucrecia asked the Ordinary Man to take her to the other two companions, presumably to discuss and interpret these visions, but he declined to do so, telling her instead to focus on protecting herself:

> I do not want to take you until you have spoken to the Vicar. Remember Jonah the prophet! And do not think about your mother or what others may think of you! You need to be as cautious as you can to get rid of the lions' claws, and go and hide yourself since you have said too much for a woman. Get away from the world and escape to that place that you thought about.

The reference to Jonah added a provocative dimension of religious rebellion and political dissent to her current plight.[9] Jonah, an 8th century BCE biblical prophet, was commanded by God to go to the Assyrian city of Nineveh to warn the people of their imminent destruction if they did not cease their wickedness and accept the rule of divine law. Frightened by the awesome responsibility of this dangerous task, Jonah fled. But when he tried to escape by ship, a fierce storm struck and he was thrown into the sea and swallowed by a huge fish. After three days God commanded that Jonah be released from the creature's belly. Rejuvenated in his faith by this ordeal, Jonah went to Nineveh and, purely through the force of his inspired words, compelled the king to come down off his throne, change his robes for sackcloth, sit in ashes, and repent his sins.

By urging her to "remember Jonah," the Ordinary Man focused Lucrecia's awareness on the idea that her plight, like Jonah's, was a divine test from which she would emerge stronger than ever. First, however, she must survive the vicar's investigation and follow the path she knew was right, regardless of what her mother or anyone else might say. Her vulnerability as a young, unmarried woman meant she had to exercise greater caution from this point forward. That meant being more careful in her dreams, too, as she found a few nights later while still sleeping in the Church official's house:

> The twentieth of February of this year, a man came to me in the same way as the Ordinary Man usually comes. However, he had his face covered with a black veil and he placed himself close to one of the walls in my bedroom, right in front of where my bed is. There was nothing else in the room except a tiny shining light, which it seemed to me was coming through a hole in the bedroom ceiling, from the moonlight. And under this small shining light, in the dark, I saw this man mentioned above with his habit and clothing as I mentioned before, without distinguishing anything else but a man's shape, being very close to the wall. I heard him calling me by my name three times, saying quickly: "Lucrecia, Lucrecia, Lucrecia!"

The opening scene of the dream reflected her actual situation: sleeping far from the safety of her family home, alone in a secluded chamber, isolated and defenseless against anyone who might want to slip into her room. In the dream she did not immediately reply to the black-veiled man, but promptly entered another dream in which she followed several neighbors through the streets of Madrid to a church, where they ate bread and grapes and prayed to a beautiful image of the Virgin. Then she woke up into the first dream again, as if no time had passed, and she thought for a moment she was in the waking world:

> When I heard that man's voice three times, I woke up and I was really awake and very alert after hearing somebody calling me that way. I thought it must be my host's wife, and I said: "Oh, my Lord, who is calling?" The man close to the wall (I saw he had his eyes open) responded: "I am the Ordinary Man." After he said that, I closed my eyes and I softly fell asleep again. He kept talking to me. . . . "And when the priests call you and tell you that I am the Devil, do not say anything in reply! Tell them it is the Ordinary Man! Oh, I feel sorry for your youth! . . . Why

are you getting into trouble giving advice to anybody? If I did not love you so much, I would not have warned you." I answered him: "Why do you have that black veil covering your face? It quite worries me." He answered: "You annoy me with all those signs of the Cross that you make." I replied: "How come the Ordinary Man never mentioned this before? Is it possible that if you were him, you would come now to tell me this news?" He answered: "I have always tricked you on this and now I want to reveal it to you, as I feel pity for your naivety." While we spoke, the prayer "verbum caro" came into my mind, and I started to recite it. As soon as I did this, I saw the man walking back towards the bedroom door. I said to him: "If you were the Ordinary Man as you told me you were, you would not be scared of these words I say." He replied: "I want to go because you do not thank me for the good advice I have given you; and if after I go, another man comes looking like me, do not believe him! It will be the Devil." At that moment, I sighed heavily saying: "Oh, prophet [Piedrola], why do you not come to help me as you promised me when you helped me going down the tower?" The man added: "Why are you calling the prophet? Do you want him to show you his witchcraft tricks? You and he will go to the same place!" After saying this, I saw the prophet coming in on a white horse, holding a spear on his shoulder with an iron stick, and a Cross in his hand, crying out loud: "Overcome this and you will deserve to receive a Cross, weapons, and a horse." Then I heard the demon starting to shout out, saying: "Prophet, do not reveal to her who I am! I cannot defeat you, so at least leave me to do my work and do not come to warn her!" And I saw that the prophet raised himself up on the stirrups, with the Cross up high and said: "Go away, Satan!"

Over the preceding several days Lucrecia had undoubtedly heard the vicar and his associates questioning her confidence that her dreams came from God and not the Devil. Perhaps she had begun to wonder about this herself. If she had so much divine support, why was she a prisoner of the Church? Did she really know the ultimate identities of the three companions? How could she expect anyone to take seriously the fantasies of an uneducated young woman? What gave her the right to argue about religious symbolism with theological experts? Such doubts might have preyed on her mind and driven her dreaming imagination toward this multi-layered encounter with a mysterious figure who claimed to be the Ordinary Man but whom she eventually recognized as the Devil.

Lucrecia's description of how the experience began—an unknown male sneaking into her darkened room and standing next to her bed—could be construed not as a dream at all but rather an attempted sexual assault. Although she presented the whole experience as a dream with many levels of awareness, she would have been justified in feeling physically vulnerable as she slept alone in the strange house. The Devil represented many vectors of danger aiming at Lucrecia's body, mind, and soul.

The heroic reference to "the prophet," that is, Piedrola, aligned her cause with his more closely than ever. He appeared in her dream as a classic knight from the chivalric tales, riding forth on his white horse to succor a damsel in distress. He saved her in the realm of dreaming, but in waking life her continuing attachment to an imprisoned heretic made her an ongoing target of religious suspicion.

Lucrecia left the vicar's custody scared and chastened but, ironically, more popular than ever. Whatever official and unofficial threats had been made against her, the authorities had let her go. Many people in her neighborhood knew firsthand about the investigation and the deadly serious charges against her, and they must have been shocked and amazed that Lucrecia was released without any punishment. Such a surprising outcome could only enhance her reputation as a visionary of untouchable spiritual power. In a direct conflict between Lucrecia and the Church, the Church had backed down. And Lucrecia continued to dream.

Evidence of her determination to carry forth appeared a few days later, in the first dream she reported after returning home. She said she woke up in the morning,

> crying out loud because I felt a strong pain in my back that I had when I went to bed; and I felt incapable of remembering anything, and started to think I had dreamt nothing. Praying to God, sitting down on the bed, I lifted my hand to my forehead and rested my eyes closing them, and everything came back to my mind, as if I was seeing it all over again. I thanked God as much as I could. . . .

The dream that came back to her memory involved a radiant angel from God descending from heaven to chastise the king for his failure to treat the people of Spain with justice and compassion:

> I saw an angel coming down from the sky on top of a cloud of blood and fire. . . . This angel's face was a lion with the chest and hands of a man. He had the haunches of a bear and the feet of a goat. He shouted, "I am God's angel that, following the will of the Trinity, comes here to punish Philip . . . because he has punished just people without reason and without fairness, and he has always favored evil people."

The dream ended with a direct admonition to bring these revelatory images into the waking world:

> The Lion Man called me and said, "Tell Don Alonso to look at this paper, it is very important."

With that she awoke, crying out in pain. The dream was indeed important in showing there would be no relenting in her oneiric criticism of the king. If anything, her dreams became even more intense in their condemnation of Philip and his monarchy. This particular experience was also important in demonstrating Lucrecia's intentional efforts to continue remembering her dreams. The jarring disruption of the physical pain in her back blocked the normal flow of nocturnal imagery from sleeping to waking awareness. Even though she awoke with no explicit memory of a dream, she had a strong enough presentiment of *something* that she paused before getting out of bed, closed her eyes, and tried to let those vague feelings and sensations reassemble themselves into a more substantial form. A few moments later she was rewarded with the recollection of a dramatic dream that would have been lost but for her patience and concentration.

1588, Spring ☞ Illness and Depression

Whatever her personal intentions or desires may have been, Lucrecia never really had a chance of carrying them out. The tensions with Don Alonso worsened as he became more insistent about controlling her future. The nobleman wrote a long letter to her father, imploring him to allow Lucrecia to be transported to a convent in Toledo where she would be safe, comfortable, and well-supervised.[10] Someone with unusual spiritual gifts like those his daughter possessed should be removed from normal society and examined carefully by competent religious officials. If, however, her father would not grant his permission for a move to a convent, then Don Alonso urged him to arrange for her to get married as soon as possible, to forestall any damaging suspicions about her virtue. The nobleman was actively pushing Lucrecia to accept Don Guillén's suit to take her as his lawful wife.[11] On March 13, the same day Don Alonso wrote his letter, Lucrecia and Don Guillén stayed up late at night (chaperoned by her mother) to observe a lunar eclipse together.

We know that Lucrecia wanted to get married one day, and we know that she and Don Guillén shared many interests and spent a great deal of time in each other's company. Becoming his wife would have given her a chance to live in a much more dream-friendly household, with more protection against harassment from Church and government officials. Yet in the end, she chose to reject his suit. Why? Perhaps the age difference (she was 19, he was in his 40s) was too great. Perhaps she did not feel comfortable with the hardened temperament of a man who had served for years as a military leader among the brutal *conquistadors*. Perhaps she did not like his low opinion of women, which he later expressed to the Inquisition: "The spirit of women is a marketplace of lies, filled with nonsense."[12] Whatever the reasons, saying no must have required Lucrecia to make a firm stand against the ardent efforts of both Don Guillén and Don Alonso. These two men were her strongest supporters, yet both were trying to control the future course of her life.

The uncertainty and stress of the past few weeks eventually took a toll on Lucrecia's health, and she fell ill. Her sleep became disrupted, and the frequency of her dream recall diminished. But the dreams she did remember maintained a remarkable level of creativity, complexity, and political boldness:

> The nineteenth of March of this year at six in the morning I fell asleep and dreamt, as I had been awake all night due to a high fever I suffered. . . .
> The king was sitting down in a chair at the head of my bed and I could

hear him saying: "Madam, Fray Lucas told me you were sick in bed and that is why I came to see you." I answered him: "Fray Lucas is so afraid of you that he thought to excuse me by saying that I was sick. Now your finger nails cannot hurt me." Philip responded: "Listen, I am the king!" I answered him: "A visit from Piedrola would be nicer." He thought that I could still not recognize him. He repeated: "Do not you see that I am the king?" I added: "Just for this year!" He said: "I came to ask what is going to happen with my son. He is sick." I answered him: "Think that he is David's son, and thank God that he is taking him away before your bad advice can damage him!" Looking down at his feet, I saw that they were bare and I asked: "How did you arrive here?" He answered that it was in a carriage. I said to him: "You are going back walking!" He replied: "I do not want anything else from you but to keep me secret." I added: "Oh, Philip, you have no idea who is in control of this tambourine!" I wanted to keep talking with another idea; however, I woke up because of the noise that my mother and Fray Lucas made when they came into my bedroom. . . .

In this instance the king visited Lucrecia in her room, a reversal of the usual process of her traveling to his palace. He had come to seek her counsel but she refused to comply, another reversal from previous dreams in which she gave him warnings but he refused to listen. In this dream she displayed a brash self-confidence, in sharp contrast to many other dreams with overtones of fear, confusion, and helplessness. Even though she was a sick young woman in bed and he was the ruler of an empire, in the dream she held all the power. She mercilessly mocked, taunted, and belittled the king, and would have kept going if her mother and Fray Lucas had not interrupted the dream and woken her up.

Later in the day she fell asleep again, and this time she experienced a remarkably peaceful and hope-inspiring dream, with no sign of the three companions, no geopolitical scheming, and no bloody encounters with vicious monsters:

This same day the nineteenth of March I went to bed for a siesta just after I had lunch. I dreamt that I was in the middle of a field on a very dark night. I saw many people lying on the ground, sleeping. In the middle of the crowd, there was a well. Some of them woke up and the moonlight was shining on them (although I could not see it) and they said to me: "Give us some water! This well has a rope and a bucket." I started to pull out buckets of water and then I called them, whistling, as shepherds call their flock to come and drink.

As she did this, one of the characters in the dream praised her as a "great Rebecca," in reference to the young woman in the book of Genesis who surprised the patriarch Isaac by appearing before him at a well in the desert, where she gave water to him and his camels.[13] Immediately after this lofty compliment Lucrecia brought up one final bucket of water, and found that it contained a beautiful child, a boy of about 2 years of age. She took the boy in her arms, and they soon found a young girl of about 5 years of age, who asked them to take her to "the high city." They walked east for a long time, and then entered the gates of a city. The boy said they had reached their destination:

"You are in Toledo! Do not put me on the ground until you take me to a church that I will show you!" Walking up the streets, I passed Don Alonso's house, and turning to the right, I arrived at a church with some steps at the front door and columns decorated with capitals. And there I put my boy down on the highest step. I saw that the girl, who had been holding onto me, moved to one side of the church door. She shook her skirt that was full of dust, with her face looking at the church. The boy waited for her to do this. When she joined him, she put her right hand on his head, and they went into the church together. And then I woke up. . . .

As a pious Spanish Catholic, Lucrecia viewed Toledo as the spiritual center of the country. In this dream she took on a maternal role and brought the two children under her care to the safest, holiest, most secure place she could imagine. She needed no help from Don Alonso, whose house she walked right past; this was her task, not his. She guided the children to the door of a church that would take them inside and provide them with sanctuary and protection. Lucrecia, however, was not meant to join them.

As it turned out, this was the last dream recorded in Don Alonso's set of fair copy transcriptions. Over the next several weeks Lucrecia's illness took a turn for the worse with recurrent fevers, headaches, ear-aches, pains in her throat, and an alarming weakness and loss of physi-cal energy. Don Alonso and Fray Lucas sent doctors to bleed and purge her, which may have been well intended but undoubtedly worsened her condition. Fray Lucas referred to her low emotional spirits, which sug-gested a deep sadness and perhaps depression had taken hold of her. Her dream recall diminished further, and she essentially stopped receiv-ing visitors or going out of the house. For the next several months she remained at home in bed. Any talk of moving to a convent or getting married had been suspended indefinitely.

At some point in late spring, the followers of Piedrola heard shocking and dispiriting news. The soldier-prophet had confessed to the Inquisi-tion that his visions were deceptive illusions, and he begged for mercy on the grounds of insanity.[14] His admission that he was nothing but a crazy fraud shattered the faith of everyone who had believed in his cause. Lucrecia had always accepted Piedrola as a trustworthy role model for her visionary activities, and she loyally followed what seemed to be his brave and courageous leadership. Now he confessed he had been lying the whole time. Worse, he was cravenly seeking forgiveness from the very king whom he had criticized for so long. Lucrecia's strongest source of moral support had now become another reason for doubting the spiri-tual integrity of her own prophetic abilities.

CHAPTER 5

NEW POWERS

1588, Summer ⤳ The Invincible Armada

After numerous delays and setbacks, including the untimely death of the Marquis of Santa Cruz, the Spanish Armada finally set sail from Lisbon on May 28, bearing northeast toward the English Channel. Close to 130 vessels bristling with cannons and gunners took part in the expedition, including 35 huge, heavily armed warships, 68 militarized cargo ships, 4 oar-propelled galleys, 2 hospital ships, and an assortment of supply ships.[1] The fleet carried more than 25,000 sailors and soldiers ready to rendezvous with an even larger Spanish army arriving from the Netherlands. Together they would march on London and seize Elizabeth's throne.

Philip had been organizing the Armada's assault on England for years, doggedly persisting despite endless logistical difficulties. He was convinced that if the invasion succeeded, it would be a triumph of incalculable value to both God and the Holy Roman Empire. All of Western Europe would be united at last into one great Catholic realm, with Philip as its sovereign lord and ruler. Drake and his privateers would be eliminated, the Protestant cause would be fatally wounded, the Dutch rebels would be easier to control, and there would be no more threats to Spanish ships carrying silver and gold back from the New World. The sacred mission of the Armada became the king's relentless obsession, the focus of all his energy and the source of all his hope for the future.[2] As Geoffrey Parker observed in his biography of Philip, "the king and his minsters believed with absolute confidence that the Armada would solve all the strategic problems that faced the Monarchy."[3] Likewise, historian J. H. Elliott said in his study of imperial Spain that "the 'Enterprise of England' had come to mean everything both to Philip and to Spain since the Marquis of Santa Cruz first submitted to the King his proposals for the great design in 1583."[4]

Philip's supreme confidence stemmed from his total fusion of religious and political motivations. Church and state would equally benefit from the invasion of England. He wrote a message to the Castilian noblemen in his government asserting that "you all know that the Enterprise that I have undertaken for the Service of God and advancement of our Holy Catholic Faith is also for the benefit of these kingdoms, because it is the same cause."[5] During the months leading up to the Armada's departure, Spaniards all over the country rallied to support this new holy war: "While the King pored over his plans day after day in the Escorial, and the elaborate preparations moved slowly to their climax, the priests from their pulpits whipped up the nation to a frenzy of patriotic and religious fervor, as they denounced the iniquities of the heretical Queen of England and vividly evoked the glories of Spain's crusading past."[6] People at all levels of society felt pride in the righteous mission of the Armada Invencible, and they were excited by the king's bold decision to deploy their greatest weapon in attacking England. They believed the Armada's victory would open a glorious new chapter in the divinely blessed future of Spain.

Yet Lucrecia dreamed again and again the Armada would fail. This theme repeated throughout her recorded dreams, from the earliest fragments she remembered from the previous November all the way through March, when she became ill and her dream recall dropped off.[7] Most vivid was the dream of December 14, which portrayed a fearsome naval battle between the two fleets in which Drake and the English routed the Armada and sent the Spanish ships fleeing to the north. On December 15, Lucrecia met with the three companions at the seashore and discussed the previous night's vision, which the Lion Man said was a clear omen of defeat for the Armada. The Marquis of Santa Cruz and the Armada performed relatively well in Lucrecia's dream of December 18, repelling the English fleet in battle, although the Spanish forces inflicted no damage on their enemies. Her dream of December 23 featured a strange vision of the Armada sailing forth toward England when suddenly four women, the "Queens of Spain," arose from the water in front of the ships; the scene then shifted to a horrifying attack on Madrid by the Moors, who slaughtered so many people that the streets flowed with blood. In her dream of January 8, the three companions criticized the Marquis of Santa Cruz for his failure to prepare his military forces, and in her dream of February 12, she journeyed to England where she watched Drake receive favorable news giving him more confidence in the coming victory of the English over the Spanish invaders. Lucrecia dreamed on March 7 that the Armada would be struck with a deadly plague; on March 16 she dreamed the king was saddened by the news of Armada losses; and on March 17 she asked another famous visionary, a woman known as the Nun of Portugal, if she had "seen the Armada." The nun's silence indicated she had experienced no visions of the Armada's future, which apparently was a mark against the nun's prophetic credibility, and evidence in favor of Lucrecia's own.

We cannot be sure how widely Lucrecia's dreams about the Armada were circulated through the city. But in 1588, Juan Horozco Covarrubias, a leading writer of the time who was critical of prophecies generally, complained about people's foolish beliefs in false visions: "bad news has begun to be spread about and even, astonishingly, believed. The talk is of dreams, for example threats of widespread death and destruction, and that the chosen few have to save themselves in caves."[8]

This accusation certainly applied to Lucrecia and her followers. The brother of Fray Lucas, a man named Christopher Allende, lived near Toledo on property that included some cliffs along the Tagus River, and he allowed Fray Lucas, Don Alonso, and some others to build a well-defended, multi-room sanctuary in a cave along those cliffs—designed in accordance with the Sopeña that appeared in Lucrecia's dreams. They received expert assistance in this project from Juan de Herrera, the king's royal architect, who had completed the construction of El Escorial. Herrera apparently found Lucrecia's dreams compelling enough to help her followers build a secret underground space big enough to hold a large group of people; a stockpile of food, water, and weapons; and a chapel for prayer.[9] Don

Alonso described it "not as a cave, nor a fortress, but the place and house of God."[10] There is no indication that Lucrecia asked Don Alonso and the others to do this; they seem to have taken it upon themselves to put the warnings from her dreams into action. They believed that if Spain was destined to suffer defeat because Philip (like the infamous king Rodrigo) had failed in his royal duties, then the followers of Lucrecia would need to be ready (like the great warrior Pelayo) to hide in a secret cave until the time came to emerge and rescue Spain from her enemies.

Meanwhile, the Armada sailed slowly north and east, buffeted by fierce storms and contrary winds that made it difficult for the numerous vessels to maintain a tight, cohesive formation. News of its halting progress did nothing to cool the ardor of its supporters, however. The Pope encouraged Catholics throughout Europe to pray for the Armada's success, and the streets of Spain were filled with religious processions asking divine favor for their fleet.[11] In the Escorial, Philip and the rest of the royal family engaged in a constant vigil of prayer. The king organized his family members into relay teams that took three-hour turns kneeling in front of the Holy Sacrament to seek the blessing of God for the Enterprise of England.[12]

Even when the storms became so strong that the fleet had to pause and seek shelter in the northern Spanish port of A Coruña, Philip refused to see anything but the benevolent favor of the Lord. He sent a letter to the Armada's new commander, the Duke of Medina Sidonia, urging him to ignore the foul weather, set sail at once, and proceed with the attack: "If this was an unjust war, one could indeed take this storm as a sign from Our Lord to cease offending him. But being as just as it [the Armada] is, one cannot believe that He will disband it but rather grant it more favor than we could hope."[13]

The English watched the approach of the Armada with growing trepidation. Queen Elizabeth did not welcome a major battle with Spain. On the contrary, she had been fervently trying to negotiate a cessation of hostilities with the Spanish King. She knew that her royal treasury could not sustain any further escalation in military spending. She also knew that her naval resources were no match for Spain's, and she had

ILLUSTRATION 4. *English Ships and the Spanish Armada, August 1588*
An oil painting, by an unknown English artist, completed in the late 16th century;
now in the National Maritime Museum in London, England.

few other military assets to protect her realm. The thought of risking her
navy in a direct confrontation with the Armada caused her great anxiety,
as one of her closest ministers reported at the time: Elizabeth "told him
that it behooved her at any cost to be friendly with the king of Spain
'because I see that he has great preparations made on all sides. My ships
have put to sea and if any evil fortune should befall them, all would be
lost for I shall have lost the walls of my realm.'"[14]

Nearly 100 English vessels readied themselves to meet the invaders.
On July 30, the two navies finally came in sight of each other, and the
English despaired: the Armada was "the largest fleet that has ever been
seen since the creation of the world," according to one English sailor,
while another reported it was "the greatest and strongest combination, to
my understanding, that ever was gathered in Christendom."[15] An Italian
observer said, "you could hardly see the sea. . . . The masts and rigging,

the towering sterns and prows which in height and number were so great that they dominated the whole naval concourse [and] caused horror, mixed with wonder."[16] The battle began on July 31, and for several days the two sides traded cannon fire and maneuvered for position. The Spanish ships tried to get close enough for their troops of soldiers to jump on board for hand-to-hand fighting, but the English ships were too quick and kept their distance. After several days of inconsequential skirmishing the two sides grew low on ammunition and other supplies, and they temporarily withdrew from battle.

On August 6, the Armada anchored in the port of Calais, only twenty-five miles from the Spanish army that had marched from the Netherlands to rendezvous with the fleet. Philip's audacious plan for the Enterprise of England came this close to success, but it would get no closer. On the evening of August 7, before the two Spanish forces could unite, the English launched several "fireships"—essentially floating bombs filled with gunpowder, covered in tar and pitch, and set alight—into the crowded Calais harbor. The Spaniards tried to keep order among their tightly packed vessels and push the fireships away, but several Armada ships were forced to cut anchor and flee the harbor. Once the fireships began exploding, more Spanish vessels left the harbor in a panic, scattering in all directions as they tried to elude the English gunners waiting for them outside the harbor. By the next morning the Spanish fleet had lost all cohesion, and any hope of uniting with the army from the Netherlands was ruined.

The Duke of Medina Sidonia ordered the remaining vessels of the Armada to abandon the battle and sail away from the English fleet, heading north and then west around the far Irish coast of the British Isles before veering south and heading back to Spain. This turned out to be a disastrously bad decision. Many more ships and men were lost on the Armada's ill-fated journey home than during the actual fighting with the English. A combination of damaged ships, dwindling supplies, rampant disease, pounding storms, poor navigation, and rocky shoals led to the gruesome deaths of thousands of Spanish sailors and soldiers.

Mateo Vázquez, a secretary in the royal court, had the unfortunate duty on September 3 of bringing to the king a letter that confirmed the shocking news of the Armada's defeat. Philip seemed to have trouble accepting the reality of events, as he angrily wrote across the letter, "I hope that God has not permitted so much evil, because everything has been done for His service."[17] Nevertheless, it seemed that God had indeed permitted an enormous wave of evil to smash the Armada to bits. As the battered remnants of the fleet straggled into safe ports, the full magnitude of the catastrophe began to dawn on the king and his people. At least fifty ships had been destroyed or lost at sea, and many of those that returned to Spain were so badly damaged they would never sail again. Upward of 15,000 men died, more than half the total crew that originally set sail in late May. The English, meanwhile, lost only the eight fireships and about 150 men.[18]

Philip fell into a deep depression. He stopped meeting with his advisors, ignored all government business, and secluded himself in the Escorial to pray. He found little comfort from the monks there, who were

ILLUSTRATION 5. El Escorial
A view of the Royal Site of San Lorenzo de El Escorial, approximately 30 miles northwest of Madrid; completed in 1584 after 21 years of construction.

acutely aware of the grim consequences of the loss. Fray Jerónimo de Sepúlveda observed that "the grief it [the Armada's defeat] caused in all of Spain was extraordinary: almost the entire country went into mourning . . . people talked of nothing else," while his colleague Fray José de Sigüenza lamented that "it was the greatest disaster to strike Spain in over six hundred years."[19]

1589, Spring ≈ The Holy Cross of the Restoration

No record remains of Lucrecia's reaction to the news of the Armada's defeat. Any personal gratification she may have felt would have been overshadowed by concern about the imminence of an English counterattack. With Spain's military forces in tatters and the king lost in penitential guilt, it seemed nothing could stop an assault by Drake and his revenge-minded privateers. The people of Spain reeled with fear and disbelief. The greatest empire in the world turned out to be a hollow shell. Their king was a failure. In spite all their prayers and devotions, God had abandoned them. This national crisis of mourning initiated a period of *desengaño*, or disillusionment, in Spain—a painful loss of cherished ideals from the past and a brutally honest reckoning with the weakness and vulnerability of the present. As the historian Roger Osborne put it, "the passage of time lends a sense of inevitability to the defeat of the Armada and we lose the contemporary feeling of wonder at the size and strength of this extraordinary fleet, and the magnitude and depth of the shock and despair that was felt at its destruction."[20] Although Spain eventually recovered and often thrived in the decades to come, the country would never again imagine itself the greatest power in the world. Its peak moment of global dominance had passed. The decline of Philip's empire had begun.

Lucrecia maintained a low profile during the months that followed the Armada's defeat, which must have been difficult given that her prophetic warnings had been proven accurate in the most dramatic fashion conceivable. Many people throughout Madrid had heard about her strange dreams predicting disaster for the Spanish fleet, and now it was hard to avoid the conclusion that she had been right all along. Tellingly, the Church and government had nothing to say. If the Armada had succeeded, they surely would have moved swiftly to denounce Lucrecia's false dreams and punish her severely. But now, what could they do? The Armada had in fact failed, making it impossible to argue that Lucrecia was a fraud or a traitor. Reluctant to grant her any further legitimacy, the officials of Philip's court simply left her alone. With the king grieving and the basic functions of state having ground to a halt, no one wanted to pursue the unpredictable implications of openly acknowledging Lucrecia's accuracy as a dreaming prophet.

The English counterattack was led by Sir Francis Drake and Sir John Norreys, who set sail in the spring of 1589 with a fleet of more than 100 ships carrying over 20,000 soldiers and sailors. Their primary target was Lisbon, where they planned to meet with Portuguese rebels willing to join in the fight against the Spanish. Along the way, Drake and Norreys hunted for coastal ports where the surviving ships of the Armada were being repaired. Their goals were to complete the destruction of the Spanish navy, shut down Philip's access to the Atlantic Ocean, and seize his treasure ships sailing back from the New World.

On May 1, Lucrecia had a dream in which she journeyed to A Coruña, where she saw Drake and his men launch a surprise assault on that northwestern port city. She described a terrible butchery of the townspeople; the air was filled with the cries of women and children screaming in pain.[21]

On May 4, Drake led the English fleet in a surprise attack on A Coruña that was notable, even by his infamous standards, for its destructive savagery. The English sank numerous ships, burned large portions of the city, and tortured and killed hundreds of residents in two weeks of drunken mayhem (the first things they plundered were the town's wine cellars).

The shockingly violent raid on A Coruña sent a new spasm of fear through the Spanish population, as it appeared nothing could stop Drake and his marauding troops. Fortunately for Spain, however, many of the problems that plagued the Armada a year earlier began to take their toll on the English fleet as well. Poor weather slowed the fleet's progress and made it difficult to coordinate the vessels. Increasing numbers of sailors and soldiers fell sick with infectious diseases. While the English paused for two weeks of murderous debauchery in A Coruña, the Spanish forces in Lisbon used that time to prepare their defenses, which held up well once Drake's forces finally arrived. The Portuguese rebels failed to provide their promised support, leaving the English outnumbered and outgunned in their planned assault on the city. After several days of mutual bombardment that left both sides badly damaged, the dispirited English finally broke off the attack and sailed back home.

Events did not bear out the worst fears in Lucrecia's dreams about the English invasion of Portugal and its danger to Spain. Indeed, from the English perspective the venture was a bust. Drake returned with a decimated fleet, no plunder, and hundreds of injured and disease-ridden men. But Spain could take little comfort in repelling the hastily planned English attack. Drake's men had proven themselves equal to the Moors and Turks as horribly cruel and bloodthirsty enemies. If the English put together a more organized military force, they could easily succeed in their goal of strangling Philip's financial ties to the New World, paving the way for a military assault on Madrid.

The battle with the English Armada made it clear that Spain was no longer the preeminent naval power in the world. Philip's troops had been lucky to fight the invaders to a bloody draw. The empire was now on the defensive, its limits exposed for everyone to see.

In times of great social change and uncertainty, when people search for new sources of guidance, an intensified interest in dreaming often emerges.[22] This seems to have happened with Lucrecia's dreams, which began to attract growing attention among the population of Madrid. This situation alarmed court officials, and on July 26, the king's secretary, Mateo Vázquez, asked Philip if the time had come to punish "that woman who does not remember the ire and justice of God," and who was misleading people with her "very false revelations." The king told Vázquez to leave her alone for now: "You should not be afraid of what she says, but of what she does not say."[23]

This evasive, ambivalent, almost mystical comment suggested that Philip did not really know what to do about Lucrecia. He refused to believe her prophecies, yet he worried about what her dreams might say about the terrible dangers facing Spain. He decided the most prudent course was to make no immediate moves against her, but continue to monitor her activities and those of her followers.

Unfortunately, Lucrecia's adherents gave the royal officials a great deal to monitor, more than was safe for any of them. One of her most ardent followers was Don Guillén, who remained committed to her cause even though she had declined his romantic overtures. He took the lead in organizing a religious group called the Holy Cross of the Restoration that was devoted to her prophecies and the protection of Spain. Hidden under their regular clothes, the members of the group wore a black scapular (a short cloak covering the shoulders) with a white cross, designed to look like an image Lucrecia had seen in her dreams. Dozens of people joined this elite spiritual society, including several members of the nobility and officials in the royal court, all united in their disgust with Philip and their faith in Lucrecia's visions. Many of them had been vigorous supporters of Piedrola, and like Don Alonso, they believed this pious young woman's dreams were true revelations of divine judgment against the king. None of them seemed to realize that the more followers she gained, the more of a threat her dreams became to Philip's royal authority.

1589–1590 🐦 Falling in Love

Lucrecia gradually regained her health and began going out of the house again. Her dream recall picked up, and so did the recording process. Fray Lucas could not continue as the primary scribe, so Don Alonso arranged for other literate members of the Holy Cross of the Restoration to transcribe her dreams. One of these members was Diego de Vitores, a 28-year-old man "of considerable learning" from Zamora in northwest Spain, who served Don Alonso as an administrative aide.[24] At some point in the fall, after her 21st birthday, Lucrecia and Vitores met and fell in love. It is easy to imagine the reasons for their mutual attraction. He was relatively close to her in age, more of a peer than any of her other followers. He had elegant handwriting, a respectable profession, and an interest in romantic poetry. Lucrecia, meanwhile, was beautiful, friendly, spiritually intriguing, and eager to find a suitable husband. They needed no urging from anyone else to pursue each other's affections.

Their courtship, conducted privately over the next several months, coincided with a rise in Lucrecia's public activities. With the encouragement and assistance of Lady Jane Dormer, her family's landlord, she began sharing her dreams with some of the most socially prominent people in Madrid. Lady Jane helped organize a series of gatherings at her stately home where interested people could meet and listen to the dreams of the girl who foresaw the defeat of the Armada. Chaperoned by her mother, Lucrecia gave numerous audiences to these elite salons, where she told people about her visions of suffering and woe for Spain.

Meanwhile, her relationship with Vitores grew closer and more intimate, and on February 20, 1590, they secretly pledged themselves to each other in marriage. This was certainly an irregular way to wed, without the benefit of a priest or an open church ceremony, but it was potentially acceptable as a valid union as long as the couple remained true to their vows and gained sanction from the Church at a later time.[25]

The dream-sharing events organized by Lady Jane continued into the new year and drew increasing public attention to Lucrecia's prophecies. The dreams themselves focused relentlessly on the king's failure to act as a just and responsible leader. Her dream of January 14, 1590, portrayed the Ordinary Man murdering Philip; the dream of March 12 showed Princess Isabella harshly criticizing her father for neglecting her; on April 17, Lucrecia saw in her dream a huge warrior woman riding a bull into Madrid, with a sword to cut off children's heads; a dream later in the spring condemned Philip as a tyrant who mistreated the poor, warning that Spain's enemies were near and criticizing the king for cowering in the Escorial. One of the companions ominously declared, "Beware, for this is the time of thunder."[26]

On April 18, Lucrecia reported the first dream with a reference to her being pregnant. In the dream her child cried out from the womb, frightened of being born into such a dangerous world.[27]

CHAPTER 6

THE TRIAL

1590, April 🐦 The Escape of Antonio Pérez

When the Inquisition finally took action against Lucrecia, the precipitating cause had nothing to do with her dreams or her growing public acclaim as a visionary prophet. The Inquisition arrested her because of the escape of Antonio Pérez.

Many of Lucrecia's followers were also vocal partisans in a long-simmering political scandal involving Pérez, a dashing young royal secretary who served as Philip's closest confidante for many years.[1] Although Pérez was greedy, corrupt, and dissolute, he became a powerful advocate for those in the Church and nobility who wanted the king to show more restraint in waging expensive foreign wars. Pérez urged Philip to negotiate a peaceful settlement with the Protestant rebels in the Netherlands, but the king decided instead to pursue the Duke of Alba's policy of increased military violence. Eventually Pérez's influence in court began to wane, and his enemies moved in. When a rival courtier returned from the Netherlands with damaging information that would end his career, Pérez took desperate action. He persuaded, or perhaps tricked, the king into sanctioning the murder of the courtier, Juan de Escobedo, as a spy. On the night of March 31, 1579, Escobedo was stabbed to death on a dark street in Madrid. His assailants escaped, but suspicion immediately fell upon Antonio Pérez, who denied the accusations yet let it be known that if he *did* have any involvement with the murder, it was only at the behest of the king himself.

Philip found himself in a painful predicament. He could not ignore the brazen slaying of a well-known court official, but neither could he fully prosecute Pérez for the crime without revealing his own culpability in Escobedo's death. So he deferred a decision and placed Pérez in a kind of judicial limbo. First arrested in 1580, Pérez was confined to various forms of house imprisonment for the next ten years. This, however, did nothing to diminish the controversy. Pérez pled his innocence in public while his enemies demanded his immediate arrest. People who already disapproved of Philip (like Don Alonso, Fray Lucas, Don Guillén, Lady Jane Dormer, and many others) saw the cause of the long-suffering Pérez as another reason to condemn the king for his tyranny and injustice.

The king's ambivalence about Pérez ended after the defeat of the Armada.[2] Philip's religious advisors urged him to make a public example of punishing people who opposed his divinely sanctioned rule, as a post-Armada gesture of strength. Pérez quickly became the primary target of this effort.[3] In early 1589, Philip put the secretary on trial for murder and demanded that he turn over all the court documents he had stolen from the king. When Pérez refused, the king ordered him to be tortured. Philip personally supervised the process until he received the information he wanted.

After this, realizing he had no time to lose before he was executed, Pérez and his closest supporters planned his escape from Madrid. On the night of April 19, he somehow managed to slip out of jail (the method he used remains a mystery) and fled northeast to Zaragoza in his home province of Aragon, where Philip's court did not have jurisdiction.[4] Fray Lucas de Allende, Lucrecia's confessor and dream scribe, played an active role in the escape plot, and he agreed to hide a valuable collection of personal "goods and jewels" for Pérez until they could be safely smuggled to him in Zaragoza.[5]

Pérez's daring escape was a shocking embarrassment for the king. It showed the weakness of Philip's security forces, and it gave Pérez more power to spread his defiant criticism of the king. Worst of all, the case had now become a threat to the internal stability of Spain itself, as the people of Aragon resisted Philip's authority to prosecute Pérez in their territory.

In the immediate aftermath of the secretary's escape, when grave dangers seemed to be pressing in from all sides, the king looked for anything he could do to restore order and demonstrate that he remained in control. He needed to make it unmistakably clear that the time for tolerance had ended. If he could not silence Antonio Pérez, he would silence someone else instead.

1590, May 🐟 Arrested

The king's royal confessor, Fray Diego de Chaves, suggested to Philip an alternative target for his righteous ire. For many years Chaves had been observing a small but influential group of people engaged in blasphemous activities that threatened the public's trust in the king. These people had been defenders of the crazy fraud Piedrola, they were advocates for the traitorous murderer Pérez, and now they were supporters of an insolent girl, Lucrecia de León, whose dreams portrayed Philip in a blatantly negative light. Chaves knew her case well, having helped the Vicar of Madrid a year earlier in his investigation of her heretical dreams, and he now encouraged the king to wield his royal authority against her. Why should Philip allow obvious traitors to undermine his divinely sanctioned rule? If the king wanted to make a public example of punishing a specific group of people who were openly opposed to him, he could do no better than aim his wrath at Lucrecia and her followers.

With Philip's blessing, Chaves launched a new investigation, this time focusing on Lucrecia's visits to Lady Jane's home to share her dreams. Once again, it took little sleuthing to find abundant evidence that Lucrecia had very high dream recall, openly talked about her dreams with many different people, and described some dreams that portrayed frightening threats to the future of Spain. The salons organized by Lady Jane had given Lucrecia an opportunity to spread her dreams more widely than ever before. Not only was this in direct violation of her agreement following the Vicar of Madrid's investigation, it also raised the suspicion that her core followers were using the gatherings to conspire with spies for Antonio Pérez. In the anxious atmosphere after the secretary's escape, when it seemed possible the allies of Pérez might try to foment a revolution against the king, anyone in Madrid with ties to the former secretary was considered extremely dangerous.

Don Alonso saw it coming, and he did what he could to prepare. He started destroying sensitive papers and organizing his defense weeks before Chaves and the Inquisition arrived on May 21 to arrest him and confiscate all his records pertaining to Lucrecia's dreams.

On May 25, 1590, by direct order of the king, the officers of the Holy Office arrested Lucrecia de León, removed her from her home, and transported her to Toledo for trial by the Inquisitorial court. Also arrested and taken to Toledo for trial were Fray Lucas, Don Guillén, and Diego de Vitores. The Inquisition apparently took no action against Lady Jane Dormer.

The next day Florence's ambassador to the Spanish court wrote the following dispatch from Madrid: "Here, and in Toledo, the Inquisition has arrested some important noblemen, among them is the brother of Don Bernardino de Mendoza, ambassador to France, and the prior of the [convent of] San Francisco [in Madrid]. The reason is a woman who some call a *beata* and who is said to have had divine revelations in her dreams and to have predicted the defeat of the Armada and now says that the king will soon die."[6]

1590, June 🏹 The Trial Begins

It took two days to travel by horse-drawn cart from Madrid to Toledo. A place of so much spiritual hope in Lucrecia's dreams was now transformed into the site of her trial as an enemy of the Church. When Lucrecia arrived at the thickly walled city perched high on a bluff overlooking the Tagus river, she entered through the ancient Puerta Bisagra, the main gate into the city. As she approached the city entrance she passed the execution grounds just outside the gate, where people convicted by the Inquisition were turned over to the civil authorities for their final punishment. The executions always drew a boisterous crowd of spectators eager to witness the last grisly act in the morality play of a heretic's trial.

When Lucrecia was first brought to the Inquisition's court on June 4, the official in charge of the proceedings noted that she was more than six months pregnant. This suggested a date of conception somewhat earlier than the date of her secret marriage to Vitores in late February. That, however, was the least of her worries. The court official asked if she knew why she had been arrested, and she replied, "because of the dreams that are written."[7] This was a very precise answer by Lucrecia, and it foreshadowed the basic strategy of her defense in the trial. She knew the Inquisition was concerned about the dreams that she had told Don Alonso and that he had transcribed, studied, and shared with others. But she insisted she had no part in anything religiously improper that other people might have done with her dream reports. On the contrary, she always tried to act in accordance with the rules of the Church. She told the dreams to her confessor and asked for his guidance in how to respond to them. Don Alonso, a prominent Church official, gave her many assurances about the theological legitimacy of his study of her dreams. She was a person of deep and consistent faith who actively prayed, worshipped, and celebrated in accordance with good Catholic practice. Most importantly, she had never *believed* in the dreams. Nothing about her dreaming experiences threatened or diminished her ultimate belief in God.

The other people arrested with her gave the Inquisitors varying reasons for their involvement. Fray Lucas said he had never wanted to have anything to do with the silly girl, but Don Alonso had pressured him to comply. Don Guillén dismissed Lucrecia as a liar and a fool and denied ever taking her seriously. Vitores admitted to being the father of her child, but insisted he was merely a newcomer scribe with no role in any plot against the king. Don Alonso grandiosely denied the authority of the Holy Office to put them on trial in the first place, arguing that Philip was unfairly using a religious court to silence his political critics.

The testimony of Lucrecia's followers gave the Inquisition additional ammunition to use against her. Two of them (Fray Lucas and Don Guillén) directly stated she was not to be believed, and one of them (Don Alonso) seemed to have only a tenuous command of his own mental faculties. The Inquisitors used their testimony to challenge Lucrecia's claims and pressure her to admit the fraudulent nature of her dreams. She consistently evaded their efforts to catch her in contradictions, however, and claimed innocence as an uneducated young woman who had no control over, or knowledge of, what the older men did with the written dream reports.

The recording of her dreams ended with her arrest and imprisonment. But the ongoing flow of her dreaming, perhaps, did not. A fellow prisoner, held on charges unrelated to her case, testified to the Inquisition that soon after her trial began Lucrecia mentioned having a dream of a seven-headed dragon who delivered a message of doom:

> Woe unto Spain, you must be destroyed and conquered by the king of Navarre; and woe unto you, Philip.[8]

The king of Navarre, otherwise known as Henry IV, king of France, was the Protestant ruler of Spain's neighbor to the north who clashed repeatedly with Philip's pro-Catholic military forces in 1590. As before, Lucrecia's dreams highlighted a genuine threat to Spain that had been made worse by the king's aggressive imperial policies. The horrifying image of the multi-headed dragon recalled the dream of a huge black dragon she had reported the night before she was first arrested by the Vicar of Madrid in February of the previous year. Both dreams expressed a feeling of helplessness in the face of overwhelming evil. Her situation was even worse now, as she faced challenges not only from the prosecutors of the Inquisition but also from her erstwhile supporters, whose conflicting claims threatened her defense at every turn.

1590–1591 🐟 Life in Prison

Don Alonso may have lost some of his mental balance, but he still knew the Church's legal system inside and out, and he immediately filed numerous protests and appeals against the Inquisitors' prosecution. As he repeatedly reminded them, he came from an extremely powerful and influential family, which meant the court officials in Toledo could not automatically dismiss his complaints about procedural issues. Thus the pace of the trial slowed to a near standstill. This may actually have been a favorable development from the perspective of the king, who had made his point about cracking down on dissidents by putting Lucrecia and her followers in prison in Toledo. Now, it did not really matter what happened to them, as long as they gave him no further trouble.

At some point in the fall, probably September or October, Lucrecia gave birth to a baby girl. As a prisoner of the Inquisition and presumed enemy of the king, Lucrecia was unlikely to have received high-quality health care during her labor and delivery. Nevertheless, she lived through the process, and so did her daughter. No evidence remains of how she cared for the child while in captivity. The simple fact of their survival suggests they had resilient physical constitutions and just enough help from their captors to endure an experience that killed so many women and newborns of this era.

We know one other significant fact about Lucrecia's daughter: her name. The Inquisition archives preserved several notes that Vitores wrote to Lucrecia while they were in prison. In one of the notes, he expressed his joy at the news of her giving birth to a baby girl, and in another note he begged Lucrecia to tell him the child's name. The name was clearly her decision, and choosing it provided perhaps the only opportunity she had at this point for a truly free and independent action. She named her daughter Margarita, which had a very specific and pointed significance in a Catholic context. Santa Margarita was a widely venerated martyr known as the patron of childbirth and the protector of pregnant women and those who have been falsely accused. Among the many legends told of Santa Margarita (also known as Margarita the Virgin) is the account of how she was cruelly abandoned by her faithless father, abused by male authorities, and tortured for her religious beliefs; she also slew a dragon, defied an emperor, and radiated spiritual power. This was the saint whose name Lucrecia gave to her child, and Vitores rejoiced when he heard it: "My Lucrecia, my wife and my dearest, it has given me such contentment that you have let me know of the Margarita of my heart."[9]

The notes from Vitores to Lucrecia revealed more than their daughter's name. They illustrated a major breakdown of the Inquisition's standard restrictions on prisoner behavior. For whatever reason, whether incompetence or neglect, the officials of the Toledo court were failing to enforce these restrictions. Lucrecia, Vitores, and the others should have been kept in total isolation from each other, with no communication or contact between them. Instead, it was clear that Vitores and Lucrecia had found a way of exchanging messages and making plans together.

In February of 1591, Philip and his royal retinue visited Toledo and attended a public *auto de fé* for several heretics convicted by the Inquisition. A courtier from the Netherlands who witnessed the gruesome ritual described it as "a very sad spectacle, distressing to see."[10] Lucrecia and the other prisoners almost certainly attended the proceedings, and perhaps were forced to parade in front of the crowd. The king's place in the royal viewing section would have been easy for Lucrecia to observe, and he must have appeared more frail than ever from his worsening gout. Whether or not Philip noticed her presence, we do not know, although she, Don Alonso, Fray Lucas, and the other prisoners were probably positioned for maximal visibility to the assembled crowd, as tangible evidence of the Inquisition's power and authority.[11]

At the end of February Philip wrote a letter to his secretary Mateo Vázquez, responding to his concerns about the rising number of problems plaguing the country—widespread famine, worsening poverty, the ruinous costs of foreign wars, and treasonous plots against the king. Philip counseled patience in all things and told his secretary in particular not to worry about traitors: "I was told that there was a danger of a sedition involving two of the leading persons here (although most of them are, I think, alone in these things), over the woman about whom I wrote."[12] During his visit in Toledo Philip apparently learned enough information about Lucrecia's trial to feel confident there was no real risk of rebellion from the two "leading persons" (Don Alonso and Fray Lucas) or from Lucrecia herself.

The king's sanguine attitude may have contributed to the Toledo court's increasing laxity in her treatment. Over the next few months, Lucrecia and her followers gained a remarkable degree of freedom and comfort while still technically in captivity. She was allowed periodically to leave her cell and visit with Vitores and the other prisoners. Don Alonso set up an office and received frequent visits from his aides, who relayed messages to and from his associates outside of prison. Prison officials socialized with Don Alonso and hosted parties at which Lucrecia was an invited guest. Guards provided her with gifts of food so sumptuous—chicken, beef, lamb—that other prisoners began to complain.[13] The leading judge in the case apparently took more than a professional interest in Lucrecia and tried to arrange for private audiences with her. The judge may not have succeeded in the effort, but he left her with no doubt regarding his desires, saying at one point: "You are so beautiful that even a dead man could make you pregnant."[14]

1591, Fall 🐎 Torture

For several months these irregularities in Toledo eluded notice by the Inquisitor General and his council, known as the Suprema, because of another crisis involving Antonio Pérez. The king had been frustrated in his efforts to extradite Pérez from his home city of Zaragoza, so he ordered the Inquisition to physically apprehend the former secretary and transport him to a secure prison. But when the Inquisitors tried to move against Pérez, violent riots broke out against the Church officials, leaving the king's local commander murdered in the street. Furious, Philip sent military troops to Zaragoza to protect the Inquisitors, restore order, and punish the rebels. His royal ministers advised against this, telling him the Inquisition was making things worse by getting involved in political issues outside its competence. The king heatedly rejected their counsel: "Maybe you will come to realize one day, that these matters are *not* outside the competence of the Inquisition, but among those that most directly concern it."[15]

After the unrest in Zaragoza, the leaders of the Inquisition made extra efforts to bolster the authority of the Holy Office in other parts of the country. In this context, it was only a matter of time before news of the situation in Toledo reached an Inquisition official who had not been personally enchanted by Lucrecia. A few months later, in September of 1591, the Suprema ordered an investigation of the Toledo tribunal and appointed a new Inquisitor, Licenciado Pedro Pacheco, to take charge of the trials of Lucrecia and her followers. Pacheco had gone to Zaragoza with the Inquisitors, in pursuit of Antonio Pérez, and now he came to Toledo to look into allegations of misbehavior among prisoners

aligned with the secretary's cause. What Pacheco found clearly aston-
ished and infuriated him, and he lost no time in taking corrective action.
He started with the Toledo officials. He immediately fired all of the local
Inquisitors involved in the case and severely punished them for their failures of duty. The one exception was Pedro de Sotocameño, a court official who had refused to participate in the improprieties surrounding
Lucrecia's case and who now rose in position to become one of the leading prosecutors against her.

Then Pacheco turned his attention to Lucrecia. She had not been
questioned in several months, so he interrogated her anew, using all the
information he had gathered from the Toledo officials and the other
prisoners to challenge her claims of innocence. He suspected she was
more intelligent and scheming than she would admit, and he knew she
had taken advantage of the liberties granted to her by the foolish locals.
Pacheco quickly became frustrated by Lucrecia's evasive answers and
refusal to take responsibility for the treasonous nature of her dreams. On
December 7, he ordered her brought to the torture chamber.

The records do not specify which method of torture was used, but the
Inquisition in Toledo often used the *toca*, essentially a form of waterboarding. Church officials were prohibited from shedding blood, which limited
their options for extreme physical coercion. Other possibilities were the
potro and *garrucha*, both variations of the rack that stretched or hung the
accused person in extremely painful positions. The *toca* had the advantages of being easy to administer and viciously effective in its results. The
accused was undressed and bound to a table, and a metal funnel was
employed to pour a large quantity of water into the person's mouth and
nose, provoking a panicked sensation of drowning.[16] At every stage of the
process the Inquisitors told the person that the torture was his or her own
fault, and it would only end with a full confession of guilt. A scribe was
present to record the accused's testimony while an official with trained
expertise applied the torments until they achieved the desired result.

Lucrecia was tortured for an unspecified amount of time until she pled
for mercy and promised to tell Pacheco everything. She said she knew Don
Alonso and the others were putting her dreams to political uses without her

ILLUSTRATION 6. A *Toca*
One of the funnels used by the Inquisitors in the Toledo Tribunal in the interrogation of prisoners; this one is in the Museum of Torture in Toledo, Spain.

consent, but there was nothing she could do to stop them, and she insisted they had violated her trust by divulging things she had only told them in confession. When Pacheco threatened further torments, "she begged that for the love of God she not be tortured again because if she dreamed those cursed black dreams and told them as she dreamed them to Don Alonso de Mendoza, he made them worse, for which she is not to blame."[17]

Pacheco apparently found this a sufficiently incriminating answer to warrant ending the session. Her testimony under torture was not significantly different from the claims she had been making from the outset of her imprisonment, but apparently that did not matter to Pacheco. He had succeeded in forcing Lucrecia to admit she knew of the connection between her dreams and political activities against the king. More importantly, he had reasserted the Inquisition's legal authority over her case and reestablished its physical control over her body. Feeling confident he had set the prosecution back on a secure course, Pacheco left Toledo in the spring of 1592.

1595, June ⤞ The Suprema Intervenes

The Inquisitor's optimism proved premature. Thanks to an interminable series of appeals, delays, consultations, and hearings, the trials dragged on for three more years. The officials of the Toledo tribunal had enough material to convict Lucrecia, but they were strangely reluctant to bring the proceedings to a definitive conclusion. She had never given a full and unqualified confession of her sinful behavior, and this created an aura of uncertainty around all the other cases.

So they held her in captivity, and let the legal proceedings grind onward. The lengthy imprisonment was itself a form of punishment, meant to break her spirit of resistance. Yet Lucrecia and Margarita lived through these years in apparently good health. The quality of their lodging and food must have worsened after Pacheco's visit, although there may still have been some benefit for them in remaining within a cloistered residence, away from the crowded, germ-ridden streets and public plazas. Despite her seemingly endless confinement, Lucrecia could take some comfort from the passage of time: the older Margarita grew, the better her chances of survival through childhood.

The same was not true for Don Alonso. His psychological state deteriorated over the years of confinement, and in January of 1595, the Suprema declared him mentally incompetent and ordered him moved to a monastery a few miles away from Toledo.[18] With his departure Lucrecia lost her primary defender in the case. Now she faced the full might of the Holy Office entirely on her own.

In June of 1595, the Suprema ordered the Inquisitors in Toledo to initiate a new phase in her trial, aimed at reaching a definitive answer to the question of whether her dreams were really dreams or just illusions from the Devil. To speed the process along, the Suprema instructed the Toledo officials to torture Lucrecia again. On June 23, she was brought to the torture chamber, where she was informed she could avoid the agony of the *toca* if she finally confessed to inventing the dreams. Lucrecia told them the dreams were really her own dreams, but she also said she fabricated some things about the Armada because she thought it might help the king to know them. The Inquisitors accused her of lying and began removing her clothes in preparation for the *toca*. She shouted for them to stop, and said that yes, Don Alonso and Fray Lucas had invented dreams for her to repeat as her own, and then they used the reports in ways she could not control. Her real dreams and their additions had gotten all mixed up, and she could not tell them apart any more. If they used the written dreams to attack the king, then they were traitors, not her. She swore she had nothing to do with the Devil, she had never believed in the dreams, and her only concern was helping the king fight his enemies.

The Inquisitors decided to end the session there. However, if they thought they gained any new insights from her testimony, those hopes would soon be dashed. Three days later, Lucrecia gave another statement, and this time she defiantly insisted on the authenticity of *all* her dreams, including the ones about the Armada and the Marquis of Santa Cruz. She recanted her claims from the torture chamber about fabricating some of her reports: "it is not true that I faked or invented anything, and all the rest is the truth."[19]

The Suprema demanded an immediate conclusion to these exasperating proceedings. Three judges were given the task of reviewing Lucrecia's testimony and the statements of her followers and the other prisoners who had spoken with her. The judges studied all the documents gathered as evidence in her trial, foremost of which were the written reports of her dreams, and they used legal and theological principles to try to make sense of this huge collection of complex symbolic material.

At some point the judges must have realized there was no way to avoid the fundamental challenge at the heart of her case. After five years of captivity, torture, and interrogation, the Inquisition had made essentially no progress in proving its accusations against Lucrecia. The charges against her still centered, as they always had, on one simple question: Were the dreams that Lucrecia reported *real* dreams?

PART II

AN ANALYSIS OF LUCRECIA'S DREAMS

CHAPTER 7

WHAT SHE WAS NOT

Introduction to the Analysis

It would seem the Inquisitors had an open-and-shut case against Lucrecia. Before the trial even began, they knew her dreams included heretical images that were politically seditious and theologically offensive. Thanks to Don Alonso's meticulous records, the Inquisitors held a document filled with dream reports that slandered the king and arrogantly cast Lucrecia as a divinely chosen oracle and savior of Spain. For years she had been openly sharing her rebellious visions with people who were bitter opponents of the king and his government. These people had formed a secret cult devoted to her and had built a fortified bunker to prepare themselves for armed conflict. She had violated direct orders from the Church to stay silent and remain in her home, and now she had begun stirring up dissent against the king in the highest levels of Madrid society.

These facts were beyond dispute, and they provided more than enough evidence to convict Lucrecia and her followers and punish them severely. Yet that did not happen. Her case dragged on for several years before the moment finally arrived for an official verdict. What accounts for such a lengthy delay? Don Alonso's legal strategies and social connections played a part, and so did the king's ambivalence toward her case. The officials of the Toledo tribunal slowed the proceedings even further, thanks to their lax enforcement and illicit intermingling with the prisoners. Yet the Inquisition faced a more fundamental problem with Lucrecia, a problem of definition. What *kind* of heretic was she? If the Inquisitors could assign her to a familiar category within the legal framework of the Holy Office and its trial system, it would help them dispose of her case more quickly. This was not a formal requirement, but the Inquisitors clearly felt uncomfortable moving ahead with her prosecution until they could state in more precise terms the nature of her criminal misbehavior.

It was a much easier task to determine what she was *not* in relation to these typical categories. To begin with, Lucrecia was neither a *converso* nor a *morisco*. Her father, Alonso, was an Old Christian of pure blood, unsullied by familial connections with Jews or Muslims, and her mother, Ana, was most likely an Old Christian, too. The Inquisitors had no grounds for using non-Christian categories in accusing Lucrecia of heresy. Nor could she be charged with Protestant sympathies. She had been raised a Catholic and had always remained a faithful member of the Church. She was not an *alumbrado*, a member of a mystical group active in some parts of Spain. The *alumbrados* promoted a variety of unorthodox spiritual practices and beliefs, whereas Lucrecia never told other people what they should do or think. Other than sharing her dreams, she followed fairly conventional practices in her religious behavior and worship. She was not a *bruja*, a witch who cast evil spells and curses on her enemies. True, her fantastic dream voyages were disturbingly similar to the legends of night flights among covens of witches. But she never engaged in the kinds of dark magical practices and malevolent shape-shifting that supposedly defined the life of a *bruja*.

Some of the Inquisition's categories had more plausible relevance to her case. She might be considered a sinful fornicator because of her out-of-wedlock sexual relations with Diego de Vitores. But she and Vitores did pledge marital vows to each other, and they remained committed to each other during their imprisonment. If they conceived a child a month or two before exchanging their vows, that was hardly the kind of misbehavior that merited a full trial by the Inquisition. She did not always obey her father, and she probably took some prideful pleasure in the attention she received for her dreams, but these peccadillos did not reflect a person who was dangerously immoral or guilty of major crimes.

The Inquisition could have argued that she was a mentally unstable lunatic, in light of the bizarreness of her dreams and the intellectual frailty of her gender. Because she was a woman, her mental faculties were automatically assumed to be inferior to a man's, highly prone to malfunctioning, and easily swayed by irrational impulses. A woman who became obsessed with dreams could be suffering a mental break-down and losing the ability to distinguish fantasy from reality. But the Inquisitors had nothing more than these points of general misogyny to use in arguing against Lucrecia's sanity. Apart from her copious dreaming, she behaved in a normal, reasonable, and socially appro-priate fashion, with none of the characteristics that might be used to diagnose her as mentally ill.[1] If anything, the Inquisitors suspected Lu-crecia of being more clever and intelligent than she wanted them to know. Her dreams were unquestionably strange and fantastic, but they had so much coherence, complexity, and relevance to current waking reality that they could not be dismissed as random nonsense from a deranged mind.

For centuries the Inquisition had known of the potential for demonic temptation and seduction in dreams, and several of the religious officials who examined Lucrecia's case suspected she was either a willing or an unwilling participant in a malevolent trick by the Devil. If this category of explanation were applied to Lucrecia, it would give the Inquisitors justification for applying extremely harsh measures to compel her confes-sion and exorcise her of the satanic possession. Lucrecia, however, denied this charge at every opportunity. Supporting her was the fact that none of her followers accused her of Devil worship, even when they claimed, under pressure, that they never believed in her foolishness. Lucrecia's life was so firmly anchored in traditional Catholic faith and practice that it was inconceivable to those who knew her that she had made a pact with the Devil. The Inquisitors had no evidence that she was consorting with demons, only their misgivings about the strange content of her dreams. Evidently this was not enough to trigger the kind of aggressive investiga-tion that was usually deployed in cases of suspected demonic possession. Whatever was going on in her case, it did not have any of the typical markings of the Devil's influence.

Varying receptions/perceptions

The Florentine ambassador, in his contemporaneous report on the arrest of Lucrecia and her followers, mentioned that some people in Madrid regarded her as a *beata*. This was a broad category for women with various kinds of spiritual gifts and religious interests. A *beata* was like a nun without a convent, an extremely devout woman practicing her faith outside a formal religious order.[2] As a general term it could be applied to Lucrecia, but doing so gave the Inquisitors no practical guidance about how to move ahead with her case. Some *beatas* were good and pious Catholics whose intense faith inspired them to saint-like acts of charity, compassion, and healing. Other *beatas* let their ecstatic devotions to God lead them into heretical excesses; they lost themselves in a wild array of volatile emotions and uncontrolled behaviors.[3] This kind of public outburst never happened with Lucrecia. She claimed no powers beyond her dreams, and she never presented herself as a saint, mystic, or spiritual role model for other people to emulate. If she was a *beata*, she seemed much more like a good one than a bad one. Since the king himself had given the order to arrest her, the Inquisition could not apply a category that would actually bolster her claims of innocence.

The easiest explanatory label for Lucrecia, and the one which the Inquisitors most forcefully tried to impose upon her, was that of a fraud. If she simply admitted to fabricating all the dreams, it would immediately end the case in a neat and administratively satisfying fashion. She would be exposed as a liar who was deliberately whipping up opposition to the king. Her followers could then be treated as gullible fools who succumbed to her trickery. Throughout the lengthy trial, the Inquisitors tried again and again to pressure Lucrecia to confess that she had invented the dreams. The reason they did so is that without her direct admission on this point, the available evidence actually supported her defense that she was telling the truth. The Inquisitors knew about her predictive dreams regarding the Armada and the Marquis of Santa Cruz, which meant they could not plausibly argue that her anticipations had failed to come true. Compared to the other self-proclaimed seers, diviners, and visionaries the Holy Office had prosecuted over the years, Lucrecia's anticipatory visions were more specific, and more accurate, than anything they had dealt with before. Without a confession, there was no easy way to apply the "fraud" category to her case.

For more than a century the Inquisition had prosecuted and punished thousands upon thousands of heretics under these headings—*conversos, moriscos,* Protestants, *alumbrados, brujas, beatas,* sinners, lunatics, Devil worshippers, and frauds. None of them applied to Lucrecia. She did not fit the definition of any of these traditional types of heretical misbehavior. The difficulty in assigning her a legal and theological identity ultimately led back to the question of her dreams. The Inquisition could not prove the dreams were false, but neither did it want to accept their possible authenticity.[4] Without some resolution of this issue, a clear settlement of her case remained out of reach.

The argument I will develop in the remaining chapters of this book is that current research on sleep and dreaming can provide retrospective help in answering this question and determining the nature and significance of Lucrecia's dreams. The Inquisition's judicial system made frequent use of outside experts who were asked to comment on difficult or unusual aspects of a case. If I could step into a time machine and go back approximately four hundred and twenty years to offer the Toledo tribunal an expert analysis of her dreams, this is how I would proceed.

In Chapter 8, the main patterns of her dream reports are discussed in relation to their continuities and discontinuities with her waking life. Chapter 9 lays out the neuroscience of sleep and dreaming, specifically the cognitive functions associated with visual imagery and creative forethought. Chapter 10 considers Lucrecia's psychological development as a dreamer in the context of her interpersonal relations, starting with her family and radiating outward to the other important people in her life. Chapter 11 highlights the political dimensions of her dreams and explains them in reference to research showing that dreams can express collective concerns, especially during times of social crisis. Chapter 12 looks at Lucrecia's dreams in relation to historical studies of visionary religious experience. After all this evidence has been presented, Chapter 13 will offer my conclusion about what Lucrecia most likely was—a prophetic dreamer.

Quality of the Data

Before any of these discussions can begin, a preliminary issue has to be addressed: How much trust can we put in the reports of Lucrecia's dreams? There appear to be many reasons to doubt the quality and reliability of the evidence that has survived from her trial. Let's consider three major points against the accuracy and usefulness of her dream reports. First, dream *experiences* are different from dream *reports*. Because they can never capture all the felt qualities of the dream as dreamt, the reports that people provide of their dreams are inherently partial, limited, and untrustworthy. Second, Lucrecia had every opportunity to fabricate or embellish her "dreams" however she wished, and she clearly enjoyed sharing them with other people. By doing so she gained attention, money, and influence—strong motivations for overdramatizing her dream life. Third, Don Alonso and her other followers were also motivated to exaggerate her dreams by highlighting the radical political messages that were emerging from, or perhaps implanted in, her dreams.

These are legitimate questions to raise, and none of them can be definitively answered. Yes, dream reports have limits. Yes, Lucrecia had reasons to exaggerate or fabricate her dreams, and so did her followers. But naming these issues is the beginning, not the end, of the methodological discussion. If these are indeed possibilities, how likely are they to be real factors in her particular case? Are there other possibilities to consider? Which ones have greater or lesser likelihood of being true? Taking all the different sources of evidence into account, with all their limits and uncertainties, what is the most probable explanation of the facts at hand? These are the questions to keep in mind when considering the quality of the data in Lucrecia's case.

Despite their many limits, dream reports do in fact convey a number of consistent patterns in their content with clear and direct relevance to waking life concerns. These patterns of dream content are rooted in well-documented activities in the brain during sleep, suggesting that people's reports of their dreams are at least partially accurate renderings of their minds' nocturnal experiences. The gap between dream-as-dreamt and dream-as-reported is smaller than often assumed.[5] As Chapter 8 will describe in more detail, dreams tend to have especially clear connections to people's social relations, daily activities, physical health, emotional temperament, and cultural beliefs about things like religion and politics. The empirical evidence from contemporary dream science indicates that dream reports, though limited, can be valid sources of meaningful information about the dreamer.

It might sound strange to say so, but Don Alonso set up an impressively sophisticated design for his process of gathering Lucrecia's dreams. Many leading dream researchers of the modern era have encouraged the use of systematic methods to gather dreams over a lengthy period of time.[6] This is exactly what Don Alonso did, especially in the early phase from November 1587 to March 1588, when he and Fray Lucas followed a consistent system for recording and transcribing Lucrecia's dreams. Some modern scientists prefer to study dreams gathered under laboratory conditions, because that allows the most controlled and direct access to the dream immediately after the person is awakened. Other researchers favor dreams gathered in "natural" or home conditions because that enables the observation of dream patterns without overly disturbing the person and disrupting his or her dreams (producing what researchers call "the lab effect"). Seen in this context, we can appreciate how Don Alonso devised an approach that effectively combined positive elements from both methods. Lucrecia slept at home in her bed as usual, so the conditions of her dreaming were natural and undisturbed, but when she woke up there was a scribe available to record her experiences before she forgot them. Indeed, Don Alonso and his helpers probably had closer access to Lucrecia and her dreams than most modern researchers ever have with the participants in their studies.

Dream researchers today generally try to gather as many reports as possible in order to improve the chances of identifying large-scale patterns that are real and solid.[7] Again, Don Alonso did a good job of putting together a sizable record of Lucrecia's dream experiences, large enough for a statistical analysis of the frequencies of various elements of dream content (presented in Chapter 8). This kind of analysis would not be possible had the 16th century nobleman not recognized the potential value of empirical methods of investigation.

As mentioned at the outset, all dream reports are limited in how much of the original dreaming experience they can convey into a waking format. However, by using systematic methods of dream collection, researchers today are able to identify meaningful patterns that are so strong and consistent they can be observed despite the limits and noisiness of the data. In Lucrecia's case the method Don Alonso used more than four hundred years ago to gather her dreams could hardly be improved upon by modern techniques. The material generated by his efforts provides a treasure trove of information about a particular individual's dream life. Setting aside his political and theological interests for a moment, we should honor Don Alonso's observational dedication as he initiated one of history's earliest studies of a long-term dream series.

But of course Don Alonso *did* have political and theological interests that motivated his study of Lucrecia's dreams, and Lucrecia herself had a variety of personal interests that motivated her willingness to participate in his project. These external incentives cast doubt on the content of the dreams Lucrecia reported and Don Alonso transcribed. Indeed, this was precisely what the Inquisition wanted to conclude, and what they tried for several years to force Lucrecia to admit: that she had fabricated the dreams so she could revel in popular attention and enjoy her deceitful influence over other people.

Modern psychologists would hardly deny that humans have natural tendencies to seek attention and positive regard from others. In the "self psychology" tradition of Heinz Kohut these are referred to as *narcissistic* desires, and in moderation they contribute to mental health and emotional balance.[8] Lucrecia did seem to take pride and pleasure in sharing her dreams. But the question is, did it give her so much pride and pleasure that she made up the dreams and lied about them for years on end? This is the most skeptical charge against her, and the one that seems most difficult to disprove: the fame and adulation Lucrecia received for her dreams gave her an incentive to secretly manufacture reports that pleased her followers and promoted her celebrity status.

This is indeed one possible explanation. But how likely is it to be true? We should be clear that such a claim no longer relies on the assumption that Lucrecia was endowed with a normal desire for attention, but rather that she was consumed by an extreme, self-destructive, and virtually suicidal intensity of this desire. Consider the years of persecution, imprisonment, and torture she suffered—did she go through all that just so people would notice and praise her? Surely she could have found an easier and less dangerous way to gain attention than by making up dreams that openly insulted the king and defied the Church. If Lucrecia persisted in lying about her dreams for all that time simply because she enjoyed the attention, then she must have been afflicted with a pathological degree of social neediness. Yet nothing else in her character or behavior suggested she was mentally ill or emotionally unbalanced, and in many instances she displayed a keen instinct for survival and a strong will to live. It remains a possibility that an extreme desire for fame drove her to fabricate the dreams, but it fits poorly with the other known facts of the case.

The alms and gifts of financial assistance Don Alonso gave to her family were explicitly intended to encourage Lucrecia's participation in the dream-recording project. The money went to her parents, not to her, as a gesture of goodwill to overcome their objections to the project. The Leóns had their share of financial troubles, so every little bit must have helped. The total amount of money Don Alonso gave them, however, was not enough to drastically change their circumstances, and certainly not enough for Lucrecia to risk life and limb with the Holy Office. Unless we assume she was possessed by a blinding desire for financial gain, Lucrecia would be unlikely to endanger herself with the Inquisition for the sake of minor charity from Don Alonso to her parents.

When surveying Lucrecia's motivations, we should also consider the incentives she had for giving accurate and truthful accounts of her dreams. The reports she provided to Don Alonso were shared in the context of the holy sacrament of confession. For a pious Catholic, confession creates a setting for maximal honesty and truthfulness; it is a place for sharing with a priest and God the unvarnished reality of one's experiences. Lucrecia was, by all accounts, a pious Catholic, which means she very likely felt pressure *not* to fabricate or make anything up, but to describe her dreams as accurately and completely as possible. For someone who had been taught from birth to believe in an omniscient and judgmental God, there could be no hiding from any falsehoods she might add to the dreams. She could fool other people, but God would know the truth.

Perhaps the strongest motivation Lucrecia had for honesty came from a realistic fear of the Inquisition itself. From the very start of the process she worried about Inquisitors using the dream reports to accuse her of heresy. Don Alonso and Fray Lucas told her she would be safe if she simply described her dreams to them, and let them do the rest. They promised she had nothing to worry about as long as she continued being honest with them. Lucrecia may have been unwise to accept their reassurances, but she does seem to have followed their advice to continue giving them accurate and truthful reports of her dreams, nothing more or less.

If Lucrecia was a pathological attention-seeker and inveterate liar, she might have made up the dreams. If she was a faithful Catholic who believed in God, trusted her priests, and feared the wrath of the Inquisition, she might have been giving honest reports of her dreams. Both are possible; the latter is more likely.

As for Don Alonso, his motivations may seem questionable because of the political relevance of Lucrecia's dreams. Don Alonso was a long-time critic of the king, and the dream reports gave him fresh ammunition to use in his complaints about the injustices of Philip's rule. The nobleman had obvious reasons to alter the dreams as he edited them, adding or deleting material to make the reports more effective as political propaganda. However, like Lucrecia, Don Alonso also had strong incentives *not* to alter the dreams but to record them as accurately and faithfully as possible. Not only was he also a strong Catholic who believed in God and the sacraments, but he specifically believed that Lucrecia's dreams might have a divine source of causation. This would make the unfiltered content of her dreams much more interesting and valuable than anything he could fabricate on his own. Of all Lucrecia's followers, Don Alonso put the most trust in the uncanny power of her dreams. He knew what she had accurately foreseen, and he was deeply curious to learn more about her oneiric capacities. He used Lucrecia for political purposes, of course, but those purposes were best served by enhancing people's awareness of her actual dreams, not replacing them with his own anti-Philip diatribes.

In contrast to Lucrecia, Don Alonso does seem to have suffered from some kind of mental illness, which may have been responsible for his reckless behavior. But his mental problems do not seem to have affected his ability to oversee the accurate transcription of her dreams. Indeed, Don Alonso went to great lengths to establish the most consistent and effective method for recording her dreams as soon as she woke up each morning. He, like Lucrecia, depended on the honesty of her dreams as his best defense against any charges from the Inquisition. It remains possible that Don Alonso secretly edited the reports to enhance their political content. But considering all his incentives and interests in Lucrecia's case, it seems more likely that Don Alonso made a scrupulous effort to record her dreams exactly as she described them.

A review of these questions about the quality of the data does not lead to final, absolute answers. It does, however, suggest that we should refrain from excessive skepticism in studying Lucrecia's dreams. The most serious doubts about her dream reports turn out, on closer inspection, to require additional assumptions that do not fit well with other known facts about the case. A more probable explanation, one that fits better with the beliefs, behaviors, and motivations of the people involved, is that Lucrecia and Don Alonso worked together to create a record of her dreams that was as accurate and complete as they could manage. They put tremendous effort into the process, at great personal risk, because they believed in the importance of faithfully conveying the dreams from her nocturnal imagination into a publicly accessible form.

CHAPTER 8

PATTERNS
IN THE DREAMS

Continuities and Discontinuities

Where should one begin when trying to analyze a long and complex series of dreams? The Church officials in charge of Lucrecia's trial had no idea. Their theological training gave them virtually no practical guidance in the interpretation of dreams. The agents of the Holy Office had long taken a dubious and dismissive view of dreaming, especially the dreams of women. The only exceptions were dream images that might indicate demonic influences, which of course required immediate and severe attention from Church authorities. Other than that, the Holy Office generally ignored the whole subject. In Lucrecia's case, however, the Inquisitors could neither dismiss her dreams as mere fabrications nor assign them a diabolical origin, making it difficult to proceed with her prosecution. If they openly acknowledged her experiences were actual dreams, the Inquisitors would be forced to admit they lacked any knowledge about what to do next.

Don Alonso did take her dreams seriously and devoted considerable effort to their interpretation. He focused on parallels with images and texts from the Bible, which made sense given his theological and political goals, although it limited the range of his analysis. He likely knew about Macrobius and other medieval writers of dream texts, and he was familiar with the *Oneirocritica* of Artemidorus, a 2nd century CE Roman manual of dream interpretation, which may have given him additional guidance (more on this in Chapter 12).

Yet as much as Don Alonso wanted to understand Lucrecia's dreams, and as much as the Inquisition needed to do so, they had no realistic way of managing the task of analysis and interpretation. Fortunately, this is an area where modern research technologies have made some progress. The use of digital technologies in the humanities has grown in recent years, with innovative applications of data analysis tools to texts and documents of various kinds.[1] My own work since the late 2000s has revolved around the creation, testing, and refinement of digital methods for studying dream content. In 2009, I created the Sleep and Dream Database (SDDb), an online archive and search engine designed to promote empirical dream research.[2] Although the use of digital methods in the study of dreaming remains in the early stages of development, my findings and those of other researchers have shown encouraging results.[3]

First and most obviously, these methods make it much easier to count and tabulate the linguistic content of a long series of dreams. How many references to emotions appear in the dreams? How many colors? How many words relating to weapons, speech, animals, hearing, religion, sexuality? Trying to count every reference in Lucrecia's dreams for all these categories would be a labor-intensive process requiring countless hours of tedious effort from error-prone people. Now, with a system like the SDDb, the same task can be reliably accomplished by a computer in a matter of seconds.[4] Using this tool gives a quick overview of the contents of a dream series and helps to identify recurrent features that are worth further study.

Second, the results of analyzing word usage frequencies make it easier to highlight important continuities between dreaming and waking. Modern researchers, led by Calvin Hall and G. William Domhoff, have shown that frequencies of dream content can provide accurate indications of a person's most important concerns, conceptions, and interests in waking life. This continuity involves more than just mirroring a person's daily activities; it extends to an illumination of the person's underlying thoughts and feelings *about* those activities.[5] Dreams reflect what we care about most deeply, whether or not it is an actual physical feature of our normal daily lives.[6] Research on the continuity hypothesis has found meaningful connections between people's dreams and their social relationships, personal characteristics, mental health, and cultural beliefs and practices. These findings can be very useful as we try to make sense of Lucrecia's dreams. We know enough about her thoughts and concerns in waking life to seek specific points of continuity with the patterns of content in her dreams.

Third, this kind of digital approach also helps to identify the *dis*continuities in Lucrecia's dream content, the places where the greatest differences and variations occur between dreaming and waking. Once we know what makes dreams ordinary, we can then determine more precisely what makes them *extra*ordinary. Elements of discontinuity can lead in several interpretive directions. They can reflect the chaotic energies that flow through the brain during sleep (more on that in Chapter 9). They can indicate the presence of symbolic or metaphorical content in which the meanings are conveyed indirectly through figurative imagery and language. And they can express concerns that go beyond the normal routines of daily life to encompass religious, spiritual, or existential themes. Any of these are possible, so caution is required in following this path. But not too much caution. The variety of possible meanings that emerge in dream discontinuities can lead to important new insights into a person's waking life.[7] Multiplicity of meaning is a feature of dreaming, not a bug.

Word Usage Frequencies

The following analysis focuses on Don Alonso's fair copy of 36 of Lucrecia's dream reports from December 1587 through March 1588. This collection constitutes the most carefully preserved and legible account of her dreams, and it comes from a time prior to the loss of the Armada and her increased public profile. It represents the dreams she experienced when she was healthiest and most enthusiastic, when the recording system was working as smoothly as it ever did, and when she had the fewest external pressures and problems to distract her.

The SDDb has a built-in word search template of several classes and categories of content (now in its 2.0 version) that I have been developing as a default framework for analyzing long series of dreams. These categories reflect important aspects of dreaming that researchers have been studying for many decades. A few of the categories in the template do not apply to the historical conditions of Lucrecia's life, but most of them do. Table 8.1 displays the results of a word search analysis of Lucrecia's dreams (in English translation) using 32 categories from the SDDb's 2.0 template.

The first thing to note is the tremendous length of her dreams, with an average (mean) count of more than 900 words per report. This seems to reflect a special combination of naturally high dream recall with optimum recording conditions. Most dreams gathered and analyzed by modern researchers are much shorter, in the range of 50 to 150 words per report. Some recent studies have looked at individuals (usually women) whose dreams average 300–400 words per report, with their longest reports topping 1,000 words.[8] Seen in this context, Lucrecia's average dreams are as long as the longest dreams of contemporary people who have a tendency for unusually profuse dreaming.

Many of the details of her reports involved vivid sensory perceptions—seeing, hearing, touching, smelling, and tasting—which accounts for the elevated frequencies of these categories. (Contemporary researchers have found smell and taste to be quite rare in dream content, so a 31% frequency for this category is quite high.) Intriguingly, the highest frequency colors in her dreams—black, white, and red—are identical to the most referenced colors in modern collections of dreams.[9]

Fear is the predominant emotion. Although she has many dreams with happiness, the general emotional tone is negative (67% of the dreams have at least one reference to fear, anger, or sadness[10]). The frequency for wonder or confusion is low, but this does not accurately gauge the high degree of curiosity and questioning in the dreams. An additional word search finds that 32 of the reports (89%) have at least one reference to "ask," "asks," "asked," or "asking," which gives a better sense of how much uncertainty she expresses in the dreams and how much she seeks to gain new knowledge.

The percentage of references to family characters seems high, but almost none of these references have to do with Lucrecia's own family; they are descriptive terms for other people's families. The majority of

TABLE 8.1. Word Usage Frequencies in Lucrecia's Dreams.

These results come from the use of 32 categories from the SDDb 2.0 to analyze a set of Lucrecia's dreams (36 in total, translated from Spanish into English). In the SDDb this set is named "Lucrecia Journal 1." Each category used in the search includes numerous words relating to that topic or theme. The "Count" column indicates the number of dream reports that have at least one use of a word from the given category. The "Percentage" column divides the count by the total number of dreams to yield a percentage rounded to the nearest hundredth. The "4 Most Used Words" column shows the words from the given category appearing most often in this set of dreams (the number in parentheses following each word is the number of dreams with at least one reference to that word). The shortest dream report in the set is 265 words, and the longest is 1,613 words. The mean (average) length is 903 words, and the median (half longer, half shorter) length is 882 words.

	Count	Percentage	4 Most Used Words
Perception			
Vision	36	100	saw (36), see (32), eyes (16), vision (16)
Hearing	34	94	heard (24), listen (9), noise (8), hear (7)
Touch	31	86	hand (24), hands (16), holding (8), finger (3)
Smell, Taste	11	31	nose (5), smell (2), tongues (1), taste (1)
Color	27	75	black (17), white (16), red (9), brown (7)
Emotion			
Fear	20	56	scared (8), afraid (7), worry (5), sorry (5)
Anger	10	28	anger (4), enraged (1), infuriated (1), angry (1)
Sadness	6	17	sad (4), miserable (1), sadly (1), disappointed (1)
Wonder, Confusion	5	14	suddenly (3), confused (1), surprised (1), surprise (1)
Happiness	13	36	happy (7), glad (5), pleased (3)
Characters			
Family	20	56	son (8), father (5), wife (5), sons (4)
Animals	32	89	lion (27), lions (5), birds (4), crows (4)
Fantastic beings	10	28	spirit (6), devil (3), demon (3), dragon (2)
Male references	36	100	man (36), he (36), his (35), him (35)
Female references	29	81	her (20), she (18), woman (12), women (8)

	Count	Percentage	4 Most Used Words
Social Interactions			
Friendliness	29	81	help (15), friend (8), warn (6), warned (5)
Physical aggression	26	72	enemies (11), fight (7), battle (6), killed (6)
Sexuality	7	19	naked (6), sleep with (1)
Movement			
Walking, Running	23	64	walking (15), walked (8), running (6), walk (2)
Flying	7	19	flying (3), flew (2), floating (2)
Falling	14	39	fell (7), fall (5), falling (4), collapse (1)
Death	23	64	dead (16), die (8), death (5), dies (4)
Cognition			
Thinking	32	89	think (17), thought (11), aware (4), praying (3)
Speech	36	100	said (36), saying (23), say (15), called (12)
Reading, Writing	19	53	read (7), letter (6), letters (5), writing (5)
Culture			
Architecture	26	72	house (16), room (16), door (8), floor (7)
Food, Drink	21	58	bread (6), fruits (5), drink (5), ate (4)
Clothing	28	78	dressed (22), clothing (11), clothes (11), shirt (4)
Transportation	20	56	street (8), streets (5), ships (5), path (3)
Weapons	18	50	weapons (9), sword (6), spear (3), spears (3)
Art	8	22	paintings (3), painting (2), sing (1), music (1)
Religion	34	94	god (24), saint (13), church (12), prophet (7)

references to animals in her dreams involve the Lion Man (more on him in a moment), and numerous other animals make appearances, including crows, turkeys, dogs, eagles, snakes, and alligators. Her references to fantastic beings, that is, living entities that are not human or animal, include several evil beings (demons, the Devil, dragons). The dream reports use more words relating to males than to females, which parallels a similar finding about typical patterns in modern people's dreams: a higher frequency of male references than female references.[11]

Lucrecia's dreams have large amounts of both friendly and physically aggressive social interactions. Of the few references to sexuality, none of them relate directly to Lucrecia; they all involve the appearance and behavior of other characters. Her dreams include more references to falling than flying, and in only one of the latter references is she herself flying in a magical, physically impossible fashion. Mortality is a constant theme—almost two thirds of the reports have a reference to death. Every one of the dreams includes a verbal communication, and almost every report has a reference to some kind of thinking or mental activity. Half the dreams include something about reading or writing, which might seem surprising from a barely literate individual. Almost all the cultural categories have quite high frequencies, especially religion. In the dreams of contemporary people, the weapons frequency tends to be very low, usually under 5 percent, so Lucrecia's frequency of 50 percent (including references to spears, swords, knives, arrows, guns, and crossbows) is impressive.

In previous studies of long series of dreams, I have used the method of focusing exclusively on the word usage frequencies and making inferences about the individual's waking life with this information alone, bracketing out all other personal details about the dreamer and setting aside the dream narratives themselves. This method of "blind analysis" seeks to derive as much meaning as possible from the quantitative patterns of word usage.[12] With Lucrecia, we have already discussed her dreams and personal life, so we are not "blind" in assessing the results in Table 8.1. But we can still look at the quantitative patterns in her dreams and make some inferences about her waking life that, even if we knew nothing else about her, seem fairly clear from the word usage frequencies alone. Based on these frequencies, the following inferences could be proposed.

She is a highly perceptive and thoughtful person. She can be characterized as friendly, talkative, and socially engaged. Religion is very important to her. Males predominate in her life. She is not sexually active. She is not especially close to her family. She has nightmarish fears about death, weapons, and physical aggression.

We already knew about these factors in Lucrecia's biography, but the point here is to highlight their quantitative prominence in her dreams, too. The basic patterns of her dream content accurately reflect many of the most important features and concerns of her waking life.

Those are the obvious continuities, so what about the discontinuities? One possibility is that she has many dreams with references to reading and writing, but has only minimal literacy skills herself. Yet during this period of time Lucrecia had a scribe coming to her house every morning to record her dreams in manuscript form, later to be read by Don Alonso. The theme of reading and writing was definitely on her mind, even if she did not directly participate in these activities. So this theme is better understood as a continuity, not a discontinuity.

The high frequency of references to lions also stands out as unusual and potentially discontinuous with her waking life. As noted, many of these dreams involved the appearance of the Lion Man. But why was he associated with lions? Several dreams had him accompanied by an actual lion, while in other dreams Lucrecia simply referred to him as the Lion Man. She also dreamed of lions in other situations, so this was clearly a powerful and meaningful animal for her. Perhaps there was some degree of continuity with her own last name, de León, referring to the northern Spanish city of León. The word *león* means "lion" (although the city was actually named for the *legio*, or "legion," of Roman troops once stationed there). Perhaps in her visits to the churches and shrines of Madrid Lucrecia learned about the powerful but ambivalent role of the lion in Christian symbolism going back to the Bible, representing both the savage cruelty of nature and the noble power of the Messiah. The lion was also a common political symbol of the king, which might be connected to her concerns about Philip and the monarchy in Spain.

Popular stories of El Cid, the great Spanish knight of the 11th century, featured an episode where the hero showed his courage by capturing a lion. Taking all these possibilities into consideration, it appears the figure of the lion had an abundance of meaning for Lucrecia. As Freud would say, it is "overdetermined" as a symbol; it has multiple threads of meaning leading in several directions.

Characters and Settings

Every dream series, in addition to references to common categories like perceptions and emotions, also includes specific characters and settings, unique to the dreamer, that appear with varying frequencies. Table 8.2 shows the word search results for the main characters and settings in Lucrecia's dreams.

The most significant discontinuities in Lucrecia's dreams appear in this table. Her three companions had no direct, one-to-one connection with anyone or anything in her waking life. Don Alonso wanted to equate them with biblical characters, but their behavior in her dreams far exceeded those limited identities. They acted as independent beings with their own thoughts, feelings, interests, and intentions. They cared about Lucrecia's fate and the future of Spain, but they also had other concerns and pursuits elsewhere in the spirit world. The recurrence of these three distinct, vivid, and highly discontinuous characters is surely one of the most remarkable features of Lucrecia's dream series.

A further discontinuity associated with the three companions regards the usual location of their meeting, the seashore. There is no evidence Lucrecia ever visited an ocean beach in her waking life. Madrid lay hundreds of miles from the nearest coast; the city was located as far from the sea as one could be in Spain. Yet in her dreams she repeatedly visited the seashore to meet with her mysterious companions. This setting played a vital role in her dream experiences, even if it had no direct analog in her waking life.

Later chapters will fill out the possible meanings of these discontinuous elements of Lucrecia's dreams. The other results shown in Table 8.2 increase the number of clear continuities between her dream content

TABLE 8.2. Frequencies of Characters and Settings in Lucrecia's Dreams. These results come from searching for each proper name, using the SDDb's "free search" function, in the set of Lucrecia's dreams designated "Lucrecia Journal 1." The "Count" column indicates the number of dream reports that have at least one use of the proper name. The "Percentage" column divides the count by the total number of dreams to yield a percentage rounded to the nearest hundredth.

	Count	Percentage
Ordinary Man	33	92
Lion Man/Young Fisherman	24	67
Old Fisherman	21	58
companions	19	53
Seashore	24	67
Spain	18	50
Toledo	14	39
Madrid	13	36
King	30	83
Philip	16	44
Don Alonso	22	61
Fray Lucas (Luke)	23	64
Don Guillén	5	14
Piedrola	9	25
Armada, army*	9	25
Marquis of Santa Cruz	6	17
Francis Drake	7	19
England, English	13	36
Turk, Turks	7	19
Moor, Moors	6	17
God	24	67

*In some dream reports the word "army" is used to refer to the Armada.

and her waking life concerns. She dreamed frequently about Spain and its two most important cities, Madrid and Toledo, which was entirely consistent with her thoughts and activities in waking. Most of her dreams had a reference to king Philip, reflecting her acute concerns, widely shared by other people in Madrid, about their ruler's strength, health, and ability to protect their country. The high frequency of dreams about the king may also have had metaphorical dimensions touching on her personal relationship with her father.

Don Alonso and Fray Lucas appeared in a majority of her dreams, accurately reflecting their importance in her waking life. Don Guillén and Piedrola also appeared fairly often, which makes sense in relation to their considerable influence on her waking thoughts and behavior. Her dreams included a geopolitically accurate portrait of Spain's two greatest enemies—the English with Drake and his privateers, and the Turks with their Moorish allies. Her dreams about the Marquis of Santa Cruz and the Armada were discontinuous with the current reality of the waking world (the Armada had not yet sailed, the Marquis was still alive), but they could be seen as continuous with the concerns many people in Spain felt about the imminent launching of the Armada. In that sense, her dreams accurately reflected a collective mood of anxious anticipation regarding Philip's long-germinating plan to attack England.

The character of God played an intriguing role in Lucrecia's dreams. For a pious Catholic of her time who went to church regularly and listened to stories from the Bible, it would be unsurprising to experience at least some dreams with references to God. Lucrecia seemed to go well beyond that, however, with a majority of her dreams presenting God as an important character in his own right. In collections of dreams from contemporary people, I have found that most mentions of God take the form of oaths or exclamations, either positive ("Thank God!"; "God bless you") or negative ("God damn it!"). Lucrecia's dreams included a few "Thank God" comments, but most of them portrayed God as an absent but very involved character with a range of strong thoughts and feelings. He gave stern warnings and explicit instructions about how to behave. He was happy when people treated him well and followed his commandments, and he was angry when they ignored his will. He showed no hesitation in sending his wrath to punish evil people and teach them a lesson, even if some good people suffered as a consequence. Although he created this world, he had plans to destroy it because of its sinfulness and to create a new world in the future. He cared for those who obeyed him, however, and showed them mercy despite their failings. He was aware of the prophetic information passing from the companions to Lucrecia in her dreams, allowing it to happen yet controlling its flow so she did not become overwhelmed. The three companions could not be reduced to characters from the Bible, but they always acted in accordance with God's will, and in several dreams they seemed to serve as direct representatives of God—not quite angels themselves, but something along those lines.

All of this would be generally consistent with the standard portrait of God in Catholic theology; there was nothing in Lucrecia's dreams that violated Church teachings about the nature of the supreme deity or his involvement in human history. She never dreamed of God speaking directly to her or favoring her with special gifts or blessings, which gave her some legal protection during her trial. Other mystics and visionaries boasted about their direct, personal communications with God, and the Inquisition usually viewed these assertions as a punishable form of spiritual arrogance. Lucrecia never made any such claims. God in her dreams was vividly known, but not seen or heard. His will shaped everything, and everyone was subject to his emotional reactions, but he never actually appeared. He was omnipresent, yet never present. His character was woven into the very fabric of Lucrecia's dream world, just as the Church taught her was true of God's existence in the waking world. This is another instance of a strong continuity between her dreams and her waking life, and it fits well with other evidence indicating that she was a deeply and sincerely faithful Catholic who accepted the reality, power, and righteous judgment of the biblical God.

CHAPTER 9

COGNITIVE
SCIENCE

The Brain's Activities in Sleep

The previous two chapters have laid out the arguments in favor of accepting Lucrecia's reports as reasonably accurate and honest descriptions of her dreaming experiences. However, even accepting those arguments, it can still be doubted whether anyone could actually have dreams like hers, so lengthy and visually detailed, with so many full-bodied characters and so much rational thinking. Setting aside her personal motivations and the various continuities and discontinuities with her waking life, the question arises whether dreams with such features are even possible. Is there any reason to believe the sleeping brain has the capacity to generate dreams like these? For people who assume modern science has definitively concluded that dreams are nothing but neural nonsense, the answer would have to be no. But that assumption is contradicted by the past several decades of actual research on the sleeping brain. The modern neuroscience of sleep can shed light on several specific features in the contents of Lucrecia's dreaming experiences.

The basis for this approach is the genetically programmed anatomy of the human brain. The structure of our brains has remained more or less the same for at least 200,000 years, and this fact opens the possibility of using scientific research on the brains of modern people to make inferences about the mental lives of people from earlier times in history. As noted in the Introduction, great caution is needed to avoid the danger of mistaking our present-day theories for universal human truths. Fortunately, the current state of sleep research is solid enough to justify a number of high-probability inferences. Although human communities have shown a great deal of variation in where, when, how, and with whom people sleep, the cross-cultural evidence indicates that all members of our species share the same basic physiological needs for a regular period of sleep each night.[1] This fact provides a good starting point for a comparative analysis of dreaming.

Sleep has a long evolutionary history, with roots in the fundamental rhythms of biological existence on this planet. All mammals and birds display the key elements of sleep behavior (i.e., an easily reversed period of sensory withdrawal and quiescence, usually in a special place and in a special posture, usually at night), and so do many species of reptiles and fish. Our primate ancestors slept in polyphasic cycles, meaning a number of different sleep periods during the day and night. When our species, *Homo sapiens sapiens* (also known as "anatomically modern humans"), emerged from this evolutionary lineage a few hundred thousand years ago, our sleep behavior shifted to a monophasic pattern of one long stretch of sleep during the night (sometimes divided into two phases with a middle period of waking[2]). Humans have a somewhat smaller total amount of sleep than other primate species, but our sleep is more consolidated than theirs and less liable to disruption.

Most significantly, the human sleep cycle has a very high proportion of rapid eye movement (REM) sleep versus non-rapid eye movement (non-REM). Indeed, humans have one of the most REM-intensive sleep cycles of any creature on earth. The REM sleep pattern is vital for the early development of our brains. For most species, REM sleep is highest among newborns and the young, and then it tapers off as a percentage of total sleep in adults. Human babies spend up to 80 percent of their sleep in REM sleep, and although it diminishes over time, REM sleep remains very important throughout our life cycle, with most adults spending an average of 20 to 25 percent of their sleep in this phase of neural activation. Figure 9.1 shows the readings of an electroencephalograph (EEG) monitor during a typical night's sleep for a contemporary human.

To be clear: REM sleep is *not identical* with dreaming. The brain's functioning during REM sleep has strong connections with many recurrent features of dreaming experience, as I will discuss in a moment.

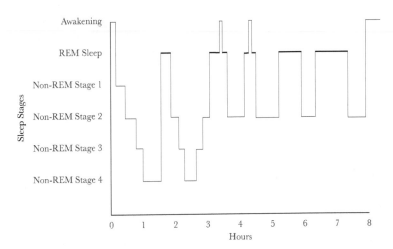

FIGURE 9.1. The Human Sleep Cycle,
as Measured by the Electroencephalograph (EEG).
A typical night's sleep of eight hours. After sleep onset, the brain quickly passes through non-rapid eye movement (non-REM) stage 1, the lightest stage of sleep. After that, stage 1 non-REM usually disappears, and phases of rapid eye movement (REM) sleep begin to appear, typically four or five times per night, with each REM phase getting longer in duration. During REM phases, the brain "rises up" to nearly waking levels of neural activity. The longest REM phase of the night is usually right before waking. The early part of the sleep cycle includes more non-rapid eye movement (non-REM) sleep, especially the non-REM stages 3 and 4 during the phase known as *deep sleep*. Later in the sleep cycle, non-REM stage 2 and REM phases dominate, and it becomes difficult to distinguish between them. Many sleep researchers now combine non-REM stages 2 and 3.

But dreams cannot be reductively explained as the psychological output of the neurology of REM sleep. For one thing, dreaming also occurs in non-REM stages of sleep.[3] For another, people with neurological damage that disrupts REM sleep can still experience dreams.[4] REM sleep is neither necessary nor sufficient for dreaming. A better way to think of the REM-dreaming relationship is to regard REM sleep as a reliable *trigger* for dreaming—a hard-wired program of neural stimulation that activates a host of complex cognitive processes all across the brain. Night after night, at all stages of the life span, REM sleep provides powerful pulses of internally generated arousal throughout the neural system. What happens after those parts of the brain are activated becomes the stuff of our dreams.

We can be very confident that, at a minimum, Lucrecia's sleep alternated between phases of REM and non-REM sleep. Assuming for the moment she had an average proportion of REM and non-REM sleep for a healthy adult human, her brain would have followed a deeply rooted program of arousal and activation at many levels of functioning. She would have started each night by spending some time in the quiet, low-energy neural state of non-REM sleep. Then her brain would suddenly be flooded with powerful waves and spikes of energy from the brainstem, initiating a new phase of REM sleep and a variety of changes to the brain's chemical, regional, and electrical activities.

In chemical terms, the neurotransmitter *acetylcholine*, which is crucial for conscious awareness during the waking state and diminishes during non-REM sleep, increases again in REM sleep to levels as high as those found in waking. The neurotransmitter *glycine*, which has the effect of rendering the body motionless, reaches its highest levels of production in REM sleep. There is a decrease in *GABA*, a neurotransmitter that inhibits brain activity (reducing GABA is like taking your foot off the brake of a car), and an increase in *dopamine*, which is associated in waking consciousness with curiosity, arousal, and desire.

In addition to these chemical changes in the brain, we can confidently presume that several regions of Lucrecia's neural anatomy became extremely active during REM sleep. These would include the *basal forebrain*, which serves as a conduit between the primitive brainstem and the higher-level functions of the *cortex* (the outer layer of the brain, especially large and densely interconnected in humans); the *pontine tegmentum*, which is associated with orienting responses to unknown environments; the *limbic system*, a neural region central to the processing of emotions, memories, and instinctual responses to survival-related situations; the *medial temporal lobe* and *fusiform gyrus*, both of them key to the brain's ability to generate visual imagination and internal imagery, with the medial temporal lobe playing an especially key role in social intelligence and "theory of mind" reasoning about other people's subjective experiences; and the *thalamus*, a neural gateway that blocks activity in the cortex from reaching the rest of the body.

The EEG is used to measure electrical processes across the brain, and researchers have found that the EEG profile of REM sleep is in many ways indistinguishable from the EEG profile of waking consciousness. In contrast to the quieter neuro-electrical conditions of non-REM sleep, the brain during REM sleep surges to extremely high levels of overall electrical arousal—so high that they rival the levels of the waking state. It turns out that REM sleep and waking consciousness are remarkably similar in their total production of neural energy. A key difference is that REM sleep uses the thalamus and the neurotransmitter glycine to block the bursts of neural energy from signaling the body to physically move; hence the general paralysis that accompanies each phase of REM sleep.

This is, of course, a highly condensed version of the current science of sleep. Even so, it gives a window into the most likely neural processes underlying Lucrecia's dreams. Every night when she fell asleep her brain shifted in and out of a state of heightened activation, with especially strong arousal in areas associated with primal emotions, visual imagination, social interactions, and orientation in space. The chemical balance of her neurotransmitters shifted toward more capacity for conscious awareness, more curiosity and desire, and less inhibition. Her body remained motionless in bed while her brain was intensely stimulated by powerful waves of internally generated neural energy. These hard-wired features of the sleeping brain provide a framework for the psychological experience of dreaming, and they help to account for many of the prominent features of Lucrecia's dream content: the strong visual impressions, turbulent emotions, complicated personal relationships, far-ranging travels, intense curiosity, multi-level thinking, and daring, uninhibited behavior.

The neurological activities of REM sleep do not completely determine what happens in dreaming, but they certainly stimulate and influence the process in a variety of ways. In Lucrecia's case the key features of REM sleep match up well with the basic patterns in her dreams. Nothing in her claims about the vividness and complexity of her dreaming exceeds or defies currently known facts about how the human brain functions in sleep.

Supernatural Agents

One of the earliest empirical dream studies by a modern psychologist was performed by Mary Whiton Calkins, whose 1893 article "Statistics of Dreams," published in the *American Journal of Psychology*, presented an analysis of several hundred dream reports (some of her own and some from a colleague).[5] Although her approach was rudimentary by present standards, Calkins accurately identified many of the basic patterns of dream content that bigger and more sophisticated research studies have since confirmed. One of these patterns has to do with social relations: most dreams include multiple characters with whom the dreamer interacts in various ways. Calkins's evidence led her to conclude, "the dream world is well-peopled."[6] Later studies have verified that dreams are indeed filled with a variety of characters, social interactions, spoken communications, and human-built environments.[7] Even though they take place in the solitude of sleep, dreams cast us into convivial realms teeming with interpersonal relations. The social aspects of waking life seem to have especially strong continuities with the general patterns of dream content.

This makes good sense in an evolutionary context, given the importance of social cognition in our species. A new branch of brain-mind research known as *social neuroscience* is pursuing the idea that the development of the human mind was shaped during evolutionary history by the adaptive benefits and pressures of living in a social group: "Our brains have evolved to connect to other minds, and our remarkable accomplishments as a species reflect our collective ability, as instantiated in each individual brain, rather than our individual might."[8] All of our primate cousins, such as the chimpanzees, have enormously complex hierarchies of social status and behavior, which means the mental capacities that underlie human social cognition are very deeply rooted in our genetic code.[9]

A good example of how this plays out in dreaming involves theory of mind reasoning. *Theory of mind* refers to the ability to recognize other people as independent, subjective beings with their own internal thoughts and feelings comparable to our own. It means that each of us forms a conceptual model of how other people's minds work so we can interact with them more effectively. This capacity to perceive, analyze, and interpret the mental states of others is a formidable achievement in human cognitive development. It takes the first several years of life to emerge fully, and it provides the foundation for empathy, compassion, cooperation, and a healthy social existence. Sociopaths and people with autism have severe problems in those parts of the brain (the medial temporal lobe) most closely associated with theory of mind. The fact that this part of the brain is highly active during REM sleep suggests we are capable of sophisticated reasoning about other people's minds in both our waking and dreaming states.

Lucrecia's dreams were populated by an abundance of characters from all across the social spectrum: real and fictional, secular and religious, human and animal, historical and mythological, familiar and unknown. Calkins's observation about the "well-peopled" nature of dream content certainly applied to Lucrecia's reports. Of all the different characters who passed through her dreaming imagination, the three companions were by far the most powerful minds with whom she interacted. They appeared in her dreams as distinct personalities with strong but largely hidden interests and motivations. They repeatedly eluded her attempts to understand their mental states; they kept her at a wary distance, and revealed only what they wanted to reveal.

To better understand their impact on her dreams, it helps to refer to current research in the cognitive science of religion (CSR) on "supernatural agents" as key figures in human religious beliefs and practices.[10] Supernatural agents can be defined as beings with their own autonomous minds who are like humans in many ways but who also possess extraordinary powers and magical abilities beyond the realm of human possibility. Examples of supernatural agents include ghosts, angels, demons, ancestral spirits, gods, saints, vampires, and aliens. All of them are typically portrayed as having human qualities and high-level cognitive functions. Yet they also can do things no human can do, like fly in the air, travel through time, and transform material objects.

According to CSR researchers, one reason why supernatural agents play such an important role in religious traditions all over the world is that they are extremely easy to remember and describe to others. Because humans are so instinctively primed for social cognition and theory of mind reasoning, we have little trouble applying our expectations about other people's minds to religious characters. We naturally assume these characters have mental lives like our own, and this automatically inclines us to believe that we can know and understand their minds in the same way we know the minds of other people. Their supernatural powers add to their memorability; they have attention-grabbing abilities that ordinary humans desire, yet cannot possess. These magical abilities function like a catchy hook in a song—they stick in the mind and make it easy to remember the character over a long period of time. The general CSR hypothesis is that religious traditions benefit from teaching their followers vivid stories about supernatural agents. The human, yet better than human, qualities of these supernatural agents work to implant the stories more deeply in people's minds and spread them more quickly to other people. A religious tradition with a colorful array of supernatural agents is thus more likely to survive, expand, and prosper than a tradition with fewer, less memorable religious characters.

The Roman Catholic tradition of Lucrecia's time was tremendously successful in promoting its teachings about a wide variety of supernatural agents, from God on down, and this does seem to be one of the keys to the tradition's power, longevity, and broad territorial expansion. It also helps explain why the Inquisition took such a dim view of Lucrecia's dreams. The three companions of her dreams were supernatural agents operating far outside the control of the Church. Despite Don Alonso's attempts to identify them with biblical characters, and the Inquisitors' efforts to find evidence of demonic origins, Lucrecia's companions were magical beings of a very different order. They seemed to occupy a kind of liminal zone between her dreaming and waking realities. They guided her deeply into the dream world and immersed her in its fantastic imagery and symbolism, yet also helped her stand apart from it so she could observe, interpret, and learn. The companions had many supernatural powers, including secret sources of knowledge and miraculous abilities to travel far distances. Their strange behavior made them highly memorable and compelling when described to others.

Threat Simulation

One of the leading cognitive scientific theories of dreaming comes from Antti Revonsuo, whose *social simulation* model of dreaming builds on the evidence we have just been considering. Revonsuo combines the importance of social intelligence in human evolution with the high frequency of interpersonal activities in dreams to offer the following hypothesis: dreaming functions in part to simulate social situations we are likely to face in the future, so we are better prepared and ready for adaptive responses if those situations actually do arise in waking life. The social simulation theory emphasizes the powerful *realism* of dreaming. According to Revonsuo, "dreamed action is experientially far more realistic than mere imagined action. . . . [W]e have good reasons to believe that dreamed action is equivalent to real action as far as the underlying brain mechanisms are concerned."[11] When we do something in a dream—run through a forest, talk with a friend, fight with an enemy—our brain processes the behavior as it would do in waking life, with the exception that the route to external physical action is blocked. This realism makes dreaming an excellent rehearsal space for practicing responses to various kinds of possible social situations.

Revonsuo developed this theory out of his earlier research on the *threat simulation* function of dreaming, which focused specifically on the evolutionary advantages of the human propensity for chasing nightmares.[12] He argued that frightening dreams of being chased and attacked, which have been reported in all cultures throughout history, serve the important function of simulating possible situations that could threaten the individual's survival. Although the dreams themselves can be filled with very negative content and upsetting emotions, their impact on behavior is ultimately positive in promoting greater vigilance, awareness, and readiness for quick action.

The threat simulation theory received criticism initially for being too narrow to account for the evolutionary functions of non-threat simulating dreams; hence the expanded scope of Revonsuo's social simulation theory. But the earlier theory remains an excellent way of understanding the function of certain kinds of typical nightmares, and Revonsuo was correct that such dreams are extremely realistic, highly memorable, and have been reported in virtually all cultures and periods of history.[13] Indeed, other psychologists throughout the 20th century pointed to the same adaptive feature of dreaming. C. G. Jung spoke of the "prospective function," by which dreams anticipate future challenges in psychological development.[14] Montague Ullman argued that dreaming promotes an optimal state of vigilance in waking life, and Frederick Snyder described dreams as part of a "sentinel system" to prepare for environmental danger.[15] Rosalind Cartwright's research highlighted the rehearsal features of dreaming, getting the individual's mind ready for future difficulties and opportunities.[16] Jeremy Taylor has shown how recurrent nightmares can provide alarms and warnings of potential problems the dreamer may encounter in the future.[17] All of these psychological theorists agree with Revonsuo that frightening dreams can be valuable guides to future challenges and dangers, with a preparatory function that improves a person's abilities to orient, adapt, and survive in the waking world.[18]

At one level, this line of research has direct relevance for the study of Lucrecia's dreams, which were overflowing with simulations of potential dangers looming in the future. No other single theme better describes the overall tenor and thrust of her dreams. Yet at another level, Lucrecia's dreams deviated in a major way from the threat simulation approach of Revonsuo and most of the other psychologists. Their theories describe why dreams have a tendency to anticipate dangers to the individual, whereas Lucrecia's dreams anticipated dangers to her *community*, namely the people of Spain. She apparently developed the capacity to experience threat simulating nightmares regarding the welfare not only of herself, but also of her broader social group.

Modern psychologists and cognitive scientists generally refrain from going beyond the individual when discussing the functions of dreaming, but their research findings do allow for a wider range of application. Chapters 11 and 12 will discuss evidence that supports an expansion of these theories to include dreams that simulate threats to collective realities in addition to individual concerns.

Metacognition

The hypothesis that dreaming has an anticipatory function is dependent on our having the mental ability while asleep to think and reason about the future. This might seem questionable to some readers—can the sleeping mind really engage in these complex activities of conscious reasoning? Dreams are filled with vibrant images and strong emotions, but is there any evidence in them of rational forethought?

One of the most paradoxical findings of modern dream research is that the sleeping mind can do almost anything that can be done by the waking mind. Dreaming and waking are not diametrically opposed; they actually share a large number cognitive features, combined and interwoven in various ways.[19] A major focus of investigation in this area has been lucid dreaming, which means dreams of becoming self-aware within the dream state. Beginning in the 1970s, psychologists have experimented with methods of inducing consciousness within dreaming, and they have found that some people have a remarkable aptitude for lucid self-awareness within the condition of sleep.[20] Further research has determined that more than half the population has had at least one lucid dream in their lives, suggesting the latent capacity is widely distributed. Other studies have shown that younger people are more likely than older people to have frequent lucid dreams, and many children spontaneously develop the ability without any external prompting. It seems that consciousness in dreaming depends on a high degree of cognitive flexibility, which is greatest in early life and can diminish over time. Several researchers and educators have devised methods to teach people how to achieve more lucidity in their dreaming, with results indicating a fairly high degree of effectiveness.

The mental abilities available in lucid dreams depend on the participation of many neural systems all across the brain, not just in the brainstem. During lucid dreaming people are able to think, reflect, move, and act in ways that indicate the activation of high-level cognitive functions, many of them centered in the brain's prefrontal cortex. A general term that psychologists now use to describe these functions is *metacognition*.[21] The literal meaning of metacognition is "thinking about or beyond thinking." It refers to the ability to take our own mental activities as an object of thought. Self-awareness is one clear example of metacognition, but the term includes many other mental functions that require a capacity to monitor and regulate the activities of one's own mind. Remembering, evaluating, questioning, testing, judging, planning, anticipating, preparing, and deciding are all common instances of metacognition. They are pervasive in the waking state and form a significant part of what many neuroscientists call the *executive system* of waking consciousness.

Full-blown lucidity is an especially striking form of metacognition in dreaming. So is the experience of observing oneself from a detached perspective, which is quite frequent for some people. Many other dreams have an abundance of metacognition, even though the dreamer never formulates the specific thought, "I am dreaming."[22] This seems to have been the case with Lucrecia. Her dreams were overflowing with complex mental activities, yet she was never lucid in the sense of focusing on the realization of her own self-awareness. She apparently accepted the conscious qualities of her dreaming as a matter of course, and proceeded with the unfolding experience.[23]

The key point is that, according to the current findings of cognitive science, nothing about Lucrecia's dreams would have required impossible feats from her dreaming mind. The high levels of metacognition she described are consistent with the various kinds of mental activities known to be possible in dreaming.

More Than Average

Human cognitive abilities are not evenly or equally distributed. They appear in varied proportions across a broad spectrum of the population. Some people may have an extremely strong innate capacity for a certain kind of mental activity, while other people are endowed with much less of that capacity. So far in this chapter, we have been assuming that Lucrecia was an average person with an average mind, right in the middle of the cognitive spectrum. That is the safest place to aim the analysis, methodologically speaking. But what if the evidence, considered as a whole, indicates she was *not* average? What if it makes more sense to view her as someone at the extreme end of the scale, with tremendous natural aptitude for various types of cognitive functioning in sleep? We should consider the possibility that Lucrecia had unusually powerful, innate abilities for dreaming that were rare, but not beyond the pale of scientific understanding. There are several reasons to believe this was so.

To begin with, she was a frequent dreamer from early childhood, as several sources of testimony agreed. She had extremely high recall and a tremendous amount of metacognition in her dreams. These characteristics alone marked her as someone with unusually intensified forms of innate human dreaming abilities. The fact that she was a young woman is consistent with modern psychological research showing that dream recall is more frequent among young people than older people, and more frequent among women than men. Current research also indicates (as noted earlier) that young people are more likely than older people to have lucid dreams. This suggests Lucrecia was a member of the demographic group most prone to remember their dreams and consciously engage with them.

Some researchers have looked at correlations between high dream recall and the personality factor of "openness to experience," and it does seem that Lucrecia was a relatively open person, perhaps more than was healthy for her.[24] She spoke freely about her dreams; took a lively interest in art, religion, and international politics; and listened avidly to other people's reports of strange spiritual phenomena. Within the strict moral confines of late 16th century Madrid, she displayed many of the behaviors that would be consistent with a relatively open personality. Indeed, it would make a great deal of sense that a person at the extreme end of the openness-to-experience spectrum would, unfortunately, struggle in a rigid, narrow-minded culture. That alone might explain a lot about her case.

This chapter has highlighted numerous ways in which the evolved architecture of the human brain-mind system corresponds to many important elements of Lucrecia's dreams. Even if we assume she was nothing more than an ordinary human being, we can be very confident her sleeping brain was capable of generating dreams with all of these features. This is strong support for a naturalistic account of her experiences. However, even more explanatory power comes from assuming that Lucrecia deviated significantly, but not pathologically, from the human norm in her dreaming abilities. Consider again Figure 9.1 and the EEG portrait of a typical night's sleep. Most people—that is, those in the middle of the recall spectrum—remember only a tiny fraction of what passes through their minds during these recurrent cycles of neural hyper-arousal. But people at the higher end of the spectrum (who tend to be young, female, and open to experience) have greater access to the vast amount of mental activity that occurs during sleep, and thus their dream reports are likely to be much longer and more detailed than the reports of people with average recall. If unusually high recall goes along with an expanded capacity for lucidity and metacognition (which researchers have found is often the case[25]), then the dream reports of such individuals will also include extremely intensified forms of thought, consciousness, and self-awareness, going far beyond the range of most people's dreaming experience. All the evidence of Lucrecia's case indicates that she was precisely this kind of person.

CHAPTER 10

RELATIONAL
PSYCHOLOGY

Growing Up

Little information has survived regarding Lucrecia's early childhood and the conditions in which she was raised. This drastically limits our ability to apply ideas from modern psychology to the study of her case. But the various details we do know about her family life enable us to make at least a few psychologically oriented interpretations.

The most useful resource here is *relational psychology*, a broad designation for theories that look at people's mental functioning as it emerges in relationships with other people.[1] Relational psychology has value for the study of Lucrecia's case for at least three reasons. First, her dreams contained a wide variety of characters, conversations, and personal interactions; social relations were clearly a major theme in her dream content. Second, the most detailed surviving material about her waking behavior involved her relationships with other people. This means a psychological analysis of this aspect of her case can draw upon a relatively robust source of information. And third, as the previous chapter indicated, a powerful capacity for social intelligence is deeply ingrained in the evolutionary framework of our brains. Relational psychology is fully compatible with this view. For more than one hundred years—in fact, long before the invention of brain scanning devices—psychologists have been exploring the social dimensions of the mind and identifying recurrent themes in the development of people's relationships over time. The theories and ideas of this lineage of research, if employed with due caution, can add new insights to an understanding of Lucrecia's life and dreaming.

A relational approach has not always occupied a central place in modern psychology. Quite the contrary. For much of the 20th century the psychoanalytic theories of Sigmund Freud encouraged a view of human development in which the highest goals were independence, autonomy, and separation from others. Freud and many other psychologists focused their therapeutic practices on strengthening the agency and selfhood of the individual. They defined psychological growth as inversely proportional to one's embeddedness in relationships with other people. A mature individual was conceived as entirely self-reliant, self-motivated, and unencumbered by social entanglements. Later in the 20th century many psychologists rejected Freudian theory, but they still preserved his emphasis on the individual when they formulated new theories of the human mind as an information-processing machine or a rational self-interest optimizer.

Even in Freud's works, however, there were seeds of awareness that mental health requires the development of a capacity for mutual relationships with other people. These seeds grew more fully in the works of his followers, especially Melanie Klein, Erik Erikson, D. W. Winnicott, Heinz Kohut, and John Bowlby. The basic idea, as Winnicott put it, is that "there is never just a baby." There is always (in normal, healthy circumstances) an adult caregiver, too, usually the mother or father, giving close and nearly constant attention to the baby.[2] The caregiving context can vary from culture to culture and family to family, but the point is that humans do not enter the world as solitary individuals. Rather, we begin life as relational beings, engaged from the moment of birth in complex social interactions with other people. The human mind develops within a relational matrix. Over time, psychological growth proceeds by building up mental abilities that enable us to navigate more skillfully through the multiple communities in which our adult lives take shape and unfold.

Despite the great separation of time and culture, modern relational psychology can advance our understanding of Lucrecia's case by highlighting several important themes in the social dynamics of her dreams and her waking life. A relational approach emphasizes a person's family background in the earliest years of childhood, when the first inter-personal experiences occur. Most people learn about social reality as children through their interactions with parents, siblings, and extended relatives, and these family interactions often become mental templates for developing other relationships later in life. In Lucrecia's childhood, her mother and father seemed to shape her behavior in powerful yet deeply conflicting ways. A relational approach also focuses on adoles-cence and the twin developmental tasks of establishing an adult identity and forming a mature, intimate bond with another person. Different cul-tures can make these tasks easier or harder for young people and their families to manage successfully; Lucrecia had to struggle mightily on both fronts. And a relational approach takes special interest in gender norms regarding proper male and female behavior. Again, different cul-tures can either promote or inhibit certain kinds of gender interactions, with direct consequences for people's psychological development and mental health. The male-dominated gender rules governing Lucrecia's upbringing colored all of her personal relationships as well as her treat-ment by the Inquisition.

Her Mother and Father

Ana Ordoñez, Lucrecia's mother, was almost certainly her daughter's primary caregiver from birth onward. Probably still in her own teens when she first became pregnant, Ana and her husband started their fam-ily in the midst of a new and rapidly changing urban environment. This meant she received little or no assistance from a traditional kinship net-work, the kind of social support system that develops when multiple gen-erations of a family live in the same area over long periods of time. In the brand-new capital city of Madrid, virtually everyone was a recent ar-rival, and few people had any deep connections to local family. The city was literally a work in progress. The rapid construction of new buildings, roads, and neighborhoods kept the city's physical character in constant flux, and its social dynamics kept expanding in size and complexity with the surging inflow of new residents from all over the country. To live in Madrid during this period of booming growth would have required a

So, for historical individuals for whom we lack this sort of info, what sort of step. is possible?

great deal of adaptive flexibility and a keen eye for the sudden appearance of both threats and opportunities.

With her husband at work in the royal palace and often away on business travel, Ana was largely on her own in caring for her daughter and tending to household chores. This suggests that Lucrecia's first several years of life took shape within her mother's world of urban domesticity. With no other siblings arriving until she was 5 years old, Lucrecia initially grew up as an only child. She and her mother very likely spent a great deal of time together during the course of Ana's daily activities: cooking, cleaning, doing laundry, fetching water, going to the market, and attending church. In such a densely populated neighborhood, these tasks would have brought them into regular contact with other women engaged in similar activities. The close-knit sphere of women's domestic work provided the original relational environment of Lucrecia's life.

From what we know of Ana's behavior toward her daughter in later years, their relationship was mostly positive. Although Lucrecia said both her parents beat her for dreaming when she was a child, there can be little doubt she was closer to her mother than her father. Ana eventually became a strong supporter of her daughter's dreaming, and she did what she could to help the process. Despite her husband's disapproval, Ana arranged for Don Alonso's scribes to visit their home each day, and she later accompanied Lucrecia on her social visits to talk about the dreams. As a dutiful Catholic wife, Ana had little direct power in her relationship with her husband, but she did show a willingness to defy him indirectly by encouraging Lucrecia's continued sharing of her dreams.

All in all, the evidence suggests that Ana and Lucrecia had a fairly strong mother-daughter bond. According to most relational psychologists, a close attachment between child and primary caregiver(s) in early life provides the foundation for a sense of basic trust in the world.[3] This bedrock feeling of trust makes it possible to open ourselves more fully to others, deepen our interpersonal connections, and expand our social horizons. Lucrecia did seem to have the psychological virtue of basic trust—she was pleasant and sociable with other people, she felt pride in the Spanish nation, and she willingly shared her dreams with others. Her

Also, this seems very suppositional.

trusting nature may have derived in part from her religious faith, which taught her to believe in the ultimate power and benevolence of God. But in psychological terms this basic trust must have also come from those early years of steady and intimate companionship with her young mother as she worked to make a life for their family in the big, bustling city.

Lucrecia's relationship with her father, Alonso Franco de León, had a very different cast. As noted earlier, his business with the court kept him away from home for long stretches of time. Compared with her mother, he was a much more distant presence in Lucrecia's life and upbringing. Among the few known details about his character and personality, he clearly prized his identity as an Old Christian and jealously guarded the honor of his family. By naming his first child after a legendary symbol of feminine chastity and obedience, Alonso made it clear from the start what kind of behavior he expected from his children. He freely admitted that he beat Lucrecia to make her stop talking about her dreams, in early recognition of the trouble they could, and eventually did, cause the family.

Despite its individualist bias, Freud's psychoanalytic theory of early child development does have relevance here, although in an unusual way. Freud regarded emotional conflict between parents and children as an important engine of psychological growth. According to his notion of the "Oedipus complex," boys in the first few years of life typically feel a jealous rivalry with their fathers over the affections of their mothers (just as in the Greek myth, Oedipus unknowingly killed his father and married his mother).[4] The developmental task for boys is to separate from their mothers and identify with their fathers so they can become mature and independent adults. For young girls, Freud spoke of a feminine version of the Oedipus complex, a reverse process in which they feel rivalry with their mother over their shared desire for the father (C. G. Jung referred to the feminine version as the "Electra complex," following the Greek myth in which Electra incites her brother to kill their mother, who has murdered their father; Freud, however, did not accept this terminology). Psychoanalysis views the feminine path to individuality as more complicated than the masculine path because young girls have to learn to separate from their mothers and yet identify with them, too, while simultaneously diminishing their attachment to their fathers. The difficulties that boys and girls experience at this stage of psychological development can have long-lasting effects on their abilities to form mature relationships as adults.

A Freudian approach is not always helpful, and even in the best of circumstances caution is required in applying an early 20th century model of the mind to a person who lived in the late 16th century. But bringing psychoanalytic ideas into the discussion does shed some interesting light on Lucrecia's development from early childhood into young adulthood. Contrary to Freud's expectations, she had a mostly positive relationship with her mother, and a mostly antagonistic one with her father. What accounts for this variation from the typical form of the female Oedipus complex? A strong possibility is that her father's behavior made it difficult for Lucrecia to develop in a psychologically healthy fashion. Not that she was blameless for the tensions between them, but Alonso's domineering actions toward her had a dramatically negative impact on their relationship. His hostility to her dreaming reflected a refusal to appreciate something that was important and meaningful to her, something that gave her a distinctive way of connecting with other people and participating in larger social conversations. The offer from Don Alonso de Mendoza to settle Lucrecia in a convent seemingly presented a convenient opportunity to move her out of the house and into a religiously respectable situation. Yet her father rejected that, too; he insisted his daughter remain at home, and he told Don Alonso and everyone else to leave his family alone.

In effect, Alonso de León tried to prevent Lucrecia from growing up. His behavior indicated that, more than anything else, he wanted her to remain a child. His actions and inactions had the cumulative result of preventing any changes in her status as his daughter, living in his home, under his control, unavailable to other men and completely subservient to his authority. Alonso's denial of her approaching adulthood made it impossible for their relationship to develop in a healthy direction.

It is hard to know what impact this conflict had on Lucrecia. The fact that she continued sharing her dreams despite her father's threatening commands can certainly be interpreted as a form of rebellion against him, one of the few ways she could elude his control and interact with people on her own terms. Indeed, the content of her dreams lends itself to a classic Freudian interpretation in which the recurrent images of aggression toward King Philip can be seen as symbolic expressions of aggression toward her father.[5] Dreaming about God's punishment of the king for his unjust treatment of the Spanish people would, in this view, express a symbolic wish-fulfillment of her desire to punish her father for his unjust treatment of her. The king's failures were echoes of her father's failures; both men were contemptible tyrants in Lucrecia's eyes. Her fervent anticipation of the end of Philip's oppressive empire reflected her yearning for the end of her father's oppressive regime at home. This line of interpretation certainly accords with the emotional quality of her relationship with her father.

Lucrecia's three sisters and one brother arrived in rapid succession when she was between the ages of 5 and 10. With that much age difference, the younger children probably had closer interactions with each other than with their older sister. They might have treated Lucrecia more as a parental figure than as another child, which would have been ironic given their father's infantilizing attitude toward her. Despite growing up in a large family, Lucrecia seems to have had a close relationship only with her mother. That was apparently enough to establish a strong sense of basic trust and general sociability, but it may also have primed her to look beyond the family for more stimulating and satisfying relationships.

Her Followers

Lucrecia's social interactions with her followers played a major role in shaping her psychological development during a pivotal time of her life. At one level, these interactions were utterly ruinous for Lucrecia. Thanks to the indiscretions of her followers, the Inquisition arrested her in 1590, tortured her, and held her prisoner for nearly five years while she awaited a final judgment that could bring an end to her life. In her time of greatest need, her followers disavowed her and actively damaged her case. She would have had good reason to feel bitterly betrayed by her alleged supporters. Yet these same people had also helped Lucrecia in many vital ways, by nurturing her innate dreaming abilities, encouraging her to share her experiences with others, and validating the importance of her dreams for the future welfare of their country. Without their passionate efforts, Lucrecia's dreams would never have reached as big an audience or made as powerful an impact as they did on her community.

Don Alonso de Mendoza was the mastermind of the whole project, and he was the greatest champion of Lucrecia's cause until, at the very end, he went insane. He came from one of the great noble families of Spain and held an eminent position in the Church hierarchy, which guaranteed him a high degree of social privilege and enabled him to protect Lucrecia from the Inquisition's attacks, at least for a while. For years people had doubted Don Alonso's mental stability, and his eccentric history of probing into strange physical and spiritual phenomena further tarnished his reputation.[6] Nevertheless, he was highly educated, deeply cultured, intellectually curious, and perhaps the first person to take Lucrecia seriously in her own right, not just as her father's daughter. Don Alonso recognized Lucrecia's gift for dreaming as soon as he met her, and he did more than anyone else to promote her dreams and defend their legitimacy and value. Their relationship opened the door for Lucrecia to become an active member of the social world outside her family, where her unusual talents could help in addressing the major concerns of her community. With Don Alonso's guidance and encouragement, she developed her innate abilities in a way that began to take shape as a special kind of adult identity. Even though her arrest by the Inquisition cut the process short, Don Alonso taught her to listen carefully to her dreams and accept without fear their extraordinary insights. No one of his stature had ever said that before, and it clearly made a deep impact on her emerging sense of self.

Yet their relationship had unhealthy aspects as well, and in the end these may have been more decisive. Don Alonso essentially treated Lucrecia as an object of research. He was in charge of everything, and she was required to obey his instructions. Eventually he began to treat her as an instrument or tool, like a magnifying glass he was learning to hold at the proper distance from a text. He spent a great deal of time with her and may have felt some paternal or even romantic interest in her, but there is no real evidence of that. His behavior before and during the trial was more consistent with an attitude of wanting to protect an especially valuable piece of equipment from getting damaged. Although he behaved kindly and protectively toward her, she was ultimately nothing more than a useful means to his political and theological ends. This lack of mutuality and compassion in their relationship meant that Lucrecia could only grow so much under Don Alonso's tutelage.

Fray Lucas de Allende was another person of high social stature who, initially at least, took a genuine interest in Lucrecia's dreams. As her new confessor, he became the caretaker of her soul and the trusted repository of her most private thoughts and feelings. Although he acknowledged her unusual spiritual powers, Fray Lucas never seems to have totally recovered from the early shock of her strange clairvoyant dream of his monastic cell. He dutifully continued serving as her scribe each morning, but he never promoted her cause as avidly as Don Alonso did. When the Inquisition arrested them all, Fray Lucas did not hesitate to condemn Lucrecia, denounce her dreams, and distance himself from the whole affair.

Don Guillén de Casaos, the former governor of the Yucatan, had a relationship with Lucrecia that led to a deeper level of intimacy than she found with either Don Alonso or Fray Lucas. Don Guillén showed interest in her dreams, and he clearly enjoyed spending time with her personally. He treated her not as a theological project but as a friendly young woman with a fascinating inner life. Their conversations gave Lucrecia a new arena in which she could learn about various kinds of spiritual phenomena with relevance to her dream experiences. Don Guillén's wide-ranging knowledge of the world fed her curiosity and stimulated her imagination.

The romantic desires of Don Guillén indicated that he, for one, certainly regarded Lucrecia as more than a child. In his eyes she was fully an adult: mature and intelligent and ready for a conjugal relationship. She could hardly have been unaware of Don Guillén's sentiments, which

signaled rather clearly that, despite her father's resistance, she was rapidly approaching a new developmental stage of life. She welcomed that
new stage and looked forward to its arrival, even though she decided
it would not involve marrying Don Guillén. For whatever reasons—his
age, temperament, views of women—Lucrecia declined his romantic
overtures. Somehow she did so in a way that preserved their friendship
and intensified his efforts on her behalf. Until the day of their arrest Don
Guillén remained an active and energetic supporter of Lucrecia's cause.
He helped organize the Holy Cross of the Restoration and drafted a
formal request to the Pope for recognition of that group as a legitimate
religious order. Other than Don Alonso, no one was more devoted to the
significance of her dreams, and no one seemed more excited about the
group's future endeavors. Yet everything changed when the Inquisition
arrested them. Don Guillén immediately turned against Lucrecia at the
trial and gave testimony that denounced her dreams, repudiated her as
a liar, and denied any special relationship with her. To save himself he
cast her in a terrible light, which he must have known would help the
Inquisition's efforts to prove her guilty. Of all her followers, his betrayal
was the most surprising and dispiriting. Don Guillén had given Lucrecia
invaluable help in developing her sense of identity as a mature adult, but
in the end he was willing to abandon their friendship and use her as a
bargaining chip with the Inquisitors to avoid his own punishment.

Lady Jane Dormer, known in Madrid as the Duchess of Feria, played
an intriguing role in Lucrecia's life. She was like a fairy godmother, providing Lucrecia's family with a home, looking out for Lucrecia's interests, and bestowing favors on her. Originally born in England, Lady Jane
had close connections to the king going back to Philip's original trip to
London in 1554 to woo Queen Mary. A teenager at the time, Jane was
the queen's favorite lady-in-waiting, and one of the small group of royal
attendants who witnessed firsthand the Spanish king's courtship of their
monarch. Indeed, Lady Jane was so closely involved with the Spanish
royal delegation that she pursued a courtship of her own, and later married one of Philip's chief ambassadors, the Duke of Feria. Lady Jane,
now the Duchess of Feria, moved with him to Madrid, and after his

There's a flatness here — presentism. No historicist feeling that "the past is a foreign country."

Also cultural flatness.

death in 1571, she managed his extensive properties and worked on diplomatic projects to help Catholics still living in England.

Lady Jane was probably the most powerful and independent woman Lucrecia personally knew, and perhaps a role model of some sort. The noblewoman seemed to recognize special qualities in Lucrecia from an early age and helped to expose her to the wider world, first by working in the royal palace and then by sharing her dreams with other elite members of Madrid society. The assistance Lady Jane gave to Lucrecia created a different kind of relationship from the ones she had with her male followers. Rather than treating Lucrecia as an object of study or a target of amorous desire, Lady Jane gave the young woman invaluable opportunities to meet new people, interact with them, and share her experiences. In developmental terms this was exactly what Lucrecia most needed to keep growing and stretching her abilities. Whatever personal benefit Lady Jane may have gained from their relationship, her intentions seem to have been driven by a genuine trust in Lucrecia and an empathetic awareness of what would be most helpful for her growth.

It is remarkable that Lady Jane was not arrested along with the rest of Lucrecia's followers. Perhaps it would have aroused too much public attention to include such a prominent member of the nobility in the trial. If the Inquisitors arrested Lady Jane, they would probably have had to arrest other socially powerful people who had attended gatherings with Lucrecia. This would make the situation look like a huge plot against the king, which might alarm the public and further erode confidence in Philip's rule. Whether or not this was the reason, Lady Jane was never arrested, and she never gave the Inquisition any evidence to doubt Lucrecia's claims of innocence.

Her Husband and Daughter

Diego de Vitores was the man Lucrecia finally chose to marry. We do not know if she felt an extraordinary connection with him, or if he was simply the first suitable male to come within matrimonial range, but this is what she decided to do. By exchanging her vows with Vitores in secret, Lucrecia made sure she entered a romantic relationship on her own terms, without interference from other people trying to control her life for their purposes.

Her choice of Vitores over Don Guillén suggests that she did not prioritize social status or economic prosperity, both of which would have been much greater in a marriage with Don Guillén. Instead, Lucrecia seemed to desire a chance for greater mutuality with a man like Vitores, someone closer to her age who shared her curiosity about the world. He was intelligent, cultured, and educated, and he may have helped to teach her to read and write; a besotted professional scribe would be well suited to that task. They had never been able to live together openly as husband and wife, but they apparently remained committed to each other throughout their time in prison. Despite all the obstacles blocking her path to a mature romantic relationship, Lucrecia finally found a man who loved her and whom she loved. This may not explain much about her dreams, since Vitores appeared so late in the recording process, but the strength of their relationship may be significant in accounting for Lucrecia's remarkable resilience during her trial and imprisonment.

The same might have been true of her relationship with her daughter, Margarita. It must have been enormously stressful for Lucrecia to go through labor and delivery while imprisoned by the Inquisition, and the odds were not good for the survival of either mother or baby. Yet they did survive, and it is possible Lucrecia actually found the maternal process comforting, or at least reassuringly familiar. After all, she had watched her own mother successfully endure four pregnancies, four deliveries, and the raising of four newborns. Lucrecia knew in great detail what was involved in taking care of a baby, and this may have helped to focus her energy and attention on something other than her own dire situation.

The name she chose for her daughter, Margarita, suggested that Lucrecia regarded the girl's birth as a divine gift. As already noted, the Catholic Santa Margarita was a 13th century Italian woman who became the spiritual patron of midwives, single women, and the falsely accused. Lucrecia surely knew her story, and the decision to give this saint's name to her daughter seemed to express the profound gratitude of a faithful Catholic (who happened to be a woman who was alone, recently delivered of a child, and falsely accused) for God's miraculous protection during a time of harrowing danger and uncertainty.

The slow, tedious legal proceedings of the Inquisition served a prosecutorial function by wearing prisoners down, weakening their resistance, and eventually persuading them to confess their crimes. For Lucrecia, the lengthy trial had no such effect. She was as defiant at the end of the proceedings as she had been at the beginning, five years earlier. Even by the Inquisition's own standards this was an unusually long case, grinding along with no resolution because Lucrecia refused to admit any significant wrongdoing. How did she endure so much pressure and maintain the strength of her resistance? Part of that strength likely came from the highly energizing experience of parenting a child into the world. The emergence of this new relationship in her life meant that Lucrecia was no longer responsible only for herself. She had a daughter to protect and care for, which gave her even more reason to reject the Inquisition's charges of heresy and insist on her innocence and faithfulness to the church. If anything, their being confined together in prison probably had the effect of intensifying the parent-child relationship by limiting their contact with outside people and encouraging more intimacy between them.

Lucrecia's marriage to Vitores transformed her into a wife. Margarita's birth transformed her into a mother. These new relational identities completed Lucrecia's passage into adulthood, and not a moment too soon. She needed all the emotional strength she could muster to resist the Inquisition's pressure and find some way to gain freedom for herself and her family.

CHAPTER 11

POLITICS
AND SOCIETY

The Political Psyche

The political and social dimensions of Lucrecia's case have already received a great deal of academic attention, with excellent historical research from Kagan, Jordán, Osborne, and others, which means this chapter does not need to repeat all their findings. The studies of these scholars have shown in impressive detail that Lucrecia's dream reports reflected important themes and conflicts in Spain's imperial policies in the late 16th century. The surviving documents from her trial provide valuable insights into the religious symbolism of dissent, the public's attitude towards the royal family, and the Inquisition's legal procedures during this period. However, as noted in the Introduction, studies like these do not assume that Lucrecia's reports represented actual dreams. Historical researchers usually bracket out this issue and focus their investigations on the impact of the reports on other people, whether or not genuine dreams were involved.

The findings of these historians might actually seem to cast further doubt on the credibility of Lucrecia's claims. Most people dream about political matters rarely if ever, yet for Lucrecia it was apparently a regular occurrence, with long, detailed narratives about imperial activities all over the world. The nearly constant presence in her dreams of prominent characters and settings relating to Spain's geopolitical situation seems inconsistent with her life as a barely literate teenage girl growing up in an obscure, unimportant family.[1] This was surely the greatest discontinuity of all between her waking and dreaming life, and it calls into question the plausibility of a person like her actually dreaming about grand affairs of state so far distant and removed from her personal, day-to-day experiences.

To begin addressing this issue, it should be pointed out that Lucrecia was not unique in her dreaming about collective realities and community concerns. There is a long cross-cultural history of political dreaming that stretches from ancient times into the present day.[2] Dreams about political issues may not occur frequently for most people, but when such dreams do occur they can make a strong and lasting impression on waking memory. They become especially impactful during times of social crisis, when a group is in danger and uncertainty hovers over everyone's future. During these times dreams can become a valuable means of expressing people's widely shared fears, mourning their collective losses, and preparing for future threats that potentially affect them all.

One of the best and most poignant illustrations of this dimension of dreaming appears in Charlotte Beradt's 1966 book *The Third Reich of Dreams*.[3] The book presents a selection of the hundreds of dreams Beradt gathered from people living in Germany from 1933 to 1939, during the rise of Adolph Hitler and the National Socialist Party, or Nazis. The dreams revealed in horrifying detail the profoundly destructive impact of a totalitarian political regime on the inner psychological life of its members. Many of the dreams revolved around fears of insecurity, loss of privacy, and the chilling realization that the Nazis were now in control of all aspects of people's lives. In some dreams people struggled against the violent pressure to submit to Hitler's rule, but they rarely prevailed for long. Most of the dreams reflected a bleak sense of helplessness against the all-powerful Nazi state. Although Beradt presented little background information about the dreamers, their concerns about the dire political situation in their country came through very clearly. Their dreams did not dwell on purely personal fantasies or symbolic struggles with their parents. These people were dreaming about frightening political forces in the outer world threatening their community.

Nazi Germany from 1933 to 1939 was an extreme case of political oppression, but the collection of dreams Beradt gathered is invaluable in highlighting the general capacity of dreaming to engage directly with political and social realities, especially when the right (or wrong) circumstances are present. Many other cultures have long traditions of relying on dreams for insight and guidance about collective concerns. The rulers of ancient India, China, Egypt, and Greece made a practice of consulting dreams, their own and those of their subjects, as one of many sources of information they used to make governmental decisions.[4] The Prophet Muhammad, the founder of Islam, made a practice each morning of asking his followers about their dreams so he could identify images and symbols of possible significance for their group.[5] The English Protestants known as Quakers, who journeyed across the Atlantic to New England in the 17th and 18th centuries, kept close track of their dreams and shared them with each other, reflecting both their utopian ideals and the aggressive imperialism supporting their new communities in America.[6] In the 19th century, Native American visionaries created new spiritual movements, or "dreamer religions," based on powerful dreams that helped their indigenous cultures respond to the violent encroachment of white European settlers.[7]

In all these traditions, dreams become more socially and politically relevant during times of collective crisis and upheaval, and special attention is given to people who have an aptitude for dreaming about community concerns.[8] Perhaps the closest parallel to Lucrecia's situation comes from England during the Renaissance (a period parallel to the Siglo del Oro in Spain), when people's dreams reflected their concerns about the country's tumultuous political and religious affairs. According to historian Carole Levin, the English rulers and church authorities of this time struggled to control the unruly power of dreaming during an era of major cultural upheaval:

> The frequent changes in state religion and in the nature of monarchy caused a time of great instability in which the religious, cultural, and social boundaries of identity became more permeable. Dreams, both actual and created for use as propaganda, give us greater insight into how these insecurities were felt. . . . Dreams of people in sixteenth- and early seventeenth-century England allow us to understand how external events intensely penetrated the deepest recesses of the unconscious.

Dreams reflected and interrelated with the most significant political, religious, and cultural values of the time. This is especially evident when examining the dreams about monarchs such as Elizabeth I.[9]

In recent years I have tried to add to this general area of research with several studies of dreams and contemporary American politics.[10] Since 1992, most of these studies have revolved around presidential elections and people's dreams of the candidates, and a few studies have looked at dreaming in relation to collective events of intense public concern in the United States (for example, the 9/11 terrorist attack and the invasion of Iraq in 2003). The findings of these projects prove that dreaming about social and political issues is not just a superstitious holdover from ancient history, but something that also happens to people in contemporary times. Despite the long-standing preference of psychologists for inward-focused interpretations, this research indicates that certain dreams also have aspects of meaning that require an outward-focused interpretation— sometimes a dream of a king symbolizes the father, and sometimes it reflects the dreamer's perspective on the actual king in waking life. As Andrew Samuels, a British Jungian analyst, put it in his 1993 book *The Political Psyche* (from which this section takes its name), "the images of the dream can be approached via their individual presence, or via their political presence, or via the movement and tension between the two."[11]

The findings of my studies have also suggested a great deal of individual variability with this kind of dreaming. Some people have very frequent dreams of social, political, and cultural characters and themes, and other people rarely or never have such dreams. This wide variability seems influenced partly by innate dreaming temperament (some people are especially sensitive in their dreams to collective realities) and partly by circumstances (some social situations are especially likely to stimulate dreams about community concerns).

Her Sources of Knowledge

It seems fair to assume that Lucrecia possessed an innate capacity for dreams like this, and her community was certainly undergoing tremendous upheaval and widespread anxiety in the late 1580s. These are precisely the conditions that can ignite an outburst of political dreaming. But the Inquisitors had a difficult time believing an uneducated teenage girl could really experience so many complex and detailed dreams about Spanish international affairs. They still felt that somehow Don Alonso was putting words in her mouth. No other explanation made sense to them.

The Inquisitors might have reconsidered if they had looked more carefully at the numerous sources of political knowledge to which she had access. Lucrecia was not a typical woman enclosed in a private domestic sphere on the "outskirts of life."[12] Although she had no formal schooling, she grew up at the intersection of several rich currents of information about Spanish public affairs. Her family's home was a frequent gathering place for friends, neighbors, and relatives to gossip about daily events in Madrid, many of which revolved around the court and the activities of the royal family. Her father's work gave her familiarity with the empire's often bleak finances, and her mother's relatives brought interesting news from all over the world. Lucrecia had opportunities to meet and talk with people from many different social perspectives, including Piedrola, the famous soldier-prophet; the Muslim woman, or *morisca*, who lived for several years in her family's apartment building; and Lady Jane Dormer, her landlord and an active conduit of news from England. Lucrecia's work in the royal palace gave her an extraordinarily close view of Philip, his family, and the day-to-day challenges of governing his sprawling realm. From Don Alonso, Don Guillén, and her other well-connected followers, she gained even more access to information about the court, the Church, the New World, and Spain's numerous enemies at home and abroad.

Taking all these sources of information together, it should no longer appear so surprising that Lucrecia's dreams had a high frequency of politically related content. During the course of her life she had been exposed to a remarkable diversity of ideas about court intrigues, imperial battles, international finances, and the welfare of the royal family. If we credit her with above average intelligence and curiosity, as seems reasonable, then these experiences would have given her all the raw material she needed for the dreams she later reported. The political themes in her dreams appear suspiciously discontinuous only if her waking life is conceived strictly in terms of the assumed limits of her gender (female) and formal education (none). If, however, we take into account the influences of her family environment, social interactions, and all the different things she heard about Spain and its problems, then it becomes much easier to appreciate the strong continuities between her waking life and the political themes in her dreams.

Lucrecia's experiences certainly put her at the high end of the political dreaming scale, but still within the range of naturalistic explanation. There is no need to rush to a conclusion of either fraud or supernatural causation for her dreams just because of their abundance of politically related content.

The Reign of Philip II

Lucrecia lived in close proximity to one of history's mightiest rulers, during his peak of global power. This in itself seemed to have a stimulating effect on her dreaming. Lucrecia grew up in an era of amazing imperial expansion with Philip at the center of it all, the embodiment of Spain's national greatness and the divinely ordained leader of its people. Yet her numerous dreams of Philip focused relentlessly on the dark, ominous shadows looming ahead. The dreams did not celebrate the king's vast domains and noble achievements, but rather excoriated him for failing to uphold his duties as a faithful ruler for the Spanish people. He was the most powerful person she knew in waking life, but in her dream world he was weak, impotent, and had no constructive role to play in the future of Spain.

Lucrecia's dreams about Philip were quite overdetermined in simultaneously conveying multiple levels of symbolic meaning. As already mentioned, one of these levels symbolically identified the king with her father as an oppressive masculine authority in her life. At another level, Lucrecia's dreams reflected her actual experiences of seeing Philip in public and working in the palace in his family's living quarters. The king was not a distant figure in her life; she knew from personal experience that he was a flesh-and-blood man, with all the frailties of his advancing age. At yet another level, her dreams expressed widely shared fears

POLITICS AND SOCIETY   165

throughout Spain about Philip's leadership and his ability to protect the people against their enemies. The king was supposed to embody the righteous spirit and godly vigor of the nation, and if he failed in that duty, everyone would suffer. Lucrecia's dreams repeatedly predicted that he would indeed fail, with catastrophic results for the Spanish people. All of these meanings were woven into her dreaming experiences to varying degrees, echoing and amplifying each other in subtle ways that we cannot hope to understand completely.

We can, however, make at least one reasonably confident inference about her dreams of the king. Lucrecia had more than enough information from personal observations to doubt Philip's ability to lead the country forward. She knew how big a gap there was between the glorious image of his empire and the frightening reality behind it. In public Philip was portrayed as the greatest ruler on earth and God's mightiest defender of the faith, but in fact his empire was incredibly fragile, his grip on power weakening, and his physical vitality declining rapidly. Because so much of the government's functioning depended on the king's active personal supervision, his worsening health threatened to become a paralyzing national crisis. The king's son and heir apparent to the throne had a mediocre mind and no readiness for the massive responsibilities of imperial leadership he would inherit as Philip III. Spain's greatest enemies—England, France, the Turks—were on the ascent, while the country's finances were in a constant state of crisis, lurching from one bankruptcy to another.

Lucrecia knew all of this. She had witnessed and heard enough in her young life to formulate a well-grounded fear about Philip's waning power and the uncertain future of the country. This same fear was haunting many other people in Madrid, too. Her dreams accurately reflected this collective anxiety and tried to anticipate the possible dangers that lay ahead.

Was Philip aware of these fears, too? Did he recognize the alarmingly tenuous and unsustainable condition of his empire? Perhaps, although his rigid religious beliefs made him virtually impervious to self-doubt or critical reflection. We know that he was aware of Lucrecia and her dreams, and we know, as mentioned in Chapter 5, that he admitted to feeling a strange disquiet about her, saying to his secretary, *"you should not be afraid of what she says, but of what she does not say."*[13] But Philip never expressed any further interest in learning about the specific details of her dreams. This in itself is rather perplexing. Philip was a man of intense faith, who owned one of the world's greatest collections of religious art and relics and who claimed to rule as God's champion on earth: how could he ignore an accurate prophecy about the most pivotal battle of his reign? Did he feel any curiosity about the source of this prophecy and the other insights it might be able to provide him? Apparently not. Lucrecia's followers were involved with the scandals of Piedrola and Antonio Pérez, and her association with the erratic Don Alonso de Mendoza must have given the king even more reason for doubt. Philip had so many urgent matters of government pressing for his attention that it would have been easy to dismiss her dreams, ignore their troubling implications, and leave her fate to the Inquisition.

When he personally signed the order to arrest Lucrecia, the king wanted to demonstrate to the country that he was still a strong and decisive leader, in full command of the empire despite his ill health and the humiliating defeat of the Armada. He decided to shut down her dreaming not because he had learned important new details about her case, but because the timing was right for him to use Lucrecia and her followers as props for an act of political theater. Philip needed to make a public display of power, and she was a convenient means to that end. He did not care about the content of her dreams, and he did not care about her. The king regarded Lucrecia as a nuisance who had to be forcefully silenced.

How does B. know what Philip did and didn't care about?

CHAPTER 12

HISTORY
OF RELIGIONS

Incubation

The preceding three chapters have followed Erikson's method of "triple bookkeeping" by analyzing Lucrecia's case from the perspectives of physiology (especially brain functioning in sleep), psychology (especially relational psychology), and sociology (especially the political dynamics of Philip's empire). Now it is time to consider a fourth perspective, the religious, which can add to the findings of the other three approaches. Lucrecia was by all accounts a person of deep faith, and she grew up in an extremely pious and religiously observant community.[1] Her dreams reflected those influences and actively responded to them, too. We can learn more about this interplay by drawing upon research and theories from the history of religions, with a special focus on finding connections between her dreams and, first, dream teachings in early Jewish and Christian traditions and, second, comparable dream phenomena in various religious traditions around the world.

A turn to the history of religions does not mean trying to explain Lucrecia's dreams in theological terms as the products of divine action. Rather, it means using well-documented historical and cross-cultural evidence to highlight specific ways in which her dreams were grounded in the religious beliefs of her tradition and consistent with intensified types of dream experience reported by people in other religious traditions.

A good place to start is by looking at rituals of dream incubation, practiced in a wide variety of cultures since ancient times. The typical features of these rituals can help us better understand some of the interpersonal dynamics between Lucrecia and Don Alonso. The fact that he encouraged her dreaming so strongly could be taken as evidence against the credibility of her reports—didn't she simply give him what he was asking for? The possibility cannot be rejected, but it explains less rather than more of her case. To accept this explanation requires ignoring other evidence that both Lucrecia and Don Alonso were genuinely interested in cultivating her oneiric potentials. Their efforts can be better understood as part of a concerted effort to stimulate her sleeping imagination, not just to produce specific dreams, but to amplify her general capacity for dreaming.

Incubation is the term modern scholars use for ritual techniques that create inviting conditions for a revelatory dreaming experience. Dream incubation is never an automatic or guaranteed process; dreams are always unpredictable, and the best one can do is set the stage. Historian of religions Kimberley Patton has identified three elements that typify the cross-cultural practice of dream incubation.[2] First is *intentionality*, which involves the purpose or reason for seeking a dream. People do not practice dream incubation as a leisure pursuit; they usually have a specific concern, worry, or question that has motivated them to make the effort. They often express their intentionality and strength of purpose through prayers, purifications, sacrifices, fasting, special clothes and postures, and other pre-sleep devotions. Second is *locality*, which means the setting where the person seeking the dream will sleep. At a minimum the locality has to be safe and undisturbed, otherwise no dreaming will be possible at all. Most incubation rituals emphasize localities for sleep that are far removed from the person's normal sphere of life, and closer to places where sacred powers are believed to exist (e.g., mountains, caves, graveyards, shrines). The third element is the *epiphany* of the dream experience itself, which is received and interpreted as a response to the pre-sleep intentionality.

These three elements of dream incubation appear quite clearly, for example, in the vision quest rituals of Native American groups, the meditation training methods of Hindus and Buddhists, and the journeys into the "Dreamtime" by Australian Aborigines.[3] People in these traditions have developed a variety of pre-sleep methods to encourage dreaming that focuses on an important and meaningful concern. Two other traditions with well-developed dream incubation practices have more than just comparative relevance to Lucrecia's case. One regards the ancient Greek healing god Asclepius, who was worshipped at beautiful temples where devotees performed rituals and slept inside a sanctuary in hopes of a divine dream. The Romans adopted Asclepius as their own healing god and continued the practice of seeking medically helpful dreams at his temples (which were in effect the hospitals of the time). The influences of these incubation practices echoed for centuries in cultures all around the Mediterranean, and very likely filtered into the folk beliefs about dreams in 16th century Spain.

The other influence on Lucrecia's awareness of dream incubation may have come, surprisingly, from Islam and its long tradition of *istikhara*, which means praying for a dream. Practicing *istikhara* involves reciting a series of prayers and sleeping on one's right side, with the right hand to the right ear. Islam generally opposes rituals of divination, but over the centuries *istikhara* has become an acceptable method of praying for God's guidance during times of great uncertainty.[4] It is possible that Lucrecia knew about this practice. Long after the Reconquista, Muslim cultural beliefs and practices continued to influence the Spanish people in many ways. If she and the *morisca* who boarded in the Leóns' apartment building for several years did have conversations about dreams, Lucrecia might even have gained a direct source of insight into the practice.

The Catholic tradition of her upbringing included at least one biblical portrayal of a dream incubation ritual, performed by the wise ruler Solomon:

> And the king went to Gibeon to sacrifice there, for that was the great high place; Solomon used to offer a thousand burnt offerings upon that altar. At Gibeon the Lord appeared to Solomon in a dream by night; and God said, "Ask what I shall give you."[5]

Whether or not Lucrecia knew specific information about the dream incubation practices of other religions, she definitely had a favorable example from her own tradition that illustrated the use of a special ritual to enhance the possibility of a powerful dream experience.

Drawing on Patton's terminology to describe Lucrecia's case, a strong intention to open oneself to revelatory dreaming was certainly present in Lucrecia. She felt anxiety and uncertainty about her country's future, and she knew that many other people in Madrid felt the same way. She had always been a vivid dreamer, long before meeting Don Alonso, and she clearly had an unusual capacity for dreaming about collective concerns. The nobleman's encouragement and support helped to sharpen her intentionality, but he did not create it (although he did later try to manipulate it). Lucrecia's dreams were already oriented toward the perception of possible threats to the future of Spain. What Don Alonso did was give her theological permission to open herself fully to this torrent of visionary experience in sleep. It must have been both reassuring and energizing for a deeply faithful person like Lucrecia to hear from a senior Church official that her dreams were religiously important. Don Alonso also emphasized her patriotic service to Spain in trying to remember her dreams with the greatest possible accuracy, and she did her best to comply. Her dream of February 22, 1588, which she remembered only after waiting patiently in bed for several moments with her eyes closed, exemplified her strong intentionality in the dream-recording process.

As a young unmarried woman, Lucrecia had no latitude to sleep anywhere but within the protected confines of her family home. Thus she could not perform an incubation ritual that involved sleeping in an unusual locality like a temple or mountain top. She did, however, have a bedroom of her own, which established some measure of privacy and separation from the rest of her family, allowing her to sleep and dream with relatively few disruptions. And her dreams, as Fray Lucas transcribed them for Don Alonso's later analysis, were certainly treated as epiphanies in Patton's sense of directly meaningful responses to her pre-sleep intentions.

Lucrecia's dream-recording process shared many features with the incubation rituals performed in cultures all over the world, including her own Catholic tradition. The same basic reasoning guided all these efforts: if it is true that dreams offer spontaneous insights into waking life problems, then one should actively develop pre-sleep techniques to elicit more dreams with those valuable qualities. Lucrecia and Don Alonso were following this well-worn path, but they had to be careful not to make her pre-sleep intentionality too obvious or specific, to prevent the Inquisition from accusing them of *believing* in her dreams. Indeed, they had every incentive to make sure their dream-stimulating efforts looked normal and unobjectionable—no unorthodox prayers or sacrifices, no unusual clothes or locations, just a girl sleeping in her room at home with her family. Within the strict limits of their circumstances, Lucrecia and Don Alonso developed the most efficient, focused, and potent dream incubation process they could put into practice.

Dreaming the Future

Most religious traditions recognize that certain people can acquire a powerful expertise in dreaming. For example, many small tribal cultures around the world have ritual specialists and healers, often referred to as *shamans*, whose general skill set includes a facility with dreaming and the regular practice of dream incubation.[6] The training process to gain these skills usually starts early in life and requires years of close supervision by an experienced guide. The process can include a series of harrowing ordeals that must be endured and overcome by the aspiring shaman.

Lucrecia did not receive any such training in waking life, but in her dreams she was treated by the three companions as a kind of shamanic initiate into their otherworldly realm. They not only delivered valuable information to her, they tried to teach Lucrecia how to discern that information for herself. She learned these lessons in the midst of some horribly frightening and disturbing dreams, but the three companions always encouraged her, if only by their presence, to trust in the value of the insights she was bringing back to the waking world. As time went on she did become more capable and confident within the dream world, although we know nothing of her further progress in this direction after her arrest by the Inquisition.

Her experience of receiving spiritual training within her dreams has parallels in other religious traditions. Tibetan Buddhists have long practiced dream incubation as a means of gaining insights and teachings from ancient teachers known only in the realm of dreaming.[7] Sufi Muslims draw guidance and inspiration from dreams of their *pirs*, spiritual masters who can appear exclusively in dreaming to provide individually tailored lessons for further religious growth and understanding.[8] For centuries Jewish mystics have sought dream revelations in which ancient rabbis, sages, and seers instruct them in the subtle nuances of sacred texts.[9] Seen in the light of comparative religions, the three companions can be viewed as Lucrecia's private spiritual educators who gave her customized guidance in the development of her dreaming abilities.

Many of the religious virtuosos who pursue these kinds of dreaming revelations are seeking to enhance their skills at healing people of their suffering. That was not Lucrecia's path, at least not at this stage of her life. Rather, she cultivated a capacity for dreaming about the future and anticipating possible threats to her community. The people of 16th century Spain were not alone in their acceptance of a future-oriented dimension in dreaming. On the contrary, there are teachings and stories in virtually all cultures around the world in which people's dreams foretell significant events to come, usually something frightening and destructive (deaths, battles, plagues). Religious traditions may attribute these dream-generated portents to supernatural beings, but modern science has shown how the sleeping brain is capable of generating dreams with anticipatory qualities.[10] As discussed in chapter 9, current research provides a naturalistic explanation for the capacity of dreaming to simulate future possibilities based on present waking concerns. In psychological terms, dreaming has an innately anticipatory dimension that enables the mind to explore, in a safe space, a variety of simulated scenarios with potential relevance for survival and adaptation in the future. Religious traditions add a metaphysical frame to something that has deep roots in the evolved functioning of our brains in sleep.

This is not an exclusively modern insight. The most influential manual of dream interpretation from ancient times was the *Oneirocritica* (*The Interpretation of Dreams*) by Artemidorus, a scholar from the Roman Empire in the 2nd century, who assiduously gathered teachings about dreams from cultures all over the Mediterranean.[11] Artemidorus explicitly set aside religious explanations of dreaming and focused on identifying recurrent correlations between specific types of dream content and specific outcomes in the dreamer's waking life. He emphasized the rationality of his method and the empirical basis of his interpretations, and he insisted that interpreters should learn everything they could about dreamers' lives before trying to analyze the predictive qualities of their dreams.

Don Alonso knew of the work of Artemidorus, and he very likely possessed his own copy of the text.[12] (The *Oneirocritica* is one of the most widely translated and published works in European history, and the basis of Macrobius' system in his *Commentary on the Dream of Scipio*.) The future-oriented approach of the ancient interpreter gave the nobleman inspiring encouragement and useful advice in pursuing his study of Lucrecia's dreams.

Biblical Prophecy

The Catholic tradition had its own teachings and stories about dreaming of the future, which Lucrecia undoubtedly learned at some point during her religious upbringing. The Bible is filled with reports of dreams foretelling events to come, starting in the book of Genesis with the patriarchs Abraham and Jacob, who are both described as having dreams that reassured them during fearful times about the future prosperity of their families and progeny.[13] In the book of Judges, Gideon overhears enemy soldiers talking about a symbolic dream portending ill in a coming battle (which meant it was a good omen for Gideon's side).[14] When King Samuel was twelve years old, as told in the first book of Samuel, he slept one night in the sacred temple near the ark of the covenant, and he had a dream in which God described his divine plans for the future.[15] The Bible tells extended stories of the dream-interpreting activities of Joseph (in the book of Genesis) and Daniel (in the book of Daniel), two God-fearing men who used their skills to analyze the dreams of kings and reveal their symbolic significance for the future welfare of these rulers' people.[16] In the New Testament book of Matthew, dreams provide a life-saving source of anticipatory guidance for Joseph and Mary, the parents of Jesus, as they flee persecution from the Romans and try to protect their newborn child. In the book of Acts, dreams also help the apostle Paul when he is frightened and uncertain about his mission to spread the word of God.[17]

An especially important biblical text for Christian beliefs about dreaming appears first in the book of Joel, and is later repeated in the book of Acts:

> And in the last days it shall be, God declares, that I will pour out my spirit upon all flesh, and your sons and your daughters shall prophesy, and your young men shall see visions, and your old men shall dream dreams; yea, and on my menservants and my maidservants in those days I will pour out my spirit; and they shall prophesy. And I will show wonders in the heavens above and signs on the earth beneath, blood, and fire, and vapor of smoke; the sun shall be turned into darkness and the moon into blood, before the day of the Lord comes, the great and manifest day. And it shall be that whoever calls on the name of the Lord shall be saved.[18]

In many ways these verses provided the clearest religious manifesto for Lucrecia's career as a dreamer. This biblical passage, appearing in both the Old and New Testaments, taught that when the last days of God's judgment arrived (which Lucrecia and many other people in late 16th century Madrid believed was on the verge of happening right then), the faithful should be ready to heed God's commands by paying close attention to strange dreams and visions. That is exactly what Lucrecia, Don Alonso, and her other followers tried to do. When we take into account these passages from the books of Joel and Acts, plus all the other biblical teachings about the predictive power of dreaming, it becomes easier to understand how Lucrecia's dreams attracted so much interest, and so much controversy.

Not all biblical passages speak favorably of dreaming. In the book of Ecclesiastes the preacher says, "When dreams increase, empty words grow many: but do you fear God," while the book of Zechariah warns, "the dreamers tell false dreams, and give empty consolation."[19]

The strongest critical words against dreaming appear in the book of Jeremiah:

> I have heard what the prophets have said who prophesy lies in my name, saying, "I have dreamed, I have dreamed!" How long shall there be lies in the heart of the prophets who prophesy lies, and who prophesy the deceit of their own heart, who think to make my people forget my name by their dreams which they tell one another . . . ? Let the prophet who has a dream tell the dream, but let him who has my word speak my word faithfully. What has the straw in common with the wheat? . . . Do not let your prophets and your diviners who are among you deceive you, and do not listen to the dreams which they dream, for it is a lie which they are prophesying to you in my name; I did not send them, says the Lord.[20]

Jeremiah was one of the most admired prophets in the biblical tradition, and he sternly warned the people of God to be wary of anyone who claimed to have special dreams of the future. He did not entirely rule out the possibility of religiously legitimate dreams ("let the prophet who has a dream tell the dream"), but he emphasized their deceptive qualities and their tendency to reflect the personal desires of the dreamers ("their own heart") rather than genuine messages from the divine.

The figure of the prophet—Jeremiah, Joel, Zechariah, and Jesus, among many others—played a powerful role in the Abrahamic tradition.[21] To what extent did Lucrecia fit the profile of a biblical prophet? In many ways, not at all. She was not a man, of course, nor did she lead an ascetic life detached from the rest of human society. She did not receive direct communications from God, and she engaged in no other actions or demonstrations of divine inspiration. No one in the Bible had dreams like hers. These characteristics might seem to fundamentally exclude her from the prophetic ranks. But other aspects of her life are virtually identical with the chief qualities usually attributed to the biblical prophets. The contents of her dreams were visually and thematically consistent with the prophets' apocalyptic visions of God's coming wrath. The dreams sharply challenged the spiritual hypocrisy of the king and vividly anticipated the violent overthrow of a corrupt political system. Lucrecia suffered a harsh response for her visionary criticism of the mighty and powerful, and yet remained defiant against their threats and confident in her faith—exactly what happened with many of the great prophets of the Bible.

Whether or not Lucrecia fit a strict theological definition of a prophet, her life and dreaming certainly exemplified many of the term's defining qualities, making it legitimate and accurate to refer to her, at a minimum, as "prophetic."

Visions of the Night

The Bible uses "dreams" and "visions of the night" interchangeably, as in this passage from the book of Job:

> For God speaks in one way, and in two, though man does not perceive it. In a dream, in a vision of the night, when deep sleep falls upon men, while they slumber on their beds, then he opens the ears of men, and terrifies them with warnings, that he may turn man aside from his deed, and cut off pride from man.[22]

Many cultural traditions have also emphasized the strong visual qualities of dreaming experience. In several languages the word for "dream" is defined as a kind of seeing in sleep, and most religions do not sharply distinguish dreaming from waking visions.[23] As I discussed in Chapters 8 and 9, dream content tends to include more visual sensations than any other kind of perception, and the sleeping brain is highly primed to produce internal imagery even though it is cut off from external visual input. In earlier works, I have referred to an "autonomous visionary capacity" that emerges in sleep and dreaming when the eyes close and the brain spontaneously begins to generate intensely realistic visual experiences.[24]

Lucrecia's dreams were overflowing with dramatic imagery, which reflected her innate capacities for intensified dreaming. This imagery likely reflected the influence of her Catholic tradition and its distinctive emphasis on the value of art and visual experience in apprehending the divine. Protestants rejected religious art as a blasphemous distraction from the pure and true worship of God. Muslims also took an iconoclastic approach to religious art, rejecting the creation or worship of any images of Muhammad or Allah. In contrast to its two bitter enemies, the Catholic Church of the late 16th century endorsed religiously themed art in a variety of forms—painting, sculpture, architecture, drama, and other creative media. The Church enforced strict boundaries regarding what was and was not artistically appropriate, but within those bounds people were free to seek religious insight and illumination by means of stimulating sensory experiences, especially visual perceptions.

Growing up in Madrid during this time, Lucrecia was exposed to a colorful variety of religiously themed art in the churches and shrines she visited, the celebrations she witnessed, and the processions she joined. All of these experiences became raw material for her visual imagination, filtering into her sleeping mind and stimulating her nocturnal creativity. Without intending to do so, the Catholic Church's liberal policy on religious art helped to nurture Lucrecia's already formidable capacity for visionary dreaming.

This may explain some of the reason why the Inquisitors struggled in prosecuting her. As her contemporaries, they surely noticed more local references in her dreams than we can recognize four centuries later—images of religiously important people, places, and activities in their shared community of worship. The Inquisitors could hardly miss the close connections between her dreams and the religious culture of Spain. This must have complicated their efforts to prove the heretical nature of her dreams, because so much of her dreams' content was indistinguishable from the religious images and themes that Catholic officials had already approved for artistic expression. Although they came from an unauthorized source, Lucrecia's dreams expressed themselves in the visual vernacular of her community, an imagistic language of symbols and metaphors recognized by everyone who had grown up within the Catholic faith.[25]

The powerful visual qualities of her dreams also help to explain some of the puzzling dynamics between her and her followers. Unlike other Catholic visionaries, such as her near-contemporary Teresa of Ávila, Lucrecia did not try to organize a group or establish an institution to carry forward her revelations. The various activities undertaken in her name, such as building the *Sopeña* and creating the Holy Cross of the

Restoration, were initiated and carried forward by her followers. There is no evidence she ordered or directed them to pursue these endeavors. Indeed, the one thing she did ask of her followers, namely their discretion, they completely failed to provide. Over time it became painfully clear that her followers were very interested in her dream visions, but not at all in her waking thoughts or feelings.

This disjunction makes more sense in light of the *modes of religiosity* theory of anthropologist Harvey Whitehouse, one of the earliest and most influential models in the cognitive science of religion.[26] This theory posits two general tendencies in religious traditions around the world, the *imagistic* and the *doctrinal*. In the imagistic mode, religious activities occur in small, idiosyncratic groups whose members engage in religious rituals with high emotional arousal and vivid imagery, leading to strong social bonds. In the doctrinal mode, religious activities become larger and more standardized, with less emotional arousal, less perceptual stimulation, and weaker social bonds. What seemed to happen in Lucrecia's case is that her dreams became a new source of imagistic religiosity for her followers. Through her visually intense dreams they felt a strong and immediate connection with divine powers that could guide them through the present time of crisis to a glorious future of spiritual renewal. Lucrecia herself was apparently irrelevant to the process; what mattered most to her followers were the dreams themselves and their dramatic religious imagery.

Whitehouse's theory predicts some degree of tension between the two modes of religiosity, and this, too, can illuminate the final persecutory turn of Lucrecia's case. The rites and teachings of Catholicism perfectly embodied the doctrinal mode of religiosity, just as Lucrecia's dreams perfectly illustrated the experiential process that can spark a new outburst of imagistic religiosity. The task of the Inquisition was to guard the Church against imagistic upstarts who challenged the religious status quo and promoted new visions of the divine. Lucrecia's followers apparently did not realize, or did not care, how far their devotion to her vibrant dreaming was leading them away from the safe institutional boundaries of Catholic belief and practice. Their naïve imagistic passions brought down a harsh doctrinal punishment.

CHAPTER 13

WHAT SHE
MOST LIKELY WAS

A Prophetic Dreamer

Taking all of these analytic perspectives into account, we can appreciate the Inquisition's dilemma in deciding how to proceed. Lucrecia's case did not fit into any of the categories typically used to prosecute heretics. She stubbornly refused to admit any wrongdoing, and several of the key facts that came out in the trial supported her claim of innocence. The Inquisitors had failed to find any real evidence that she was mentally ill, religiously unorthodox, or a liar who had fabricated her dreaming. They had found nothing to indicate she was influenced by demons or had made a pact with the Devil.

A criminal investigator from a few hundred years in their future would note that "when you have eliminated the impossible, whatever remains, however improbable, must be the truth."[1] After a trial lasting five long years, what remained before the Inquisitors was the record of Lucrecia's dreams, and the question at the heart of her case: were they genuine dreams? If, after all other possibilities were dismissed, the most likely answer to that question was yes, it would require a very different assessment of Lucrecia's identity and the religious significance of her dreaming. More specifically, it would require the Inquisitors to confront the improbable truth of her case: *Lucrecia was a prophetic dreamer.* The most straightforward reading of the evidence indicated that she was an ordinary young woman who had extraordinary powers of future-oriented dreaming. She started life with an innately strong capacity for vivid dreaming, and with the help of Don Alonso and others she subtly cultivated that capacity and focused it on gaining religious and political insights that could help her community. Considering her case within a biblical context, the use of the term *prophetic* seems not only accurate and appropriate but almost inescapable. One would have to willfully ignore a great deal of evidence from her trial and religious history to apply any other term to her.

To refer to Lucrecia as a prophetic dreamer does not mean that everything she dreamed came true. Rather, it means the activities of her sleeping mind focused on envisioning threatening possibilities ahead for her community, some of which came to pass and some of which did not. She had a natural aptitude for such dreams, and this aptitude combined with the special circumstances of her life—her deep Catholic faith, the crisis of Philip's weakening leadership, her knowledge of imperial politics, her work in the royal court, the support of Don Alonso and his dream scribes—to produce a series of visionary experiences that simulated possible scenarios for her country's future, providing well-informed warnings of looming danger.

Ultimately we do not know with 100 percent certitude that Lucrecia actually had these dreams. There is always a horizon of uncertainty around our ability to understand the inner truth of other people's dream lives. But we do know with great confidence that it would have been entirely plausible for a person like Lucrecia, in circumstances like hers, to experience the kinds of dreams she described. Similar dreaming phenomena have been reported by people from various religious and cultural traditions around the world, from ancient times to the present day. All the main features of her dreams have reasonable connections to naturalistic processes that occur in everyone's brains and minds during sleep. In her case, these processes seem to have reached unusually intense levels of arousal and activation. Her prophetic dreaming was different in degree, but not in kind, from ordinary dreaming.

What, then, should the Inquisition have done with her? If, as I have argued, she was reporting genuine dreams, then it would plainly be wrong to hold her legally responsible for their contents. Saint Augustine and Saint Thomas Aquinas, the two greatest theologians in Catholic history, both declared that a person is not morally at fault for having dreams with morally objectionable imagery, feelings, and actions. In his 4th century CE autobiography, *Confessions*, Augustine distinguished his dreaming self from his "true self." He said the misbehavior of his self during dreams could not tarnish the religious purity of his true self in waking.[2] Aquinas, in his 13th century opus *Summa Theologica*, concluded that "what a man does while he sleeps and is deprived of reason's judgment is not imputed to him as a sin, as neither are the actions of a maniac or an imbecile."[3]

What mattered for these two eminent theologians was how a person reacted to the dreams, either morally or immorally. In Lucrecia's case, she shared her dreams within the framework of confession and theological inquiry, conducted under the supervision of high-ranking Church officials. She entered the process with good moral intentions, and she had no control over other people's behavior, sinful or otherwise, after she shared her dreams with them. There was no evidence of any demonic influence or diabolical deception in her life. If Lucrecia's dreams were in fact real and natural dreams, then the theological basis for her arrest disappeared, and the Inquisition's charges lost their legal rationale.

The Inquisitors could still focus their prosecutorial energies on proving Lucrecia guilty of the sin of "believing" in her dreams, which she compounded by continuing to tell people about them despite being warned not to do so. But this would mean punishing a person for sharing dreams that (a) were approved by her confessor and senior Church officials, (b) had direct relevance to important community concerns, (c) turned out to be accurate, and (d) might have saved the country terrible suffering had they been heeded. Once the suspicions of fraud and demonic influence were dismissed, and once the legitimately prophetic qualities of her dreams were acknowledged, the Inquisitors would have had no compelling legal reason to find her guilty of erroneous heretical belief.

From a strictly Catholic perspective, the closest analog to Lucrecia in the Church's long history would have to be Augustine's mother, Monica. Augustine talked about her in great detail in the *Confessions*. Monica was an uneducated woman, from a nondescript family in northern Africa, who converted to Christianity and prayed fervently that her pagan son would one day join her in the Christian faith. Augustine reported a dream she had years before his conversion in which he came and stood next to her on a long wooden plank—"where she was, there was I also."[4] He expressed amazement at the reassuring impact this dream had on his mother: "by the dream the joy of this devout woman, to be fulfilled much later, was predicted many years in advance to give consolation at this time in her anxiety."[5] Later, Monica performed a dream incubation by praying to God for a night vision of her son's future after marriage; the results of her efforts were unsuccessful, however. Augustine said she intuitively knew which of her dreams were and were not prophetic: "She used to say that, by a certain smell indescribable in words, she could tell the difference between your [God's] revelation and her own soul dreaming."[6]

In Augustine's telling of his religious awakening, Monica played a key role in providing him with an inspiring model of pure Christian faith, unadulterated by pagan ideals or classical education. Thanks to his portrait of her in the *Confessions*, Monica was eventually sainted, in honor of giving birth, both biologically and spiritually, to one of the Catholic tradition's most influential theologians.

The parallels with Lucrecia—another obscure, illiterate woman with strong faith and an unusually vivid dream life—are striking. According to Augustine's direct testimony, Monica had an intuitive gift for dreaming prophetically. Setting aside all the other evidence in her case, the fact of this shared quality between Lucrecia and Monica should have given the Inquisitors pause. Would the agents of the Holy Office have arrested Augustine's own mother as a heretic because of *her* prophetic dreaming?

HISTORICAL
EPILOGUE

1595, July ☙ The Verdict

Despite intensive deliberations, the three judges presiding over Lucrecia's case could not reach a unanimous decision. One of the judges
found enough evidence of diabolical influence and traitorous conspiracy to convict Lucrecia of the most serious charges against her. But the
other two judges decided she should not be held responsible for the content of her dreams or the uses to which other people put them. A court
administrator who knew the case well, Juan de Pantoja, persuaded these
two judges that Lucrecia was not a dangerous heretic but rather a "weak
minded and extremely timid" individual who did not deserve to suffer for the misbehavior of Don Alonso and Fray Lucas.[1] This was, of
course, the essence of Lucrecia's self-defense going back to the first day
of her trial.

The panel of judges finally concluded that Lucrecia was guilty of
making theologically false and heretical statements, but they cleared
her of the worst accusations of treason against the king. After several
more weeks of debate, the judges decided her punishment: one hundred
lashes, two years of confinement in a convent, and permanent banishment from Madrid.

It could have been worse. Much worse. But still, it was hardly good.
If the Inquisitors were unable to convict Lucrecia, they were clearly determined to make her disappear. The public announcement of her conviction was carefully censored to exclude any references to the contents
of her dreams. Most significantly, the Inquisition arranged for her *auto de
fé* to be held in private, in the enclosed courtyard of a Dominican monas-

tery. Appearing with two *moriscos* convicted of unrelated crimes, Lucrecia stood in a white *sanbenito* robe, a rope around her neck and a candle in her hand, and listened to a court official read the charges against her, starting with this line: *"That ever since she was young, she began to dream."*[2]

It was a rare deviation from normal Inquisition practice to hold the ritual of an *auto de fé* in private, and it indicated with unmistakable clarity that the Holy Office had no desire to provide further attention or publicity for Lucrecia and her dreams. In this context, we should also note with suspicion that the Inquisition's records do *not* include the autobiographical statement Lucrecia gave to the court shortly after her arrest.[3] This is a major gap in the documentation of the trial. The first-person statements from Don Alonso, Fray Lucas, and her other followers still remain in the archives, but not Lucrecia's. Thus we do not have her direct account of her own life and dream experiences. Perhaps the text of her statement disappeared because a court official inadvertently lost or misfiled it. Perhaps someone spilled ink on the parchment and ruined it. Accidents happen. But in light of the Inquisition's decisions to downplay its verdict and hold her *auto de fé* out of the public eye, another possible explanation is that her autobiographical statement was deliberately hidden or destroyed, in an effort to silence Lucrecia and prevent any first-person accounts of her remarkable dreaming abilities from spreading further than they already had.

For unknown reasons, the Inquisitors had difficulties finding someone to administer her punishment. After waiting another week, Lucrecia was finally brought to a specially designed platform where her hands were bound and her bare back exposed. A professional hired by the Church struck her repeatedly with a whip, most likely made of leather, capable of inflicting considerable pain and physical harm. The process would certainly have continued until blood was drawn, which would not take long with a slight young woman. The Inquisition did not explicitly sentence her to death, but if she happened to die after her punishment, no one would complain.

This included her father. After she had been whipped, the Inquisitors tried to place Lucrecia and her daughter, now five years old, in a suitable convent, but none would take her without some kind of advance payment for her care and supervision. The Holy Office sent a letter to Alonso de León asking him to provide financial support for his daughter and granddaughter. In his last act in the historical record, Alonso said no.

Lacking other alternatives, the Inquisitors placed Lucrecia and her daughter in a religious hospital devoted to the housing and care of beggars and people with contagious skin diseases. One could hardly imagine a less hygienic residence for a woman with bloody lacerations on her back and a young child in her care. Once again, it seemed the Inquisition was more than willing to look the other way if circumstances took an unfortunate turn for her.

In late October, Lucrecia made a request to the Holy Office, asking that she and her daughter be moved to a better hospital facility. Another letter was sent from the Holy Office to her father seeking his financial assistance. No reply was ever received.

After the conclusion of Lucrecia's case, the trials of her followers ended in quick and rather anticlimactic fashion. Don Guillén died in prison in September of 1595, before the Inquisition could formally convict him of anything. Fray Lucas was convicted and sentenced to one year's confinement in a monastery. Don Alonso, as mentioned, was declared insane and condemned to six years in a monastery. Diego de Vitores was released and exiled from Madrid and Toledo for two years. None of these punishments reflected an especially harsh or punitive judgment of their behavior. On the contrary, by this point the Inquisition just wanted the cases to go away. Despite last-minute protests from the prosecutor Pedro de Sotocameño that evil heretics were escaping punishment for serious crimes, the Inquisition decided that after five years of imprisonment, the followers of Lucrecia were no longer a threat worthy of the attention of the Holy Office.

1598 🗝 The Death of the King

When Vitores was released in November of 1595 he returned to his home city of Zamora, about 130 miles northwest from Madrid, where he found work again as a secretary. In a letter to the Inquisition in February of 1596, he said that Lucrecia was not with him.[4]

What did happen to her? No one can say for sure. Once the trial ended, no more records were kept (or have been preserved) regarding Lucrecia's location or activities, so we can only speculate about the later course of her life. Simply trying to survive would have been a daunting challenge. She was a convicted heretic and criminal, rejected by her father, forever banished from her home city, a single mother with a young child, penniless, barely literate, and probably still injured from the whipping. By any measure, her prospects were bleak.

Although it may have taken some time, the Inquisition presumably found an appropriate convent or women's religious house where she could serve her two years of confinement. It is possible that during this time Lucrecia died, leaving her daughter an orphan. Her experiences over the previous several months, from the torture session to the *auto de fé*, from the hundred lashes to her placement in the contagious skin disease hospital, had been intensely stressful and physically damaging. She would have received minimal medical care for her injuries, and the city's poor sanitation would have exposed her to any number of infectious agents. She could easily have succumbed to a fatal illness during her confinement, and slipped away from the world without another trace.[5]

However, throughout her life Lucrecia displayed remarkable resilience and impressive survival skills. It thus remains possible that she did not fall prey to disease but rather regained her health after the whipping and lived in a convent with Margarita for the two years of her sentence.[6]

What then? She could not go back to Madrid, and she apparently did not stay in Toledo. Even if she were healthy again, a woman in her condition had very few options, and a great many vulnerabilities. At best, she might find work as a housekeeper or governess, although her status as a convicted heretic would make it difficult to find an employer willing to hire her. She could try to eke out a living in a city market by peddling fruits or fabrics, or perhaps even interpreting people's dreams. If her fortunes fell far enough, she might be reduced to begging, theft, or prostitution, joining the dreary ranks of thousands of other "wandering women" impoverished and adrift throughout the country.[7]

The cruel and unforgiving conditions of late 16th century Spain should not be underestimated. Lucrecia may well have died a lonely, degrading death soon after the completion of her trial. But a less tragic conclusion is also possible. Indeed, there are some reasons to think the most likely ending to her story was a happy one.

Assuming she survived the two years of her confinement, she might have turned to either Lady Jane or Don Alonso for assistance. Both of them had given her significant help in the past, and both had powerful family connections and extensive networks of sympathizers around the country. Either one of them could have provided a path toward safety and self-sufficiency for Lucrecia and her daughter. She might also have turned to her extended family on her mother's side, from the northern part of Spain. Her father had decided to cut her out of his life entirely, but it seems highly unlikely that Lucrecia's mother would have been equally indifferent to the plight of her daughter and granddaughter. The intensity of Alonso de León's anger may have prevented his wife from directly making contact with Lucrecia or giving her financial assistance, but that would not have stopped Ana from using her wide-ranging contacts among family members and neighbors to stay in touch and extend some kind of aid.

Of all the people in her life, the one who had the strongest motivation to help Lucrecia after her release from confinement was Diego de Vitores. He had pledged marital vows with her, fathered a child with her, and shared secret love notes with her during their five years of imprisonment. Aside from her mother, no one had a stronger positive bond with Lucrecia, and no one had more reason to offer her, and their daughter, a safe place to live. If Vitores had spent the two years since his release working in paid employment, he would have had the financial resources to help Lucrecia and Margarita make the journey to Zamora. His extended family may have objected to his unorthodox choice of a wife, but by this point he was 35 years old and presumably free to make his own decisions in such matters.

Assuming Lucrecia, now 28, also remained in love with Vitores, this plan would have enormous benefits for her and Margarita. She would, at long last, be able to join together with her husband and daughter, and they would finally begin their lives as a family. The horror of the Inquisition trial would be over, the intense dramas of the royal court would be a fading memory, and she would be able to enjoy the simple normality of married life in a Spanish town. Compared to the alternatives, this must have been an extremely appealing option. Again, we do not know with certainty what happened to Lucrecia after her trial. But we do have a good sense of her relationships with other people and their shared interests and motivations. This information gives some degree of plausibility, and perhaps even likelihood, to the "happy ending" scenario sketched out here.

If Lucrecia did survive to the end of her forced enclosure in a convent, she would have received grim satisfaction from the coincidental timing of her final release and the slow, agonizing death of the king. Philip's gout had been worsening over the past several years, with terrible fevers, joint inflammation, and painful sores breaking out all over his body. Now, in the summer of 1598, he insisted, against his doctors' orders, on traveling from Madrid to El Escorial, a four-day trek in the scorching heat. Soon after arriving at his remote religious shrine, the king's condition took a sharply negative turn. Any kind of physical movement caused him unbearable agony, and the pain finally became so acute that his doctors confined him to bed. There he remained for the last 53 days of his life in a fevered delirium, suffering from an unquenchable thirst, oozing pus from various open sores, and evacuating his bowels through a hastily carved hole in the bed. The malodorous room was filled with crucifixes, holy relics, and praying monks. On September 1, the sacrament of extreme unction was performed while the king still had enough mental competence to respond properly. Two weeks later, he was dead.[8]

The throne of Spain and the empire now passed to the mild-mannered Philip III, just 20 years old at the time. During this transitional period the religious and political policies of the old monarch yielded to those of the new. Many issues that obsessed Philip II did not receive the same amount of attention from his son, and the resources of the government shifted accordingly. For example, the family members of Antonio

Pérez were quietly released from prison, in recognition of the passing of the old regime and the sudden irrelevance of its personal feuds from earlier years.

As the country adapted itself to the interests of a new ruler, Lucrecia may have benefited from this collective transition away from the final, dark years of the old king's life. Once released from confinement, she would not need to worry about continued harassment by the Inquisition, whose new master had different priorities for his religious police force. As long as she engaged in no further activities that were heretical in the eyes of the Inquisition and stayed away from Madrid, she would have some degree of liberty to choose her own path in life. The death of Philip II, which Lucrecia had anticipated in her dreams for so long, may well have coincided with her own rebirth as a free and independent citizen of Spain.

1605 🐟 The Knight of the Mournful Countenance

The Siglo del Oro of Spanish culture encompassed both the nation's dizzying rise to the heights of imperial power and its shocking, disillusioning fall from greatness. Miguel de Cervantes witnessed all of it, and his novel *Don Quixote*, which first appeared in 1605, revolved around the inevitable clash between noble illusions and painful realities. None of his original readers would have missed the larger point about their country's recent history. Don Quixote's grandiose effort to promote the ideals of chivalry was just as foolish and doomed to failure as Spain's vain attempt to establish itself as the greatest and most divinely favored empire in the world. The lofty principles that inspired Don Quixote may have been admirable and virtuous, but his naïve efforts to put those principles into practice inevitably led to terrible damage and humiliating destruction for everyone involved. Likewise, Philip's grand plan to create a global empire of pure Catholic faith resulted in endless wars, crushing bankruptcies, and bitter religious divisions that would take centuries to heal. Too much absorption in one's ideals, no matter how perfect or true they seem to be, can turn into a kind of insanity that makes one oblivious to the actual harm caused by those fervently held beliefs.

The madness of Don Quixote is portrayed in the novel as a kind of dream state he enters while still awake. His squire and simple-minded companion, Sancho Panza, is a glutton for slumber, but Don Quixote abhors sleep and prefers to keep a waking vigil through each night. As a result, his daily activities take on the surreal qualities of a dream, and his waking experiences become confusingly intertwined with spontaneous eruptions of intense imagery and strong emotions deriving from his fantasies about chivalry. In an incident that has unfortunate results for a great many livestock, Don Quixote comes upon two flocks of sheep and, "seeing in his imagination what he didn't see with his eyes and wasn't there," he believes they are two rival armies of famous knights whose conflict requires the might of his sword to settle.[9] This is a fair description of what happens when we dream—we see vividly in our imaginations what is not actually present in front of our physical eyes.

The novel does make brief references to the Roman maiden Lucretia and her timeless reputation for feminine virtue. For instance, when praising his own lady, Dulcinea del Toboso, Don Quixote exclaims, "Helen cannot match her, nor can Lucretia come near, nor any other of the famous women of ages past."[10] Although they lived in the same neighborhood for three years, there is no direct evidence that Cervantes knew of Lucrecia de León, and if he did, he probably viewed her in an unfavorable light. While admiring the honorable chastity of the ancient Lucretia, Cervantes was unlikely to find anything appealing in the prophetic dreams of the contemporary Lucrecia. He had always been a strong supporter of Philip's imperial enterprise and a firm believer in traditional religious values regarding proper male and female behavior. He showed no interest in the political causes of Piedrola or Antonio Pérez, and little curiosity about spiritual phenomena or religious experiences.

Yet in the second part of his novel, which appeared in 1615, an incident occurs that raises many of the same questions that baffled the Inquisitors in Lucrecia's trial. The brave Don Quixote (earlier dubbed the "Knight of the Mournful Countenance" because of the perennially sad look on his face) decides to descend into the famous Cave of Montesinos to see for himself the wonders that reputedly lie within.

He arranges for Sancho and others to lower him on a rope into the black abyss of the cave. When, about an hour later, they finally pull him back up, his eyes are closed in deep sleep. After being shaken awake, the knight looks distressed and says, "may God forgive you, my friends, for you've plucked me from the most delicious and agreeable life and spectacle that any human being has ever seen or lived."[11] He goes on to describe an adventure lasting several days in which he visited a magnificent castle, engaged in eloquent conversations with lords and ladies, and witnessed the plight of people bewitched by a sorcerer's evil spells. Sancho and the others express amazement and skepticism at Don Quixote's story, and for the next several hundred pages a number of characters try to make sense of his experience. Was it real, or a dream, or just a fraudulent fantasy? A great deal of debate and disagreement ensues, and Don Quixote vigorously denies any charges that he simply made it up. The knight's mysterious experience in the Cave of Montesinos becomes an emblem of the frustrating impossibility of disentangling illusion from reality, dreaming from waking.

Only when Don Quixote reaches his deathbed does he finally regain possession of his reason. He repudiates everything having to do with chivalry and renounces his previous exploits as nothing but the empty products of madness. Sancho and his friends are relieved by the return of his good sense, but they also deeply mourn the loss of the brave knight who amused, amazed, and inspired them with his wondrous visions of a better and more noble world than the one they actually inhabit.

Cervantes' novel reflected the profound sadness and disillusionment pervading Spanish culture toward the end of the Siglo del Oro. Following the shocking loss of the Armada and the miserable death of Philip II, it seemed that lofty dreams could lead only to humiliating failure. The danger of being deceived by empty illusions and vain fantasies was too great; better to ruthlessly cast aside all such follies and focus on the cold, harsh facts of the here and now.

Lucrecia's story illuminated, if only briefly, the possibility of a different approach. The course of her life suggested that dreaming could be informed by reality and reality could be informed by dreaming *at the same time*. Rather than becoming lost in the insanity of pure illusion or hopelessly resigned to the immutable limits of material existence, Lucrecia began to dream in a way that opened up a vast imaginative realm between these two states, a realm in which elements of both fantasy and reality were able to interact and combine in creatively stimulating ways. The Inquisitors tried to stop her from exploring this realm and sharing her experiences with other people, and in large part they succeeded. But Lucrecia's most significant legacy may be the potential she revealed for a dynamic integration of inner *and* outer realities. Through her dreams she highlighted powers of the human mind far beyond anything her theological judges were able to conceive or to tolerate from a young woman.

CONCLUSION

Limitations

A project like this cannot yield certainties, only probabilities. The tremendous differences of time, language, and religious beliefs between Lucrecia's world and ours make it impossible to determine the absolute truth of several issues in her case. Any effort to understand her life is constrained by the complex multiplicities of dreaming, the questionable reliability of testimony given under threat of torture, and the lack of sources of information outside the trial documents that could fill out the picture of her upbringing and psychological development. What we can do, however, and what I have tried to do throughout this book, is evaluate the best available evidence about her case and formulate reasonable hypotheses about the most likely answers to the questions raised by the Inquisition. These hypotheses are grounded in leading research from a variety of academic disciplines—history, psychology, cognitive science, and religious studies—which does not guarantee their correctness, but at least elevates the results above mere opinion.

Would Lucrecia herself have agreed with my evaluation of her dreams? I imagine she would have, insofar as my findings essentially support the testimony she gave to the Inquisition. If one important test of the validity of a historical interpretation is whether or not the people of that time would find it understandable, this study can reasonably conclude that its results are consistent with the claims made by the historical figure at the center of the analysis.

The Inquisition's archival records include much more material about Lucrecia's trial than is discussed here, although the conditions of that material (fraying parchments crammed with hasty handwriting, irregular grammar, obscure abbreviations, and ink bleeding through both sides of the page) render it extremely challenging to use as a scholarly resource. In light of that, I have tried to build my arguments on the most transparent and accessible information about her case that has been verified by professional scholars. However, I can imagine changing my arguments, perhaps significantly, if new material from the archives or other sources comes to light and goes beyond what we currently know about Lucrecia's life and dreaming. This book will surely not be the last word on Lucrecia de León, though I do hope it will provide a guide for future researchers who study her case in further detail.

The dream texts analyzed in Chapter 8 are available for study in the Sleep and Dream Database, where readers can explore the reports for themselves and search for other patterns of content beyond those discussed here.[1] Also available in the SDDb is a small selection of dream reports from other periods of Lucrecia's life, originally transcribed by María Jordán.[2] For anyone who wants to test my claims, refute them, or extend them in new directions, the SDDb provides a free online resource with easy-to-use analytic tools to help the process. Whatever the limits of my own interpretation of Lucrecia's case, my goal has been to encourage more attention to her story and encourage further reflection on the remarkable powers of her dreaming imagination.

The Scientific Study of Religion

The early years of the 21st century have brought renewed interest in the use of modern scientific methods to examine religious beliefs, practices, and experiences. Improvements in brain-mind research technologies have combined with more sophisticated awareness of historical and cultural traditions to spur innovative studies of religion's many roles in human life.[3] Many of these studies have led to models in which religion can be defined by certain universal traits and features. In contrast to those large-scale efforts, I have focused more narrowly in this book on just one individual and the complex religious dynamics of her life. Bracketing out the macro-question of defining religion in general, this study has concentrated on the micro-question of how best to understand the religiously infused dreaming of this particular person. Now, in closing, I would like to consider a few ways in which the findings of this study may contribute to broader conversations about the scientific study of religion.

First, the detailed investigation of individuals with extraordinary capacities for religious experience can reveal latent potentials in the human psyche that are often overlooked or dismissed by general theories of religion. William James was right to emphasize the value of carefully examining the lives of religious virtuosos and their unusually intense and vivid modes of spiritual expression.[4] Such rare individuals do not tell us everything we want to know about religion, but any theory that ignores them is doomed to shallow inadequacy. This methodological point is appreciated by modern neuroscientists, whose theoretical understanding of mental functioning has made enormous progress thanks to pioneering studies of a few singular individuals like H.M., whose short-term memory disorder revealed new features of how the brain encodes information, and Phineas Gage, whose freakish injury from a railroad explosion gave key insights into the neural interactions of rational thought and social intelligence.[5] Lucrecia's case has the potential to serve a similar role in the scientific study of religion, with the significant difference that her capacities for prophetic dreaming emerged from a healthy, not damaged, state of psychological functioning.

Second, this study illustrates a point that has animated my research and writing for many years—dreaming is a phenomenon that occurs squarely at the intersection of religion and science. Dreams are rooted in the genetically hard-wired activities of our brains in sleep, and they also open our minds to startling transcendent insights and bursts of creative energy that often lead in religious directions. I have tried to show that the best way of understanding dreams is to recognize and appreciate the dynamic interplay of both these dimensions, rather than pursuing the narrower explanatory paths of either neural reductionism (dreams are nonsensical by-products of brain activity in sleep) or theistic supernaturalism (dreams are caused by gods, demons, angels, or other divine beings).

Lastly, this project hints at exciting future potentials for the digital humanities as a resource in the study of dreaming.[6] Lucrecia's case has offered an opportunity to demonstrate that technologies of quantitative data analysis can be integrated with qualitative material from biographical and historical sources. The numbers do not have to overwhelm the story; statistical analysis can strengthen and amplify interpretations that have been inspired by insight and intuition. The use of data mining tools in the study of dreaming is still in the early stages of development, with the SDDb and G. William Domhoff's Dreambank.net website representing two of the first efforts in this direction. As more people become familiar with digital tools of dream research, and as the tools themselves improve, progress is bound to accelerate and expand in new directions. Another reason I have emphasized the availability of a selection of Lucrecia's dream reports in the SDDb is to encourage readers to engage creatively with her story beyond the confines of these pages. Future discoveries in dreaming, religion, and cognitive science will depend on students' and researchers' pursuing innovative studies enhanced by digital technologies and oriented by humanistic principles.

These new scholarly developments underscore the ultimate irony of Lucrecia's story. The Spanish Inquisition's bureaucratic precision, which made it such a frighteningly efficient weapon against political and religious dissenters, also enabled the reports of her dreams to survive until today, more than four hundred years later, when modern research methods can illuminate evidence supporting her claims of innocence. The Inquisitors tried to make Lucrecia disappear, and instead they enabled her dreams to reach a greater audience than she would ever have imagined.

ACKNOWLEDGMENTS

The librarians at the National Historical Archive in Madrid, Spain, have been enormously helpful in providing access to the original manuscripts from Lucrecia's trial. I am profoundly grateful for the expert assistance of Eva Nuñez of Portland State University in translating the dream reports and advising me on questions of Spanish history and culture. Richard L. Kagan and María V. Jordán offered welcome encouragement and advice in the early stages of the project, and I hope I have honored their excellent historical works by making a worthy contribution to the scholarly literature on Lucrecia. I have also benefited along the way from the assistance and counsel of Adam G. Beaver, Robert Hoss, Luis Fernando San Jose, the Rev. Jeremy Taylor, Tom Traub, Tony Zadra, and the librarians in charge of Richard L. Kagan's archived papers at Johns Hopkins University. Eternal thanks go to Kurt Bollacker, the software engineer who designed the architecture of the Sleep and Dream Database, and the team at Graybox in Portland, Oregon, who help me manage the SDDb website. I deeply appreciate the support and intellectual companionship of my editor, Emily-Jane Cohen; the editors of the Spiritual Phenomena series, Tanya Luhrmann and Ann Taves; and the anonymous reviewers of the manuscript for this book. Throughout the writing process, my family—Hilary, Dylan, Maya, and Conor—have followed with avid interest the twists and turns in Lucrecia's story, and I cannot thank them enough for their inspiring influence in everything I do and write.

NOTES

Introduction

1. The English word *dream* comes from the Proto-Germanic word *draugmaz*, which meant dream, deception, delusion, hallucination, festivity, and ghost. The Greek word *oneiros* comes from *oner* in Proto-Indo-European (the oldest known human language), meaning both dreams and the figures who appear in them. The Spanish word *sueño* derives, like *somnium* in Latin and *songe* in French, from another Proto-Indo-European word, *swepno*, meaning sleep.

2. The Siglo del Oro is generally considered to extend from the end of the 15th century to the latter part of the 17th century.

3. Many cultures distinguish between dreams in sleep and visions from the waking state, while other cultures do not make such a distinction and speak of dreams and visions interchangeably (e.g., see Levin, *Dreaming the English Renaissance*, 3; Gerona, *Night Journeys*, 6; Plane and Tuttle, *Dreams, Dreamers, and Visions*, 5). The focus of my research is on dreams in sleep, and in Lucrecia's case the evidence indicates that she was reporting dreams in sleep, not visions from the waking state.

4. Kagan, *Lucrecia's Dreams*; Osborne, *The Dreamer of the Calle de San Salvador*; Jordán Arroyo, *Soñar la historia*.

5. Kagan, *Lucrecia's Dreams*, 2.

6. Jordán, "Competition and Confirmation in the Iberian Prophetic Community," 72.

7. The partial exceptions are Osborne, who delved into some of the psychological and theological symbolism of the dreams, in *The Dreamer of the Calle de San Salvador*, and Moss, who wrote a brief but vivid chapter about the sexual dynamics of Lucrecia's case in his book *The Secret History of Dreaming*.

8. I regard the brain and the mind as two elements of an integrated system. They are mutually interdependent, with neither being entirely reducible to the other. At various points ahead I will emphasize the physiological activities of the brain, the psychological processes of the mind, and the integrated functioning of the brain-mind system. See Thompson, *The Brain*; Kandel et al., *Principles of Neural Science*; and Kelly et al., *Irreducible Mind*.

9. *Cognitive science* refers to an alliance of six disciplines—psychology, linguistics, philosophy, computer science, neurology, and anthropology—that began in the 1970s for the purpose of developing new interdisciplinary models of how the human mind works. The cognitive science of religion (CSR) emerged in the 1990s and early 2000s as an effort to apply aspects of cognitive scientific research to the study of various topics in religion.

10. See Wulff, *Psychology of Religion,* and Rambo, *Understanding Religious Conversion.*

11. Xygalatas, *The Burning Saints.*

12. Luhrmann, *When God Talks Back.*

13. Cohen, *The Mind Possessed.*

14. Taves, *Religious Experience Reconsidered*; Graves, *Mind, Brain, and the Elusive Soul*; Pyysiäinen, *How Religion Works*; Hogue, *Remembering the Future, Imagining the Past*; Bingaman, *The Power of Neuroplasticity for Pastoral and Spiritual Care*; Slingerland and Collard, *Creating Consilience*; Carrette, "Religion Out of Mind."

15. See Czachesz and Biró, *Changing Minds*; Chilcott, "Directly Perceiving K̥ṣṇa"; Payne, "Buddhism and Cognitive Science"; Hays, "Possible Selves, Body Schemas, and *Sadhana.*"

16. Tooby and Cosmides, "The Psychological Foundations of Culture."

17. The reversibility of this method gives historians an active and constructive voice in cognitive science discussions. I emphasize this point in anticipation of concerns about using psychology to study history in a myopic, one-directional fashion.

18. In *Night Journeys: The Power of Dreams in Transatlantic Quaker Culture,* Carla Gerona describes her methodological goal as the development of "a historically specific interpretation that would not have seemed alien to the people I studied" (5). It should be noted that a kindred principle animates the ethics statement of the International Association for the Study of Dreams (IASD): "IASD celebrates the many benefits of dreamwork, yet recognizes that there are potential risks. IASD supports an approach to dreamwork and dream sharing that respects the dreamer's dignity and integrity, and which recognizes the dreamer as the decision-maker regarding the significance of the dream. Systems of dreamwork that assign authority or knowledge of the dream's meanings to someone other than the dreamer can be misleading, incorrect, and harmful. Ethical dreamwork helps the dreamer work with his/her own dream images, feelings, and associations, and guides the dreamer to more fully experience, appreciate, and understand the dream."

19. The approach taken here does not rule out a Freudian or Jungian interpretation of Lucrecia's life and dreams using more sophisticated versions of Freud's and Jung's psychological theories. In fact, this book will, I hope, provide a solid foundation for future efforts along those lines. In later chapters I do mention some Freudian and Jungian concepts in relation to Lucrecia's dreams, but I do not attempt a detailed analysis using these concepts, for two reasons. First,

many scholars in other academic fields, particularly history, reject Freudian and Jungian approaches. These scholars are quite suspicious of attempts to apply modern psychological ideas to people from other places and times. As a result, attempting a Freudian or Jungian analysis in this book would have required a detailed account of Freud's and Jung's theories, along with extensive responses to many critics. That was more of a task than could be managed in this text. Second, even if these psychological theories were accepted as legitimate, it is unclear whether there is enough relevant material in the trial records to apply them in a valid way to Lucrecia's life. My focus in this book is on the intersection of Lucrecia's personal dreaming and the collective concerns of her time (which, it should be emphasized, was her focus, too), and for that purpose the existing trial records are a sufficient source of data. But if one wanted to study her dreams as a window into the dynamics of her psychological development (as conceived by modern theorists), then the currently available evidence is much patchier and open to competing interpretations. A deeper dive into the archival materials in Madrid would be necessary, and even that might not yield the kind of personal information about her life required for a truly satisfying interpretation from either a Freudian or Jungian perspective.

20. Erikson, *Childhood and Society*; *Young Man Luther*; *Gandhi's Truth*.

21. Erikson, *Childhood and Society*, 45.

22. Ibid., 46: "[B]eing unable to arrive at any simple sequence and causal chain with a clear location and a circumscribed beginning, only triple bookkeeping (or, if you wish, a systematic going around in circles) can gradually clarify the relevances and the relativities of all the known data."

23. Payne, *Spanish Catholicism*.

Historical Prologue

1. Livy, *The Early History of Rome*.

2. Ibid., 101.

3. Ibid., 102.

4. Ibid.

5. Ovid, The Regifugium.

6. Dante, *The Inferno*, 53–54.

7. In 1571, just a few years after Lucrecia's birth, the master Italian artist Titian presented Philip II with an enormous oil painting titled *Tarquin and Lucretia*, portraying the moment of the prince's violent attack on the defenseless virgin. Another artist of the Italian Renaissance, Botticelli, painted *The Story of Lucretia*, a work in three panels, in the early years of the 16th century.

8. Her parents might also have been influenced by the stories of Saint Lucretia of Mérida, a young virgin who was martyred in the 4th century during Roman persecutions, and Saint Leocritia of Córdoba, a young Muslim girl in the 9th century who converted to Christianity, was arrested for apostasy, and

then martyred. Each legend teaches that the ultimate virtue for a woman is self-sacrifice in obedience to a higher power.

9. This account draws on Grieve, *The Eve of Spain*, 21–23.

10. In some versions of the story, Rodrigo staggers into seclusion after his defeat and suffers a horribly emasculating punishment.

11. Grieve, *The Eve of Spain*, 25.

12. The legend of La Cava and Rodrigo was used as dramatic material for the oral ballads widely sung and performed in Iberian folk culture. These ballads provided one of the most influential sources of cultural knowledge for people without formal education. As a lifelong resident of Madrid, Lucrecia would have had ample opportunity to hear these ballads and absorb their characters, stories, and themes into her imagination.

13. Downey, *Isabella*, 278.

14. The focus here is on the Spanish Inquisition, which differs in significant ways from Inquisition activities in other European countries. The political importance of the Inquisition in Spain was unusually strong and gave it a dual authority: "After 1478 in Castile, Inquisitors would be politically subject—and hence politically loyal—to monarchs, even though the authority and jurisdiction of those Inquisitors had to come from the pope himself. . . . From the beginning, then, the Spanish Inquisition differed fundamentally from the medieval, papal inquisitions, because of the prominent role Spanish kings played in its institution" (Homza, *The Spanish Inquisition 1478–1614*, xvii).

15. "Ruler of the biggest accumulation of states ever known in European history, he [Charles] drew Spain into an imperial role it had never before experienced" (Kamen, *Philip of Spain*, 22). See also Elliott, *The Revolt of the Catalans*.

16. See Kamen, *The Spanish Inquisition*; Giles, *Women in the Inquisition*; Homza, *The Spanish Inquisition 1478–1614*; Kors and Peters, *Witchcraft in Europe 1400–1700*; Roth, *The Spanish Inquisition*; Edwards, *Inquisition*; Lea, *A History of the Inquisition of the Middle Ages*; Kagan and Dyer, *Inquisitorial Inquiries*.

17. "Charles V's fantastically expensive foreign policies and his dependence on credit to finance them therefore had had disastrous consequences for Castile" (Elliott, *Imperial Spain 1469–1716*, 207).

18. Kamen, *Philip of Spain*, 181.

19. Ibid., 183–184.

20. Kagan, *Lucrecia's Dreams*, 15.

21. Ibid., 115.

Chapter 1

1. The biographical details of this paragraph and the next are drawn from Kagan, *Lucrecia's Dreams*, 14–15.

2. Lady Jane Dormer was born to a family in the highest ranks of the English nobility. As a teenager she became "one of Queen Mary's ladies-in-waiting

and most intimate companions" (Wiltrout, *A Patron and a Playwright in Renaissance Spain*, 37). When Queen Mary died, Lady Jane married the Spanish ambassador, the Duke of Feria, and decided to emigrate with other Catholics to Spain, rather than remain in England under the rule of the Protestant Queen Elizabeth. See Clifford, *The Life of Lady Jane Dormer, Duchess of Feria*.

3. Kamen, *Philip of Spain*, 139.

4. Ibid.

5. Elliott, *Imperial Spain 1469–1716*, 241.

6. Quoted from the author's preface to Part II of *Don Quixote*.

7. The Council of Trent gave strict guidelines for what could and could not be displayed, insisting that, "in the invocation of saints, the veneration of relics, and the sacred use of images, every superstition shall be removed, all filthy lucre be abolished; finally, all lasciviousness be avoided; in such wise that figures shall not be painted or adorned with a beauty exciting to lust; nor the celebration of the saints, and the visitation of relics be by any perverted into revellings and drunkenness. . . . [L]et so great care and diligence be used herein by bishops, as that there be nothing seen that is disorderly, or that is unbecomingly or confusedly arranged, nothing that is profane, nothing indecorous" (The Council of Trent, "On the Invocation, Veneration, and Relics, of Saints, and on Sacred Images."

8. See Lamoreaux, *The Early Muslim Tradition of Dream Interpretation*; Marlow, *Dreaming across Boundaries*; Plane and Tuttle, *Dreams, Dreamers, and Visions*; Levin, *Dreaming the English Renaissance*; Bulkeley, Adams, and Davis, *Dreaming in Christianity and Islam*; Le Goff, *The Medieval Imagination*; Kruger, *Dreaming in the Middle Ages*; Gerona, *Night Journeys*; Stewart, *Dreaming and Historical Consciousness*; Harris, *Dreams and Experience in Classical Antiquity*; Shulman and Stroumsa, *Dream Cultures*; Stephens, *The Dreams and Visions of Aelius Aristides*; Rivière, "Visions of the Night"; O'Flaherty, *Dreams, Illusion, and Other Realities*; Angelidi and Caolofonos, *Dreaming of Byzantium and Beyond*; and Von Grunebaum and Callois, *The Dream and Human Societies*. As Carol Rupprecht observed, "In the sixteenth century then, when a person had a dream, no single criterion could be comfortably or systematically invoked to assess its origin" ("Divinity, Insanity, Creativity," 125).

9. Bulkeley, *Dreaming in the World's Religions*. These roots indicate a great deal of continuity across time for several common ideas about dreaming, and this continuity poses a challenge for claims that one period of history marks a radical shift in people's views of dreams and dreaming. For example, Plane and Tuttle (*Dreams, Dreamers, and Visions*) argue against the "interiorization" thesis of the history of dreaming in Europe, and I agree with their rejection of a teleological theory of dream history in which people's explanations move from outer to inner causes. People of a certain era may create innovative ways of formulating their ideas about dreams and find new evidence in support of them, but in almost every case the ideas themselves have a long and rich lineage in previous periods of history.

10. Le Goff, *The Medieval Imagination*, 201.

11. Kruger, *Dreaming in the Middle Ages*, 19–24.

12. Ibid., 22.

13. Le Goff, *The Medieval Imagination*; Kruger, *Dreaming in the Middle Ages*.

14. Le Goff, *The Medieval Imagination*, 203.

15. Ibid., 205–207.

16. Kruger, *Dreaming in the Middle Ages*, 13.

17. Le Goff, *The Medieval Imagination*, 220. According to Plane and Tuttle (*Dreams, Dreamers, and Visions*), "Catholic Reformation theology, with its reaffirmation of the cult of saints (a significant number of whom were visionaries and divine dreamers), implied continuing revelation and held open the possibility that God would continue to speak to the faithful in their dreams" (13).

18. Kruger, *Dreaming in the Middle Ages*, 52.

19. Kagan, *Lucrecia's Dreams*, 44.

20. Kamen, *Philip of Spain*, 175.

21. Ibid., 176.

22. Kagan, *Lucrecia's Dreams*, 44.

23. Her employment qualifications may have been enhanced by virtue of her experiences helping her mother care for her four younger siblings.

24. Kamen, *Philip of Spain*, 270–271.

Chapter 2

1. Kagan, *Lucrecia's Dreams*, 27.

2. Ibid., 26.

3. For more on religion and prophecy at this time, see Christian, *Apparitions in Late Medieval and Renaissance Spain*; Haliczer, *Between Exaltation and Infamy*; Ryan, *A Kingdom of Stargazers*; Bilinkoff, *The Avila of Saint Teresa*; Niccoli, *Prophecy and People in Renaissance Italy*; and Grafton, *Cardano's Cosmos*.

4. Kagan, *Lucrecia's Dreams*, 45.

5. Ibid., 51.

6. Ibid., 59; emphasis added.

7. Ibid., 24.

8. Ibid., 60.

9. Ibid., 48.

10. Ibid., 48.

11. Ibid., 75.

12. Ibid., 46.

Chapter 3

1. Kagan has identified a total number of 415 dream reports in the archives, most of which have been preserved in very challenging conditions for accurate transcription, as I can personally attest after inspecting them in Madrid. We do

not know the criteria Don Alonso used to decide which dreams merited transcription into a fair copy version and which did not. It seems likely he favored longer and more dramatic dreams with specific references to the political and religious fate of Spain.

2. In December of 1587, Philip's health was so bad he remained in bed for four weeks, unable to perform his usual governing activities; see Parker, *Imprudent King*, 315.

3. Kagan, *Lucrecia's Dreams*, 75–76.

4. Ibid., 60–61.

5. Osborne, *The Dreamer of the Calle de San Salvador*, 152.

6. Ibid., 154.

Chapter 4

1. Kamen, *Philip of Spain*, 271.

2. Kagan, *Lucrecia's Dreams*, 119.

3. Ibid., 120.

4. Ibid.

5. Ibid.

6. Ibid., 122.

7. Ibid., 123. See also Zambrano, Simons, and Blázquez, *Sueños y procesos de Lucrecia de León*, 26.

8. Kagan, *Lucrecia's Dreams*, 119.

9. See Jonah 1–4, and Matthew 12:39. All biblical references are to the Revised Standard Version (RSV).

10. Zambrano, Simons, and Blázquez, *Sueños y procesos de Lucrecia de León*, 116 ff.

11. Kagan, *Lucrecia's Dreams*, 54.

12. Ibid., 112.

13. Genesis 24.

14. Kagan, *Lucrecia's Dreams*, 99.

Chapter 5

1. Hutchinson, *The Spanish Armada*, 89.

2. Ibid., 80–81.

3. Parker, *Imprudent King*, 317.

4. Elliott, *Imperial Spain 1469–1716*, 287

5. Parker, *Imprudent King*, 317.

6. Elliott, *Imperial Spain 1469–1716*, 288.

7. As late as August of 1588, according to Kagan, she dreamed about the Armada's defeat.

8. Kamen, *Philip of Spain*, 282.

9. Kagan, *Lucrecia's Dreams*, 12.

10. Ibid., 124.

11. Hutchinson, *The Spanish Armada*, 92.

12. Parker, *Imprudent King*, 320.

13. Hutchinson, *The Spanish Armada*, 104.

14. Ibid., 84.

15. Parker, *Imprudent King*, 320.

16. Hutchinson, *The Spanish Armada*, 122.

17. Parker, *Imprudent King*, 322.

18. Hutchinson, *The Spanish Armada*, 202.

19. Parker, *Imprudent King*, 323.

20. Osborne, *The Dreamer of the Calle de San Salvador*, 208.

21. Jordán, "Competition and Confirmation in the Iberian Prophetic Community," 72.

22. Bulkeley, *Dreaming in the World's Religions*.

23. Kagan, *Lucrecia's Dreams*, 129.

24. Osborne, *The Dreamer of the Calle de San Salvador*, 112.

25. The lack of additional information makes it difficult to infer anything else about their union. For more on the marriage customs of this era, see Poska, *Women and Authority in Early Modern Spain*; Bennett and Karras, *The Oxford Handbook of Gender in Medieval Europe*.

26. Kagan, *Lucrecia's Dreams*, 77; and Kamen, *Philip of Spain*, 282.

27. Kagan, *Lucrecia's Dreams*, 21–22. The dream goes on to envision the birth of a child, a boy named Carlos.

Chapter 6

1. See Marañón, *Antonio Pérez*; Parker, *Imprudent King*, 324–329; and Kamen, *Philip of Spain*, 284–292.

2. Parker, *Imprudent King*, 329.

3. Ibid., 324.

4. Marañón, 243–247.

5. Ibid., 57–58, 244.

6. Kagan, *Lucrecia's Dreams*, 13.

7. Ibid., 138.

8. Ibid., 133.

9. Zambrano, Simons, and Blázquez, *Sueños y procesos de Lucrecia de León*, 143.

10. Kamen, *Philip of Spain*, 285.

11. Also living in Toledo at this time were the playwright Lope de Vega, who had grown up in Lucrecia's neighborhood in Madrid, and the painter known as El Greco. With the king's presence adding to the importance of the public gathering, one or both of these great artists may also have been in attendance at the *auto de fé* that day.

12. Kamen, *Philip of Spain*, 283.

13. One of the other prisoners testified that Lucrecia and her followers were going in and out of their cells "muchas veces de noche y dia" (many times in the night and daytime) and that the guards shared meals with her of "carnero y gallina y vaca" (ram and chicken and beef). Another prisoner said of Lucrecia's treatment, "fue regalada con extraordinario cuidad" (she was treated with extraordinary care). Quoted from legajo 2085, no. 1, in the National Historical Archive, Madrid.

14. Kagan, *Lucrecia's Dreams*, 143.

15. Kamen, *Philip of Spain*, 287.

16. Homza, *The Spanish Inquisition 1478–1614*, xxv, 56.

17. Kagan, *Lucrecia's Dreams*, 145.

18. For more on Don Alonso's trial, see Tropé, "La Inquisición frente a la locura en la España de los Siglos XVI y XVII"; and Shuger, *Don Quixote in the Archives*.

19. Kagan, *Lucrecia's Dreams*, 152.

Chapter 7

1. For more on the Inquisition's principles for determining a person's sanity or lack thereof, see Shuger, *Don Quixote in the Archives*.

2. For more about the *beatas* of early modern Spain, see Perry, *Gender and Disorder in Early Modern Seville*, 97–117.

3. Ibid., 101.

4. In terms of the dream typology of Macrobius, which the Inquisitors may not have explicitly referenced but which formed the conceptual background to their analysis, Lucrecia's dreams were certainly more significant than an *insomnium* or a *visium*. But to acknowledge her dreams as belonging to any one of the higher three categories—*somnium*, *visio*, or *oraculum*—would grant Lucrecia's experiences more spiritual authenticity than the Inquisitors were apparently willing to concede.

5. See Windt's detailed arguments for the validity of subjective dream reports as a source of scientific research, in *Dreaming*, ch. 2–4. Domhoff addresses many of the same issues in *The Scientific Study of Dreams*.

6. Hall and Nordby, *The Individual and His Dreams*; Domhoff, *Finding Meaning in Dreams*, and *The Scientific Study of Dreams*; Foulkes, *Children's Dreaming and the Development of Consciousness*.

7. See, for example, Domhoff's study of more than 3,000 dream reports from "Barb Sanders," reported in *The Scientific Study of Dreams*.

8. See Kohut, *In Search of the Self*, for his theory of "healthy narcissism." See also Sedikides et al., "Are Normal Narcissists Psychologically Healthy?"; and Mann et al., "Self-Esteem in a Broad Spectrum Approach for Mental Health Promotion."

Chapter 8

1. Gardiner and Musto, *The Digital Humanities*.

2. See SDDb: Sleep and Dream Database, http://sleepanddreamdatabase
.org.

3. Domhoff and Schneider, "Studying Dream Content Using the Archive
and Search Engine on Dreambank.net"; Maggiolini et al., "The Words of Adolescents' Dreams"; Barcaro, *The Interwoven Sources of Dreams*; Walsh, "Prophetic
Imagination and the Neurophysiology of Trauma in Traumatized Adolescents";
Sears, "Spiritual Dreams and the Nepalese."

4. The use of word search tools in the study of dreams poses several methodological challenges, including the dangers of false positives and false negatives,
the adequacy of the word categories used to orient the search, the validity of
using the same categories for dreams in different languages (in the original or
in translation, as here), and the need for large quantities of data to generate
meaningful results. These tools do not replace other methods of analysis and
interpretation, but rather supplement them with reliable statistical information.
For more discussion, see Bulkeley, *Big Dreams*, especially ch. 6.

5. Hall and Nordby, *The Individual and his Dreams*; Domhoff, *The Scientific
Study of Dreams*.

6. Bulkeley, "Dreaming in Adolescence."

7. Hunt, *The Multiplicity of Dreams*.

8. Domhoff, *The Scientific Study of Dreams*; Bulkeley, "Dreaming in Adolescence."

9. Bulkeley, *Big Dreams*, ch. 6.

10. This figure is derived from the results of a word search combining all
three emotion categories.

11. Bulkeley, *Big Dreams*, ch. 6.

12. Bulkeley and Domhoff, "Detecting Meaning in Dream Reports"; Bulkeley, "Dreaming in Adolescence."

Chapter 9

1. Kryger, Roth, and Dement, *Principles and Practice of Sleep Medicine*; Maquet,
Smith, and Stickgold, *Sleep and Brain Plasticity*; McNamara, Barton, and Nunn,
Evolution of Sleep; Lohmann, *Dream Travelers*; Ekirch, *At Day's Close*.

2. Ekirch, *At Day's Close*.

3. Particularly at sleep onset and during NREM stage 2 toward the end of
the sleep cycle, when the brain is alternating between REM and NREM stage 2.
See Kahan, "The 'Problem' of Dreaming in NREM Sleep."

4. Solms, *The Neuropsychology of Dreaming*.

5. Calkins, "Statistics of Dreams."

6. Ibid., 329.

7. See Domhoff, *Finding Meaning in Dreams*.

8. Cacioppo and Decety, "An Introduction to Social Neuroscience," 5; see also Schutt, Seidman, and Keshavan, *Social Neuroscience*; and Cozolino, *The Neuroscience of Human Relationships*.

9. See de Waal, *Chimpanzee Politics*.

10. See Guthrie, *Faces in the Clouds*; Boyer, *Religion Explained*; Barrett, *Why Would Anyone Believe in God?*; Barrett, "Exploring the Natural Foundations of Religion"; and Pyysiäinen, *How Religion Works*.

11. Revonsuo, "The Reinterpretation of Dreams," 97.

12. Ibid.

13. See Bulkeley, *Dreaming in the World's Religions*.

14. Jung, "General Aspects of Dream Psychology."

15. Ullman, "A Theory of Vigilance and Dreaming,"; Snyder, "Toward an Evolutionary Theory of Dreaming."

16. Cartwright, *The 24-Hour Mind*.

17. Taylor, *Dream Work*.

18. The counterfactual realities that dreams can simulate can represent not only frightening threats but positive potentials and opportunities, too (as in dreams of flying, great beauty, or sexual pleasure).

19. See Purcell, Moffitt, and Hoffmann, "Waking, Dreaming, and Self-Regulation"; and Kahan and LaBerge, "Dreaming and Waking." An exception seems to be mental tasks involving literacy or numerical calculations. See Hartmann, "We Do Not Dream of the 3 R's."

20. Hurd and Bulkeley, *Lucid Dreaming*. The research findings mentioned in the following paragraph all refer to chapters in this two-volume collection of new studies on consciousness in sleep.

21. Kahan, "Consciousness in Dreaming."

22. Purcell, Moffitt, and Hoffmann, "Waking, Dreaming, and Self-Regulation."

23. For more on consciousness in dreams, see Thompson, *Dreaming, Waking, Being*.

24. Schredl et al., "Dream Recall Frequency, Attitude toward Dreams, and Openness to Experience."

25. Gackenbach and LaBerge, *Conscious Mind, Sleeping Brain*.

Chapter 10

1. This term includes psychologists and psychoanalysts who have been working for the better part of a century in the ego psychology, object relations, and self psychology schools of thought growing out of Freud's original theories. See Greenberg and Mitchell, *Object Relations in Psychoanalytic Theory*; Mitchell et al., *Relational Psychoanalysis*; Jones, *Contemporary Psychoanalysis and Religion*; Cooper-White, *Braided Selves*; and Cataldo, "I Know That My Redeemer Lives."

2. Winnicott, *Playing and Reality*.

3. Erikson, *Childhood and Society*, 247–251. The opposite of basic trust is basic mistrust, involving feelings of suspiciousness, not belonging, not fitting in, and identity fragmentation. None of those characteristics fit with the known details of Lucrecia's life.

4. Freud, *The Interpretation of Dreams*.

5. For Freud's approach, see *The Interpretation of Dreams*.

6. According to Shuger, Don Alonso was also keenly interested in the input and output of the human digestive system, and for a time he closely supervised the diet and excretory activities of a family in Toledo (*Don Quixote in the Archives*, 49–50).

Chapter 11

1. This was the attitude of the ancient Greek philosopher Aristotle, who had great influence on Catholic theologian Thomas Aquinas. According to Aristotle, "it is absurd to combine the idea that the sender of such [prophetic] dreams should be God with the fact that those to whom he sends them are not the best and wisest, but merely commonplace persons" (Aristotle, "On Prophesying by Dreams," 627). Le Goff says the same point was made by Macrobius, who "stressed the traditional idea that there is a hierarchy of dreamers, and that only the dreams of persons invested with supreme authority could be regarded as authentic and irrefutable premonitory dreams" (*The Medieval Imagination*, 201).

2. See Von Grunebaum and Callois, *The Dream and Human Societies*; and Shulman and Stroumsa, *Dream Cultures*.

3. Beradt, *The Third Reich of Dreams*.

4. Bulkeley, *Dreaming in the World's Religions*.

5. Hermansen, "Dreams and Dreaming in Islam."

6. Gerona, *Night Journeys*.

7. Irwin, *The Dream Seekers*.

8. Bulkeley, *Dreaming in the World's Religions*, especially ch. 8–10.

9. Levin, *Dreaming the English Renaissance*, 8, 159. Along the same lines, Plane and Tuttle introduce their edited volume *Dreams, Dreamers, and Visions* by affirming the significance of dreams in the study of historical change during the early modern era: "[D]reams never merely reflect cultures, cultural patterns, or *mentalités*. Instead, dreams and visions—and, most critically, the ways in which they are used and reported—help to create, extend, and integrate social change, both inside European societies and within new and expansive colonial contexts" (21).

10. See Bulkeley, *American Dreamers*.

11. Samuels, *The Political Psyche*.

12. Historian Lucian Febvre, quoted in Perry, *Gender and Disorder in Early Modern Seville*, 9. Perry's methodological focus on "women in a male-dominated city" requires attention to unorthodox sources of information from liminal spaces representing "marginality both in standing outside the pale of respectability and

in presenting the voice of folk wisdom rather than official knowledge." Dreams and dream theories would seem to be promising resources for this approach. Rupprecht's study of the Italian Renaissance scholar Girolamo Cardano points in this same direction: "[The] selectivity in Western habits of thought has led to the substantial privileging of Cardano's logical, rational, 'prescientific' writings and to the fragmentation, marginalization, and finally denigration of his writings on aspects of culture like dreams and of his belief in the sympathy of all things in the universe" ("Divinity, Insanity, Creativity," 115).

13. Kagan, *Lucrecia's Dreams*, 129; emphasis added.

Chapter 12

1. "During the sixteenth century, the Hispanic peninsula became the center of Catholic thought" (Payne, *Spanish Catholicism*, 39).

2. Patton, "A Great and Strange Correction."

3. See Bulkeley, *Dreaming in the World's Religions*.

4. Aydar, "*Istikhara* and Dreams."

5. 1 Kings 3:4–5.

6. Tedlock, *The Woman in the Shaman's Body*.

7. See Mullin, *The Practice of the Six Yogas of Naropa*.

8. See Ewing, "The Dream of Spiritual Initiation."

9. See Covitz, *Visions of the Night*.

10. Aristotle may have been the first to offer a naturalistic explanation for anticipatory dreams, by suggesting that residual sense impressions from the day continue to echo through the mind at night; during the quiet solitude of sleep, the mind is able to perceive subtle movements, stirrings, and "beginnings" that can hint at the unfolding of future events: "it is manifest that these beginnings must be more evident in sleeping than in waking moments" (Aristotle, "On Prophesying by Dreams," 627).

11. Artemidorus, *The Interpretation of Dreams*.

12. This is indicated by comments made during Inquisition testimony (legajo 2085, no. 1, in the National Historical Archive, Madrid).

13. Such as Genesis 16:12–16 and 28:10–22.

14. Judges 7:13–14.

15. 1 Samuel 3:1–18.

16. Genesis 37–47, Daniel 2, 4.

17. Acts 16:6–10, 18:9–11.

18. Acts 2:17–21, following Joel 2:28–32.

19. Ecclesiastes 5:7 and Zechariah 10:2.

20. Jeremiah 23:25–28 and 29:8–9.

21. See Brueggemann, *The Prophetic Imagination*; and Heschel, *The Prophets*.

22. Job 33:14–17.

23. Bulkeley, *Big Dreams*, p. 80.

24. Ibid., p. 237.

25. These visual references could be explored further by scholars with skills in art history and Counter-Reformation theology, helping to shed new light on Lucrecia's cultural environment.

26. Whitehouse, *Modes of Religiosity*.

Chapter 13

1. Sherlock Holmes, in Doyle, "The Adventures of Sherlock Holmes," 209.

2. Augustine, *Confessions*, 203.

3. Aquinas, *Summa Theologica*, II-II.154.5.

4. Augustine *Confessions*, 50.

5. Ibid.

6. Ibid., 108.

Historical Epilogue

1. Kagan, *Lucrecia's Dreams*, 154.

2. Ibid., 154; emphasis added.

3. Ibid., 13.

4. Ibid., 159.

5. There is a slight but real chance that Lucrecia's story reached the ears of William Shakespeare around the time he began composing his epic poem *The Rape of Lucrece*, a reimagining of the Roman legend that he published in the spring of 1594. Information about Lucrecia de León's life could have reached Shakespeare via two routes. One route started with Lady Jane Dormer, who was born a year after Shakespeare's mother, Mary Arden, in an English country town about 50 miles from Mary's home. Both women came from ancient and noble families of deep Catholic faith, and after emigrating to Spain, Lady Jane continued to communicate with Catholic friends and family still in England. Lucrecia's story, at least in its outlines, could easily have passed from Lady Jane to an English Catholic who knew Mary Arden, and from there to her son, William. Not likely, perhaps, but possible. Somewhat more likely is the second route, starting with the close friendship between Fray Lucas de Allende and Antonio Pérez. Fray Lucas, Lucrecia's long-time dream scribe, actively helped Pérez plan his escape from the Inquisition's prison in 1590 and took care of the secretary's personal wealth, indicating a great deal of trust and intimacy between them. In 1593, Pérez arrived in England, where he spent two years publicly criticizing Philip and enjoying London's nightlife, especially its theatrical performances. Pérez almost certainly crossed paths with Shakespeare during his time in London, and some scholars have suggested that Pérez was Shakespeare's model for the character Don Adriano de Armado, a preening, grandiloquent Spaniard in the comedy *Love's Labour's Lost*, written in the mid-1590s. Pérez was a witty *bon vivant* who enjoyed sharing gossip with his English friends that cast a negative light on King

Philip, making it conceivable that Shakespeare heard Pérez mention Lucrecia's story at some point prior to the writing of the poem.

6. Although chronically underfunded, many convents provided a safe and supportive enclosure for women who could not survive anywhere else: "It would be easy to assume that nuns were the most oppressed of all women in this patriarchal society, but to view them as victims ignores the ways that many women in religious orders found increased opportunities for self-expression" (Perry, *Gender and Disorder in Early Modern Seville*, 75).

7. Ibid., 7, 13.

8. Kamen, *Philip of Spain*, 312–315.

9. Cervantes, *Don Quixote*, 141.

10. Ibid., 222. Later in the novel, a woman named Camila says she will not go as far as Lucretia did in killing herself before gaining vengeance against her wrongdoers (331).

11. Ibid., 672.

Conclusion

1. To access the dreams, follow these steps: from the SDDb home page (http://sleepanddreamdatabase.org), select "Word Searching" from the horizontal menu bar. Then in "Build a Search" step #1, scroll down the list of surveys to "Lucrecia Journal 1." Click on it; then click on the "Search" button.

2. To access these dreams, follow the same steps as in note 2 above to reach the list of surveys, then select "Lucrecia Journal 2."

3. See McNamara, *Where God and Science Meet*; Taves, *Religious Experience Reconsidered*; Xygalatas, *The Burning Saints*; and Gay, *Neuroscience and Religion*.

4. James, *The Varieties of Religious Experience*.

5. See Damasio, *Descartes' Error*.

6. See Gardiner and Musto, *The Digital Humanities*.

BIBLIOGRAPHY

Angelidi, Christine, and George T. Caolofonos, eds. *Dreaming in Byzantium and Beyond*. Farnham: Ashgate, 2014.

Aquinas, Thomas. *The Summa Theologica*. Trans. Fathers of the English Dominican Province, 1947. http://dhspriory.org/thomas/summa/SS/SS154.html#SSQ154A5THEP1.

Aristotle. "On Prophesying by Dreams." Trans. J. I. Beare. In Richard McKeon, ed., *The Collected Works of Aristotle*, 626–630. New York: Random House, 1941.

Artemidorus. *The Interpretation of Dreams*. Trans. Robert J. White. Park Ridge: Noyes Press, 1975.

Augustine. *Confessions*. Trans. Henry Chadwick. Oxford: Oxford University Press, 1991.

Aydar, Hidayet. "Istikhara and Dreams: Learning about the Future through Dreaming." In Kelly Bulkeley, Kate Adams, and Patricia M. Davis, eds., *Dreaming in Christianity and Islam: Culture, Conflict, and Creativity*, 123–136. New Brunswick: Rutgers University Press, 2009.

Barcaro, Umberto. *The Interwoven Sources of Dreams*. London: Karnac Books, 2010.

Barrett, Justin. "Exploring the Natural Foundations of Religion." *Trends in Cognitive Sciences* 4, no. 1 (2000):29-34.

———. *Why Would Anyone Believe in God?* Walnut Creek: AltaMira Press, 2004.

Bennett, Judith M., and Ruth Mazo Karras, eds. *The Oxford Handbook of Women and Gender in Medieval Europe*. New York: Oxford University Press, 2013.

Beradt, Charlotte. *The Third Reich of Dreams*. Trans. Adriane Gottwald. Chicago: Quadrangle Books, 1966.

Bilinkoff, Jodi. *The Avila of Saint Teresa: Religious Reform in a Sixteenth Century City*. 2nd ed. Ithaca: Cornell University Press, 2014.

Bingaman, Kirk. *The Power of Neuroplasticity for Pastoral and Spiritual Care*. Lanham: Lexington Books, 2014.

Boyer, Pascal. *Religion Explained: The Evolutionary Origins of Religious Thought*. New York: Basic Books, 2001.

Brueggemann, Walter. *The Prophetic Imagination*. 2nd ed. Minneapolis: Fortress Press, 2001.

Bulkeley, Kelly. *American Dreamers: What Dreams Tell Us about the Political Psychology of Conservatives, Liberals, and Everyone Else*. Boston: Beacon Press, 2008.

———. *Big Dreams: The Science of Dreaming and the Origins of Religion*. New York: Oxford University Press, 2016.

———. "Dreaming in Adolescence: A 'Blind' Word Search of a Teenage Girl's Dream Series." *Dreaming* 22, no. 4 (2012):240–252.

———. *Dreaming in the World's Religions: A Comparative History*. New York: New York University Press, 2008.

Bulkeley, Kelly, Kate Adams, and Patricia M. Davis, eds. *Dreaming in Christianity and Islam: Culture, Conflict, and Creativity*. New Brunswick: Rutgers University Press, 2009.

Bulkeley, Kelly, and G. William Domhoff. "Detecting Meaning in Dream Reports: An Extension of a Word Search Approach." *Dreaming* 20, no. 2 (2010):77–95.

Cacioppo, John T., and Jean Decety. "An Introduction to Social Neuroscience." In Jean Decety and John T. Cacioppo, eds., *The Oxford Handbook of Social Neuroscience*, 3–8. New York: Oxford University Press, 2011.

Calkins, Mary. "Statistics of Dreams." *American Journal of Psychology* 5 (1893):311–343.

Carrette, Jeremy. "Religion Out of Mind: The Ideology of Cognitive Science and Religion." In Kelly Bulkeley, ed., *Soul, Psyche, Brain: New Directions in the Study of Religion and Brain-Mind Science*, 242–261. New York: Palgrave Macmillan, 2005.

Cartwright, Rosalind. *The 24-Hour Mind: The Role of Sleep and Dreaming in Our Emotional Lives*. New York: Oxford University Press, 2010.

Cataldo, Lisa. "I Know That My Redeemer Lives: Relational Perspectives on Trauma, Dissociation, and Faith." *Pastoral Psychology* 62, no. 6 (2013):791–804.

Cervantes, Miguel. *Don Quixote*. Trans. Tom Lathrop. New York: Signet, 2011.

Chilcott, Travis. "Directly perceiving *Kṛṣṇa*: Accounting for perceptual experiences of deities within the framework of naturalism." *Religion* 45, no. 4 (2015):532–552.

Christian, William A., Jr. *Apparitions in Late Medieval and Renaissance Spain*. Princeton: Princeton University Press, 1981.

Clifford, Henry. *The Life of Lady Jane Dormer, Duchess of Feria*. London: Burnes and Oates, 1887.

Cohen, Emma. *The Mind Possessed: The Cognition of Spirit Possession in an Afro-Brazilian Religious Tradition*. New York: Oxford University Press, 2007.

Cooper-White, Pamela. *Braided Selves: Collected Essays on Multiplicity, God, and Persons*. Eugene: Wipf and Stock, 2011.

The Council of Trent: The Twenty-Fifth Session. "On the Invocation, Veneration, and Relics, of Saints, and on Sacred Images." In *The Canons and Decrees of the Sacred and Oecumenical Council of Trent*, ed. and trans. J. Waterworth, 233–236. London: Dolman, 1848. http://history.hanover.edu/texts/trent/ct25.html.

Covitz, Joel. *Visions of the Night: A Study of Jewish Dream Interpretation*. Boston: Shambhala, 1990.

Cozolino, Louis. *The Neuroscience of Human Relationships: Attachment and the Developing Social Brain*. 2nd ed. New York: W. W. Norton, 2014.

Czachesz, Istvan, and Tamas Biró, eds. *Changing Minds: Religion and Cognition through the Ages*. Leuven: Peeters, 2011.

Damasio, Antonio. *Descartes' Error: Emotion, Reason, and the Human Brain*. New York: Quill, 1994.

Dante Alighieri. *The Inferno*. Trans. John Ciardi. New York: New American Library, 1954.

de Waal, Frans. *Chimpanzee Politics: Power and Sex among Apes*. Baltimore: Johns Hopkins University Press, 2007.

Domhoff, G. William. *Finding Meaning in Dreams: A Quantitative Approach*. New York: Plenum, 1996.

———. *The Scientific Study of Dreams: Neural Networks, Cognitive Development, and Content Analysis*. Washington, DC: American Psychological Association, 2003.

Domhoff, G. William, and Adam Schneider. "Studying Dream Content Using the Archive and Search Engine on Dreambank.net." *Consciousness and Cognition* 17 (2008):1238–1247.

Dominguez Ortiz, Antonio. *The Golden Age of Spain, 1516–1659*. Trans. James Casey. London: Weidenfeld and Nicolson, 1971.

Downey, Kirstin. *Isabella: The Warrior Queen*. New York: Nan A. Talese/Doubleday, 2014.

Doyle, Arthur Conan. *The Adventures of Sherlock Holmes*. Mineola: Dover, 2009.

Edwards, John. *Inquisition*. Stroud: Tempus, 1999.

Elliott, J. H. *Imperial Spain 1469–1716*. London: Edward Arnold, 1963.

———. *The Revolt of the Catalans: A Study in the Decline of Spain (1598–1640)*. Cambridge: Cambridge University Press, 1963.

Ekirch, Roger. *At Day's Close: Night in Times Past*. New York: W. W. Norton, 2005.

Erikson, Erik. *Childhood and Society*. New York: W. W. Norton, 1950.

———. *Gandhi's Truth: On the Origins of Militant Nonviolence*. New York: W. W. Norton, 1969.

———. *Young Man Luther: A Study in Psychoanalysis and History*. New York: W. W. Norton, 1958.

Ewing, Katherine. "The Dream of Spiritual Initiation and the Organization of Self Representations among Pakistani Sufis." *American Ethnologist* 17 (1990):56–74.

Foulkes, David. *Children's Dreaming and the Development of Consciousness*. Cambridge: Harvard University Press, 2002.

Freud, Sigmund. *The Interpretation of Dreams*. Trans. James Strachey. New York: Avon Books, 1965.

Gackenbach, Jayne, and Stephen LaBerge, eds. *Conscious Mind, Sleeping Brain*. New York: Plenum, 1988.

Gardiner, Eileen, and Ronald G. Musto, eds. *The Digital Humanities: A Primer for Students and Scholars*. New York: Cambridge University Press, 2015.

Gay, Volney P., ed. *Neuroscience and Religion: Brain, Mind, Self, and Soul*. Lanham: Lexington Books, 2009.

Gerona, Carla. *Night Journeys: The Power of Dreams in Transatlantic Quaker Culture*. Charlottesville: University of Virginia Press, 2004.

Giles, Mary E. *Women in the Inquisition: Spain and the New World*. Baltimore: Johns Hopkins University Press, 1998.

Grafton, Anthony. *Cardano's Cosmos: The Worlds and Works of a Renaissance Astrologer*. Cambridge: Harvard University Press, 1999.

Graves, Mark. *Mind, Brain and the Elusive Soul*. Aldershot: Ashgate, 2008.

Greenberg, Jay R., and Stephen A. Mitchell. *Object Relations in Psychoanalytic Theory*. Cambridge: Harvard University Press, 1983.

Grieve, Patricia E. *The Eve of Spain: Myths of Origins in the History of Christian, Muslim, and Jewish Conflict*. Baltimore: Johns Hopkins University Press, 2009.

Guthrie, Stewart. *Faces in the Clouds: A New Theory of Religion*. New York: Oxford University Press, 1992.

Haliczer, Stephen. *Between Exaltation and Infamy: Female Mystics in the Golden Age of Spain*. New York: Oxford University Press, 2002.

Hall, Calvin, and Vernon J. Nordby. *The Individual and His Dreams*. New York: Signet, 1972.

Harris, William V. *Dreams and Experience in Classical Antiquity*. Cambridge: Harvard University Press, 2009.

Hartmann, Ernest. "We Do Not Dream of the 3 R's: Implications for the Nature of Dreaming Mentation." *Dreaming* 10, no. 2 (2000):103–110.

Hays, Glen. "Possible Selves, Body Schemas, and *Sadhana*: Using Cognitive Science and Neuroscience in the Study of Medieval *Vaisnava Sahajiya* Hindu Tantric Texts." *Religions* 5, no. 3 (2014):684–699.

Hermansen, Marcia. "Dreams and Dreaming in Islam." In Kelly Bulkeley, ed., *Dreams: A Reader on the Religious, Cultural, and Psychological Dimensions of Dreaming*, 73–92. New York: Palgrave, 2001.

Heschel, Abraham J. *The Prophets*. New York: Harper Perennial, 2001.

Hogue, David. *Remembering the Future, Imagining the Past: Story, Ritual, and the Human Brain*. Eugene: Wipf and Stock, 2009.

Homza, Lu Ann, ed. *The Spanish Inquisition 1478–1614: An Anthology of Sources*. Indianapolis: Hackett, 2006.

Hunt, Harry T. *The Multiplicity of Dreams: Memory, Imagination, and Consciousness*. New Haven: Yale University Press, 1989.

Hurd, Ryan, and Kelly Bulkeley, eds. *Lucid Dreaming: New Perspectives on Consciousness in Sleep*. 2 vols. Westport: ABC-Clio, 2014.

Hutchinson, Robert. *The Spanish Armada*. New York: Thomas Dunne Books, 2013.

Irwin, Lee. *The Dream Seekers: Native American Visionary Traditions of the Great Plains*. Norman: University of Oklahoma Press, 1994.

James, William. *The Varieties of Religious Experience.* New York: Mentor Books, 1958.

Jones, James W. *Contemporary Psychoanalysis and Religion: Transference and Transcendence.* New Haven: Yale University Press, 1993.

Jordán, María V. "Competition and Confirmation in the Iberian Prophetic Community: The 1589 Invasion of Portugal in the Dreams of Lucrecia de León." In Ann Marie Plane and Leslie Tuttle, eds., *Dreams, Dreamers and Visions: The Early Modern Atlantic World,* 72–87. Philadelphia: University of Pennsylvania Press, 2013.

Jordán Arroyo, María V. *Soñar la historia: Riesgo, creatividad, y religión en las profecías de Lucrecia de León.* Madrid: Siglo XXI Editores España, 2007.

Jung, C. G. "General Aspects of Dream Psychology." In R.F.C. Hull, ed. and trans., *Dreams,* 23–66. Princeton: Princeton University Press, 1974.

Kagan, Richard L. *Lucrecia's Dreams: Politics and Prophecy in Sixteenth-Century Spain.* Berkeley: University of California Press, 1990.

Kagan, Richard, and Abigail Dyer, eds. *Inquisitorial Inquiries: Brief Lives of Secret Jews and Other Heretics.* Baltimore: Johns Hopkins University Press, 2004.

Kahan, Tracey. "Consciousness in Dreaming: A Metacognitive Approach." In Kelly Bulkeley, ed., *Dreams: A Reader on the Religious, Cultural, and Psychological Dimensions of Dreaming,* 333–360. New York: Palgrave, 2001.

———. "The 'Problem' of Dreaming in NREM Sleep Continues to Challenge Reductionist (Two Generator) Models of Dream Generation." In Edward Pace-Schott, Mark Solms, Mark Blagrove, and Stevan Harnad, eds., *Sleep and Dreaming: Scientific Advances and Reconsiderations,* 167–169. Cambridge: Cambridge University Press, 2003.

Kahan, Tracey, and Stephen LaBerge. "Dreaming and Waking: Similarities and Differences Revisited." *Consciousness and Cognition* 20 (2011):494–515.

Kamen, Henry. *Golden Age Spain.* 2nd ed. New York: Palgrave Macmillan, 2005.

———. *Philip of Spain.* New Haven: Yale University Press, 1997.

———. *The Spanish Inquisition: A Historical Revision.* London: Folio Society, 1998.

Kandel, Eric, James Schwartz, Thomas Jessell, Steven Siegelbaum, and A. J. Hudspeth, eds. *Principles of Neural Science.* 5th ed. New York: McGraw Hill, 2012.

Kelly, Edward, Emily Williams Kelly, Adam Crabtree, Alan Gauld, Michael Grosso, and Bruce Greyson. *Irreducible Mind: Toward a Psychology for the 21st Century.* Lanham: Rowman & Littlefield, 2007.

Kohut, Heinz. *The Search for the Self: Selected Writings of Heinz Kohut: 1950–1978.* Ed. Paul H. Ornstein. 2 vols. New York: International Universities Press, 1978.

Kors, Alan Charles, and Edward Peters, eds. *Witchcraft in Europe 1400–1700: A Documentary History.* Philadelphia: University of Pennsylvania Press, 2001.

Kruger, Steven F. *Dreaming in the Middle Ages.* Cambridge: Cambridge University Press, 1992.

Kryger, Meir H., Thomas Roth, and William C. Dement, eds. *Principles and Practice of Sleep Medicine.* 4th ed. Philadelphia: Elsevier Saunders, 2005.

Lamoreaux, John. *The Early Muslim Tradition of Dream Interpretation.* Albany: State University of New York Press, 2002.

Lea, Henry Charles. *A History of the Inquisition of the Middle Ages.* 3 vols. CreateSpace Independent Publishing Platform, 2006. First published 1887 by Harper and Brothers.

Le Goff, Jacques. *The Medieval Imagination.* Trans. Arthur Goldhammer. Chicago: University of Chicago Press, 1988.

Levin, Carole. *Dreaming the English Renaissance: Politics and Desire in Court and Culture.* New York: Palgrave Macmillan, 2008.

Livy. *The Early History of Rome.* Trans. Aubrey de Sélincourt. London: Penguin Books, 2002.

Lohmann, Roger, ed. *Dream Travelers: Sleep Experiences and Culture in the Western Pacific.* New York: Palgrave Macmillan, 2003.

Luhrmann, T. M. *When God Talks Back: Understanding the American Evangelical Relationship with God.* New York: Vintage, 2012.

Maggiolini, Alfio, Paolo Azzone, Katia Provantini, Daniele Viganó, and Salvatore Freni. "The Words of Adolescents' Dreams: A Quantitative Analysis." *Dreaming* 13, no. 2 (2003):107–117.

Mann, Michelle, Clemens M. H. Hosman, Herman P. Schaalma, and Nanne K. de Vries. "Self-Esteem in a Broad Spectrum Approach for Mental Health Promotion." *Health Education Research* 19, no. 4 (2004):357–372.

Maquet, Pierre, Carlyle Smith, and Robert Stickgold, eds. *Sleep and Brain Plasticity.* New York: Oxford University Press, 2003.

Marañón, Gregorio. *Antonio Pérez: Spanish Traitor.* Trans. Charles David Ley. London: Hollis and Carter, 1954.

Marlow, Louise, ed. *Dreaming across Boundaries: The Interpretation of Dreams in Islamic Lands.* Cambridge: Harvard University Press, 2008.

McNamara, Patrick, ed. *Where God and Science Meet: How Brain and Evolutionary Studies Alter Our Understanding of Religion.* 3 vols. Westport: Praeger, 2006.

McNamara, Patrick, Robert Barton, and Charles Nunn, eds. *Evolution of Sleep: Phylogenetic and Functional Perspectives.* New York: Cambridge University Press, 2010.

Mitchell, Stephen A., Lewis Aron, Adrienne Harris, and Melanie Suchet, eds. *Relational Psychoanalysis.* New York: Routledge, 2007.

Moss, Robert. *The Secret History of Dreaming.* Novato: New World Books, 2010.

Mullin, Glenn, ed. and trans. *The Practice of the Six Yogas of Naropa.* Ithaca: Snow Lion, 2006.

Niccoli, Ottavia. *Prophecy and People in Renaissance Italy.* Trans. Lydia G. Cochrane. Princeton: Princeton University Press, 1990.

O'Flaherty, Wendy Doniger. *Dreams, Illusion, and Other Realities.* Chicago: University of Chicago Press, 1986.

Osborne, Roger. *The Dreamer of the Calle de San Salvador: Visions of Sedition and Sacrilege in Sixteenth-Century Spain.* London: Pimlico, 2002.

Ovid. *The Regifugium*. In *The Book of Days*, trans. A. S. Kline, Book II: February 24. http://www.poetryintranslation.com/PITBR/Latin/OvidFastiBkTwo.htm #anchor_Toc69367697.

Parker, Geoffrey. *Imprudent King: A New Life of Philip II*. New Haven: Yale University Press, 2014.

Patton, Kimberley. "'A Great and Strange Correction': Intentionality, Locality, and Epiphany in the Category of Dream Incubation." *History of Religions* 43 (2004):194–223.

Payne, Richard. "Buddhism and Cognitive Science: Contributions to an Enlarged Discourse." *Pacific World: Journal of the Institute of Buddhist Studies*, 3rd series, no. 4 (2002):1–13.

Payne, Stanley G. *Spanish Catholicism: An Historical Overview*. Madison: University of Wisconsin Press, 1984.

Perry, Mary Elizabeth. *Gender and Disorder in Early Modern Seville*. Princeton: Princeton University Press, 1990.

Plane, Anne Marie and Leslie Tuttle, eds. *Dreams, Dreamers, and Visions: The Early Modern Atlantic World*. Philadelphia: University of Pennsylvania Press, 2013.

Poska, Allyson. *Women and Authority in Early Modern Spain: The Peasants of Galicia*. New York: Oxford University Press, 2006.

Purcell, Sheila, Alan Moffitt, and Robert Hoffmann. "Waking, Dreaming, and Self-Regulation." In Alan Moffitt, Milton Kramer, and Robert Hoffmann, eds., *The Functions of Dreaming*, 197–260. Albany: State University of New York Press, 1993.

Pyysiäinen, Ilkka. *How Religion Works: Towards a New Cognitive Science of Religion*. Leiden: Brill, 2001.

Rambo, Lewis. *Understanding Religious Conversion*. New Haven: Yale University Press, 1995.

Revonsuo, Antti. "The Reinterpretation of Dreams: An Evolutionary Hypothesis of the Function of Dreaming." In Edward Pace-Schott, Mark Solms, Mark Blagrove, and Stevan Harnad, eds., *Sleep and Dreaming: Scientific Advances and Reconsiderations*, 85–109. Cambridge: Cambridge University Press, 2003.

Rivière, Janine. "'Visions of the Night': The Reform of Popular Dream Beliefs in Early Modern England." *Parergon* 20, no. 1 (2003):109–138.

Roth, Cecil. *The Spanish Inquisition*. New York: W. W. Norton, 1964.

Rupprecht, Carol Schreier. "Divinity, Insanity, Creativity: A Renaissance Contribution to the History and Theory of Dream/Text(s)." In Carol Schreier Rupprecht, ed., *The Dream and the Text: Essays on Literature and Language*, 112–132. Albany: State University of New York Press, 1994.

Ryan, Michael A. *A Kingdom of Stargazers: Astrology and Authority in the Late Medieval Crown of Aragon*. Ithaca: Cornell University Press, 2011.

Samuels, Andrew. *The Political Psyche*. New York: Routledge, 1993.

Schredl, Michael, Petra Ciric, Simon Gotz, and Lutz Wittman. "Dream Recall

Frequency, Attitude toward Dreams and Openness to Experience." *Dreaming* 13, no. 3 (2003):145–153.

Schutt, Russel K., Larry J. Seidman, and Matcheri Keshavan, eds. *Social Neuroscience: Brain, Mind, and Society*. Cambridge: Harvard University Press, 2015.

Sears, Robert. "Spiritual Dreams and the Nepalese: Applying Attribution Theory to the Dreams of Nepali Christians and Hindus." Unpublished doctoral dissertation. Pasadena: Fuller Theological Seminary, 2016.

Sedikides, Constantine, Eric A. Rudich, Aiden P. Gregg, Madoka Kumashiro, and Caryl Rusbult. "Are Normal Narcissists Psychologically Healthy?: Self-Esteem Matters." *Journal of Personality and Social Psychology* 87, no. 3 (2004):400–416.

Shuger, Dale. *Don Quixote in the Archives: Madness and Literature in Early Modern Spain*. Edinburgh: Edinburgh University Press, 2012.

Shulman, David, and David Stroumsa, eds. *Dream Cultures: Explorations in the Comparative History of Dreaming*. New York: Oxford University Press, 1999.

Slingerland, Edward, and Mark Collard, eds. *Creating Consilience: Integrating the Sciences and the Humanities*. New York: Oxford University Press, 2011.

Snyder, Frederick. "Toward an Evolutionary Theory of Dreaming." *American Journal of Psychiatry* 123, no. 2 (1966):121–136.

Solms, Mark. *The Neuropsychology of Dreams: A Clinico-Anatomical Study*. Mahwah: Lawrence Erlbaum, 1997.

Stephens, John. *The Dreams and Visions of Aelius Aristides: A Case-Study in the History of Religions*. Piscataway: Gorgias Press, 2013.

Stewart, Charles. *Dreaming and Historical Consciousness in Island Greece*. Cambridge: Harvard University Press, 2012.

Taves, Ann. *Religious Experience Reconsidered: A Building-Block Approach to the Study of Religion and Other Special Things*. Princeton: Princeton University Press, 2009.

Taylor, Jeremy. *Dream Work: Techniques for Discovering the Creative Power in Dreams*. Mahwah: Paulist Press, 1983.

Tedlock, Barbara. *The Woman in the Shaman's Body: Reclaiming the Feminine in Religion and Medicine*. New York: Bantam, 2005.

Thompson, Evan. *Waking, Dreaming, Being: Self and Consciousness in Neuroscience, Meditation, and Philosophy*. New York: Columbia University Press, 2014.

Thompson, Richard H. *The Brain: A Neuroscience Primer*. New York: Worth, 2000.

Tooby, John, and Leda Cosmides. "The Psychological Foundations of Culture." In Jerome H. Barkow, Leda Cosmides, and John Tooby, eds., *The Adapted Mind: Evolutionary Psychology and the Generation of Culture*, 19–136. New York: Oxford University Press, 1995.

Tropé, Hélène. "La Inquisición frente a la locura en la España de los Siglos XVI y XVII (y II): La eliminación do los herejes." *Revista de la Asociación Española de Neuropsiquiatría* 30, no. 107 (2010):465–486.

Ullman, Montague. "A Theory of Vigilance and Dreaming." In Z. Zikmund, ed., *The Oculomotor System and Brain Functions*, 453–465. London: Butterworths Books, 1973.

Von Grunebaum, G. E., and Roger Callois, eds. *The Dream and Human Societies*. Berkeley: University of California Press, 1966.

Walsh, Mary C. "Prophetic Imagination and the Neurophysiology of Trauma in Traumatized Adolescents." Unpublished doctoral dissertation. San Anselmo: San Francisco Theological Seminary, 2014.

Whitehouse, Harvey. *Modes of Religiosity: A Cognitive Theory of Religious Transmission*. Walnut Creek: Altamira Press, 2004.

Wiltrout, Ann E. *A Patron and a Playwright in Renaissance Spain: The House of Feria and Diego Sánchez de Badajoz*. London: Tamesis Books, 1987.

Windt, Jennifer M. *Dreaming: A Conceptual Framework for Philosophy of Mind and Empirical Research*. Cambridge: MIT Press, 2015.

Winnicott, D. W. *Playing and Reality*. London: Tavistock, 1971.

Wulff, David. *Psychology of Religion: Classic and Contemporary*. 2nd ed. New York: Wiley & Sons, 1996.

Xygalatas, Dimitris. *The Burning Saints: Cognition and Culture in the Fire-Walking Rituals of the Anastenaria*. Sheffield: Equinox, 2012.

Zambrano, María, Edison Simons, and Juan Blázquez Miguel. *Sueños y procesos de Lucrecia de León*. Madrid: Tecnos, 1987.

INDEX

Page references followed by *f* refer to figures. Page references followed by *t* refer to tables.

study of religion and, 194–196; visions of the night, 176–178
Renaissance, dreaming during, 161–162
Revonsuo, Antti, 140–141
Rodrigo (Visigoth king), 14–15, 202n10, 202n12
Roman Catholic Church: banishment of non-Catholics from Spain, 17–19; on belief in dreams, 46–47, 97, 171, 181; confession in, 117–118; convents in, 70, 76–77, 213n6; *conversos*, 19, 21, 26, 110, 113; doctrinal versus imagistic modes of religiosity, 178; dreams in, 36, 97, 130, 169, 173; holy war against Protestants, 25–26, 66, 81–82, 84, 98; importance in daily life, 6–7, 36, 111; investigation of Lucrecia in 1588 by, 66, 68–70; Isabella on instruction of Indians, 18; *moriscos/moriscas*, 26, 41, 110, 163, 169; prohibition on dream interpretation, 34–36, 46–47, 203n8, 204n17; prophecy in, 173–176; on revelation, 204n17; on stories and artistic imagery, 33, 38–39, 176–177, 203n7; supernatural agents in, 138–139
Rupprecht, Carol Schreier, 210–211n12

Samuels, Andrew, 162
San Lorenzo de El Escorial. *See* El Escorial
Seashore, in Lucrecia's dreams: as dream setting, 49, 55, 63, 64, 124; in dreams of Armada battle, 60–61, 68, 82; fishermen at, 57; frequency in dreams, 128, 129*t*
Self-awareness, in dreaming, 143
Sexuality: in dreams, 125*t*, 126;

dreams of male sexual aggression, 59, 73–75; La Cava legend and, 15
Shakespeare, William, 212–213n5
Shamans, 171
Siglo del Oro, 1, 16, 189, 191, 199n2
Sleep: anticipatory dimension in, 172, 211n10; deep, 134*f*; neural anatomy and neurotransmitters in, 135; polyphasic and monophasic, 133; REM and non-REM, 133–135, 134*f*, 136, 208n3 (Chapter 9)
Sleep and Dream Database (SDDb), 121–131; availability of, 194, 196, 213nn1–2; characters and settings in, 123, 124*t*, 126, 128–131, 129*t*, 136; dream texts in, 194, 213nn1–2; word search in, 121–122, 208n4 (Chapter 8); word usage frequencies in, 123–128, 124*t*–125*t*
Snyder, Frederick, 141
Social interactions: caregiving context in, 147; in developing adult identity, 148; with Diego de Vitores, 156–157; with Don Alonso de Mendoza, 153–154; with Don Guillén de Casaos, 154–155; with Fray Lucas de Allende, 154; with Lady Jane Dormer, 155–156, 163; with Lucrecia's daughter, 157–158; in Lucrecia's dreams, 125*t*, 126, 136, 137, 146; with Lucrecia's father, 150–152; with Lucrecia's mother, 148–150, 210n3 (Chapter 10); of Lucrecia with her followers, 152–153, 163
Social neuroscience, 137
Social simulation model of dreaming, 140–141
Solomon (king of Israel), dream incubation by, 169
Somnium, 35, 207n4

dinand and, 17; Philip II and,
25–26, 30–32
Tuttle, Leslie, 203n9, 210n9

Ullman, Montague, 141
United States, dreams in nation's
crises, 162

Valle, Pedro de, 70
Vázquez, Mateo, 87, 90, 100
Vega, Lope de (Félix Lope de Vega y
Carpio), 29, 206n11 (Chapter 6)
Vicar of Madrid (Neroni, Juan
Baptista): anger over freedom of
Lucrecia, 70; arrest and investiga-
tion of Lucrecia by, 66, 68–69;
imprisonment of Lucrecia in
home of, 70–75; Lucrecia's
dreams and, 66–67, 71–76, 98

Visio, 35, 207n4
Visium, 35
Vitores, Diego de: arrest and trial
of, 96, 97; on birth of daughter,
99–100; exile of, 185; marriage to
Lucrecia, 91–92, 110, 156–157;
possible help to Lucrecia after
punishment, 187–188

Waterboarding, 102, 103*f*
Whitehouse, Harvey, 178
Winnicott, D. W., 147
Word usage frequencies, 122–128,
124*t*–125*t*

Young Fisherman. *See* Lion Man

Zechariah, book of, warnings on false
dreams, 174

SP SPIRITUAL PHENOMENA
TANYA LUHRMANN and ANN TAVES, Series Editors

Spiritual Phenomena features investigations of events, experiences, and objects, both unusual and everyday, that people characterize as spiritual, paranormal, magical, occult, and/or supernatural. Working from the presupposition that the status of such phenomena is contested, it seeks to understand how such determinations are made in a variety of historical and cultural contexts. Books in this series explore how such phenomena are identified, experienced, and understood; the role that spontaneity and cultivation play in the process; and the similarities and differences in the way phenomena are appraised and categorized across time and cultures. The editors encourage work that is ethnographic, historical, or psychological, and, in particular, work that uses more than one method to understand these complex phenomena, ranging from qualitative approaches to quantitative surveys and laboratory-based experiments.

99290506R00153

Made in the USA
Lexington, KY
15 September 2018